© 1983, AWP

SURVIVING AWAY FROM HOME

Dedicated to our mothers, Betty Rae Frandsen, Jean Jenkins, and Mabel Shoemaker, and to all our moms who started teaching us in our cradles and who never stopped.

WHERE'S MOM NOW THAT I NEED HER?
SURVIVING AWAY FROM HOME.

By Betty Rae Frandsen
Kathryn J. Frandsen
Kent P. Frandsen

ASPEN WEST
PUBLISHING & DISTRIBUTION
8385 Sandy Parkway, Suite 129, Sandy, UT 84070
(801) 565-1370

32nd printing, October 1995

Copyright © 1983, Aspen West
Publishing Co., Inc.

Aspen West Publishing Co., Inc.
P.O. Box 1245
Sandy, Utah 84091

TX 1-504-973
Hardcover ISBN: 0-9615390-0-3
Paperback ISBN: 0-9615390-1-1

This publication is designed to be an informational guide in
regards to the subject matter covered. It is sold with the
understanding that the publisher is not engaged in rendering
medical or other professional services. Where professional
services are required, the services of a competent
professional person shall be sought.

CONTENTS

The nutritional war has been waged for centuries: children, eager to be tumbling on the warm front lawn after a battered baseball, sit instead, lower lip stuck out, stubbornly refusing to eat a plateful of soggy canned peas. But everyone knows that kids have to eat vegetables. Mother's voice drifts in from the confines of the steamy kitchen: "And if you don't eat them now, you'll eat them—cold—for supper."

We remember from our childhoods: we had to eat meat. Drink milk. Savor vegetables. Even choke down liver.

But why?

Easy: good nutrition builds body cells, which enables us to grow. And, when we're finished growing, it keeps us healthy, helps us resist disease and infection, enables us to stay mentally alert.

There is a lot of complex chemistry behind nutrition—which chemical agents work and how—but the basics are really quite simple.

A LOOK AT THE BASIC NUTRIENTS

Five basic nutrients make up a well-balanced diet: proteins, carbohydrates, fats, vitamins, and minerals.

Proteins

Protein is essential: you need it to fight infection, grow, and maintain tissue. Protein has been called the body's "building block," because it plays an essential part in the healing process (both for tissue and for bone). Unfortunately, most Americans eat far too much protein—some estimate that we eat four to five times more protein than we need every day! Does too much protein hurt us? Not literally—but it causes us to sacrifice some of the other important nutrients that we need, like vitamins and minerals.

While the body has the ability to store some nutrients—like carbohydrates or some of the vitamins—it cannot store protein.

1

What that means for you is this: you must evenly space your protein intake throughout the day to keep your body well fueled.

There are two major sources of protein: animal sources and plant sources.

Animal sources of protein—eggs, dairy products, cheese, meat, fish, and poultry—are the most popular, probably because they provide complete protein. In other words, if you eat a chunk of cheese, you've completed your protein requirement for that meal. Ditto for a juicy hamburger, a breast of chicken, or a tender steak.

It's not that easy with plant sources of protein: they are incomplete, which means that you have to combine two or more sources in order to get a complete protein.

How does it work? The combinations have to be of certain plant sources in order to work: soy and whole grains; soy and seeds; dried

---

Vitamins from a Jar: Do You Really Need Them?

With so many different vitamin and mineral supplements on the market, you've probably wondered whether you really need to take a vitamin pill. While you shouldn't really need vitamin supplements if you're getting a balanced diet, there are some people who *do* need supplements—among them dieters, women who are pregnant or nursing, women who are using contraceptive pills, people who drink or smoke heavily, people who are about to undergo surgery, people who take medication regularly, or people with chronic illness (such as cancer, anemia, or jaundice).

If you decide you need a vitamin supplement, follow these guidelines in choosing one:

Choose a multivitamin. You're better off to pick a multivitamin tablet than to buy separate vitamin supplements; you require much lesser amounts of certain vitamins than others, and multivitamin supplements have been balanced for you.

Watch the level. Some people think that if a little is good, a lot must be great! Not necessarily so with vitamins—some of them are stored in the fat and can build up to toxic levels. Find a vitamin supplement that provides you with 100 percent of the recommended daily allowance of about ten vitamins. Be careful not to get too much vitamin A or D.

Store them carefully. Keep vitamin supplements in a dry, cool place, away from the sunlight. Your kitchen cabinet is ideal. The bathroom cabinet is a bad spot: too humid. And the fridge is too cool.

Take them correctly. Take your vitamin with a full meal; if you don't eat much at breakfast, you'll lose more than half of its benefits within the first three or four hours: it dissolves and is eliminated in your urine.

2

beans and grains; dried beans and dairy; whole grains and nuts; whole grains and dried beans; nuts and dairy; dried beans or peas and seeds.

Sound complicated? It doesn't have to be. For example, whole grains and nuts combine to create a complete protein: spread some peanut butter on a piece of whole wheat bread. Nuts and dairy combine to make a complete protein: pour some milk over some nutty granola.

With all the computing that's necessary, why do plant sources of protein have an advantage over animal sources? There are several reasons. For one, animal sources contain cholesterol, which has been implicated in coronary disease. For another, animal sources are higher in calories. And for still another, plant sources are richer in fiber, vitamins, and minerals.

For the best bet in protein, take the best of both worlds: get some of your protein from animal sources, but try some plant sources, too.

Carbohydrates

Carbohydrates—contained in most of the sugary and starchy foods we eat—provide us with energy, essential for function and critical to the performance of protein. Without protein, the body can't grow and maintain and heal itself; without carbohydrates, the protein can't work.

You can get carbohydrates in foods that contain sugar: syrup, jams, jellies, candy, cake, pie, and other sweet foods are rich in carbohydrates. But if you're interested in limiting your sugar intake, you can also get carbohydrates in dried fruits (such as raisins), cereals, potatoes, dried beans, dried peas, lima beans, corn, bread, and fresh fruits. Honey, too, is a good source of carbohydrates.

Fats

At first glance, it would seem that we'd want to eliminate fats from our diet—but fats play an essential role in health. First, fats supply energy in a higher concentration than any other food. Fats keep our skin soft and supple and our hair in good condition. Fats also carry the fat-soluble vitamins (A, D, E, and K) and enable the body to utilize them. Fats, in fact, are part of the structure of every cell in the body.

The most common sources of fats include butter, cream, salad oil, salad dressing, shortening, and fatty meats, such as sausages.

Vitamins

Approximately twenty vitamins that are essential to health have been identified by researchers; if you eat a well-balanced diet, you are likely to get all of them but vitamin D, which is formed in the skin as a result of the ultraviolet rays of the sun. Some of the vitamins are water-soluble and easily dissolved and utilized by the body; others, listed above, are fat-soluble, and must be utilized by the body along with fat.

While each vitamin is valuable, no vitamin works alone: nature has designed a delicate balance, and the vitamins and minerals are dependent on each other for proper assimilation by the body.

Some of the major vitamins include the following:

Vitamin A. Well-known for promoting good vision, vitamin A helps maintain the health of the body's mucous membranes, including the linings of the nose, mouth, intestinal tract, and digestive tract. By maintaining the mucous membranes, vitamin A helps protect the body against infection. Vitamin A is also important for maintaining the health and vitality of the skin.

Good sources of vitamin A include liver, egg yolks, butter and margarine, cheese, deep yellow vegetables (especially carrots and sweet potatoes), and dark green vegetables.

A fat-soluble vitamin, vitamin A is stored in the body.

Vitamin B-1. Called thiamin, vitamin B-1 enables the body to utilize carbohydrates, promotes normal appetite, and helps the nervous system function efficiently and well. Vitamin B-1 contributes to overall health by increasing the ability of the body to digest food.

Good sources of thiamin include meat, fish, poultry, pork (three times richer in thiamin than other meats), eggs, whole grain breads, potatoes, fortified cereals, broccoli, dried beans and peas, and liver.

Vitamin B-2. Also called riboflavin, vitamin B-2 enables the body to use oxygen. Critical to the health of the skin, eyes, lips, and tongue, riboflavin helps the body utilize the energy from other foods.

Good sources of riboflavin include milk, ice cream, cheese, cottage cheese, liver, meat, fish, poultry, eggs, yogurt, enriched

4

cereals, whole grain breads, and peanuts.

Niacin. Critical for the assimilation of other vitamins, niacin promotes the health of the nervous system and enables the digestive system to function smoothly. Niacin also works to help keep the skin, mouth, and tongue in good condition.

Rich sources of niacin include liver, meat, fish, poultry, milk, fortified cereals, whole grain breads, and peanut butter.

Vitamin C. Also called ascorbic acid, vitamin C was the first vitamin successfully separated from food. Vitamin C is literally the

Pass the Salt

Pass it up, that is!

We eat far too much salt: on the average, each of us downs about fifteen pounds a year.

It's easy to identify the salt in some of our favorite foods—like potato chips, salted peanuts, and pretzels. But did you know that there is salt lurking around in plenty of other things, too—like Jello, cream of mushroom soup, canned beans, and dill pickles?

More than half the salt you eat comes from processed foods, but you need to watch out for natural foods, too: cottage cheese is high in sodium, as are spinach, beets, celery, and turnips. Even your drinking water might be loaded with sodium!

So how can you cut back on salt? Try these hints:

Cook without salt. If people want to add it at the table, they can, but it's pretty tough to take salt away once it's in the food!

Taste before you salt. Too many of us automatically pick up the salt shaker and give our food a good dousing before we even taste it.

Check the labels on medication. Some medication contains alarmingly high levels of sodium; antacids are notorious offenders. If you're concerned about sodium, ask your doctor to recommend

medication that is low in sodium.

Watch out for processed foods. Most contain more salt than they should. Opt for "low-sodium" foods, or buy frozen meats and vegetables. If you use canned produce, rinse it and cook it in fresh water. Use unsalted butter or margarine, and choose cheese low in sodium.

Try seasoning with herbs and spices. Raid your spice cupboard, and see what you can find. Lemon juice is delicious—or try a delicate sprinkle of white pepper, garlic powder, or dry mustard.

cement mixture of the body: it holds the cells together, tones the walls of the blood vessels, helps heal wounds and broken bones, and helps the body resist infection. Vitamin C deficiency—called scurvy—leads to swollen painful joints, weak muscles, and bleeding gums.

The most famed source of vitamin C is citrus fruit—oranges, tangerines, grapefruit, lemons, and limes. Other valuable sources include tomatoes, tomato juice, green peppers, broccoli, cabbage, brussels sprouts, kale, spinach, potatoes, sweet potatoes, strawberries, and cantaloupe.

Vitamin D. While there are some food sources of vitamin D, the leading source is sunlight, which enables the body to manufacture vitamin D in the skin. An essential vitamin, it enables the body to utilize calcium in building strong, straight bones and good teeth.

Some of the food sources of vitamin D include tuna fish, sardines, salmon, and other oily fish; egg yolks; butter; and milk that has been fortified with vitamin D.

Vitamin E. Critical for healthy reproduction and lactation, vitamin E is necessary for growth and helps build resistance to degenerative diseases. A deficiency in vitamin E can lead to miscarriage and sterility and is believed to contribute to the development of certain degenerative diseases, among them cancer, arthritis, heart disease, and some kinds of paralysis.

The best sources of vitamin E are the plant oils, including margarine and vegetable oil. Other sources include wheat germ, whole grain breads, whole grain cereals, dried beans, green leafy vegetables, and liver.

Vitamin K. Essential to clotting of the blood, vitamin K helps maintain proper bone formation and metabolism; a shortage of vitamin K can lead to hemorrhage and the loss of calcium from the bones. People who are taking antibiotics for a prolonged period of time and those with cancer or kidney disease require extra vitamin K.

The best sources of vitamin K include liver, potatoes, green leafy vegetables, cabbage, cauliflower, peas, and cereals.

Folic acid. A vitamin that acts with vitamin B-12 in the building of genetic material (determinants of heredity), folic acid is critical to the formation of hemoglobin in red blood cells. Women who use oral contraceptives require extra folic acid; a deficiency of folic acid during pregnancy can lead to abnormalities in the baby.

6

Good sources of folic acid include liver, kidney, dried beans and peas, wheat germ, and dark green leafy vegetables. Folic acid is stored by the body.

Pantothenic acid. A nutrient that helps form hormones, pantothenic acid is essential to the health of the nervous system and helps the body use fats, proteins, and carbohydrates. Manufactured by intestinal bacteria, pantothenic acid is destroyed in foods that are heavily refined and processed.

Excellent sources of pantothenic acid include dark green vegetables, whole grain breads and cereals, eggs, nuts, liver, kidneys, and, to some extent, all plants and animals.

Biotin. Essential to the formation of fatty acids, biotin helps the body derive energy from carbohydrates. Biotin, too, is produced by intestinal bacteria and, interestingly, can be destroyed by raw egg whites.

Good sources of biotin include dark green vegetables, green beans, egg yolks, liver, and kidneys.

Minerals

Minerals are present to some extent in every food we eat. There are two basic categories of minerals: macrominerals, which we need a fairly substantial supply of, and trace minerals, which we need only a small supply of.

Calcium. Essential to life, calcium helps regulate the heart rhythm, helps the nerves function, and helps the body build strong bones and teeth. Calcium is also critical to the absorption of vitamin B-12 and the activation of certain enzymes in the body. Calcium helps the blood clot, enables the muscles to contract, and helps maintain the cell membranes.

As you get older, your body is less capable of absorbing calcium, so you need to increase the amount you get in your daily diet. Other factors that can increase your need for calcium are diets rich in fats, proteins, or phosphorus (common in soft drinks and meats). Women who are pregnant, nursing, or going through menopause also require greater amounts of calcium.

The best source of calcium is milk; others include yogurt, ice cream, cottage cheese, Swiss cheese, eggs, macaroni and cheese, oranges, lentils, and walnuts. Calcium is contained in smaller concentrations in dark green leafy vegetables, salmon, and sardines.

Iron. Essential to the formation of hemoglobin in the blood, iron also makes up part of several proteins and enzymes. Without enough iron, you can experience weakness, fatigue, shortness of breath, and anemia.

How Sweet It Is: Cutting Down on Sugar

As a nation, we eat far too much sugar: on the average, every man, woman, and child in this country eats about a third of a pound every day!

So what?

Here's what: sugar has been blamed for a variety of ills and implicated in a host of conditions—among them overweight, heart disease, diabetes, and tooth decay.

If you'd like to cut back on the amount of sugar you eat, try some of the following suggestions:

Avoid snacks. Most of the snacks we eat, unfortunately, are loaded with sugar. If you're an inveterate snacker, try something less sweet: unbuttered popcorn is a good bet, as are fresh fruits and vegetables.

Get creative with desserts. For too many of us, the word "dessert" connotes gooey sundaes, rich pies, or our favorite German chocolate cake. Look again: there are plenty of sweet things you can serve for dessert without overloading on sugar. Try a bowl of fresh raspberries, a sliced peach drizzled with cream, or a cluster of firm, sweet grapes. Or how about a crisp apple with a few slices of creamy cheese?

Get back to home cooking. Most of the prepared foods we buy have too much sugar (and salt, for that matter). Start making your own food, and watch what you put in. For a good natural sweetener, try unsweetened apple juice. Substitute it for the liquid in a recipe, and eliminate the sugar—it's a safe and nutritious way to sweeten!

Cut out soft drinks. Did you know that the average 12-ounce soft drink contains the equivalent of *nine teaspoons* of sugar? Yuk. Try unsweetened fruit juices, or sip some mineral water with a twist of lime.

Read labels religiously. You'd be surprised at the number of foods that contain sugar: saltine crackers do, for example, and there's hardly anything sweet about them! Ingredients are listed in order of their relative amounts—steer away from foods that list sugar high on the list. Some breakfast cereals are almost *half* sugar, for instance, and a 1-ounce chocolate candy bar contains the equivalent of seven teaspoons of sugar.

Discover other seasonings. If you need to sweeten something, try sprinkling a little unsweetened shredded coconut on it. Or try experimenting with herbs and spices—plenty of spices, such as ginger, basil, coriander, and nutmeg, are sweet and add a delicious flavor to foods.

The best sources of iron include red meats, liver, kidneys, egg yolks, blackstrap molasses, whole grain cereals, dried beans and peas, potatoes, and green leafy vegetables.

Phosphorus. Phosphorus is critical to the body's ability to utilize the energy it can obtain from other nutrients. Essential to the formation of genetic material, phosphorus also helps maintain the cell membranes, bones, and teeth. Prolonged use of antacids may endanger phosphorus levels in the body.

Good sources of phosphorus include milk, cheese, cottage cheese, fish, poultry, meat, eggs, and dried beans and peas. Phosphorus is also found in a number of processed foods, including soft drinks.

Potassium. Also critical to the body's ability to utilize energy, potassium helps maintain the body's fluid levels and enables the nerve impulses to transmit. Potassium also enables the muscles to contract. Those who exert themselves in hot weather, those who have chronic diarrhea, and those who take diuretics run the risk of potassium deficiency.

Good sources of potassium include bananas, dried fruits, orange juice, peanut butter, potatoes, dried beans and peas, bran, meats, tea, coffee, and cocoa.

Magnesium. Also essential to the body's ability to utilize energy, magnesium helps conduct nerve impulses to the muscles, helps the body utilize proteins, and helps build bones. Those with chronic disease, such as diabetes, kidney disease, and epilepsy, run the risk of magnesium deficiency, as do alcoholics and those who take diuretics.

Good sources of magnesium include soybeans, seeds, almonds, cashews, whole grains, and leafy green vegetables eaten raw.

Copper. Critical to the formation of red blood cells, copper is an essential part of several respiratory enzymes. The best sources of copper include corn oil, nuts, liver, and dried beans and peas.

Zinc. An ingredient in more than 100 enzymes, zinc helps the body grow and heal. The best sources are liver, meat, eggs, seafood, and poultry; zinc is found in lesser concentrations in milk and whole grain breads.

Iodine. Essential to normal reproduction, iodine is a part of the thyroid hormones; deficiency in iodine results in goiter, an enlargement of the thyroid gland. Iodine is found naturally in seaweed, sea salt, saltwater fish, and seafood; you can buy table salt that has had iodine added to it.

THE BASIC FOUR FOOD GROUPS

Now that you know some of the individual constituents, how do you grab all the nutrients and fit them together in a meaningful way?

Don't worry—nutritional researchers have done it for you, and have categorized all the things you need to eat into four basic groups.

Milk Group

As an adult, you need two servings each day from the milk group, a category made up of dairy products such as milk, ice cream, cottage cheese, cheese, yogurt, and pudding. A "serving" is one cup of milk or yogurt; an equivalent would be two cups of cottage cheese, two slices of cheddar cheese, one cup of pudding, or almost two cups of ice cream.

As an adult, you require less than teenagers—who need four servings from this group—or children, who require three servings.

Meat Group

Regardless of your age, you should have two servings from the meat group—or an equivalent of four ounces of cooked boneless lean meat. Other foods in the meat group include poultry, fish, seafood, eggs, dried peas and beans, nuts, and peanut butter. Servings vary, depending on the amount of protein in the food: a "serving" of peanut butter, for example, is four tablespoons, while a "serving" of cottage cheese is about half a cup.

Fruit–Vegetable Group

Regardless of your age, you need four servings each day from the fruit–vegetable group, with each "serving" counted as one cup of raw vegetables, half a cup of cooked vegetables, or a medium-sized piece of fruit (such as a medium peach, medium apple, or medium banana).

Besides getting your four daily servings, you need to vary the items you eat from this group in order to get the proper balance of vitamins and minerals. Researchers recommend that you eat one citrus fruit each day, three or four dark orange vegetables each week, and three or four dark green leafy vegetables each week.

Grains–Cereals Group

Made up of a variety of foods such as grains, cereals, breads, pasta, rice, pancakes, and grits, the grains and cereals group provides important carbohydrates without excessive sugar. When you can, you should eat cereals and breads that have been fortified or enriched.

Regardless of your age, you should eat four servings of grains per day—with each serving equivalent to a slice of bread, one cup of dry cereal, or half a cup of cooked cereal.

Hold the Pickles, Hold the Lettuce . . .

We're all familiar with the fast-food jingles—but are you familiar with the fast-food calories?

It's a real temptation to dash into a fast-food restaurant, sink your teeth into a delicious double burger, gobble up some golden fries, savor a creamy malt, and be on your way again. After all, they're convenient, not too expensive, and—well, the food is usually pretty good!

But if you're watching your weight, you'd better beware: a single fast-food meal can tally up as many calories as you should consume in an *entire* day.

Sound unreal?

Here are the hard, cold facts:

A double burger with fries and a shake is about 1,050 calories.

A ten-inch cheese pizza is about 1,000. Add pepperoni, tomato sauce, mushrooms, olives, green pepper, and sausage, and you add another 300 calories.

Or how about some good old fish and chips? Two pieces of deep-fried fish, fries, and a serving of cole slaw tally up to 950 calories. Add another piece of fish (for those who are really hungry), and you add another 350 calories.

How about roast beef? A fast-food roast beef sandwich with fries, cole slaw, and a shake adds up to 1,200.

Even chicken isn't immune. You'll get more than 1,000 calories with three pieces of fried chicken, a serving of mashed potatoes with gravy, some cole slaw, and a roll—forget the butter. Add a shake, and you have 350 more.

FINDING THE BEST FOOD BUYS

Y ou've got your shopping cart or basket, and you're standing in the middle of a crowded shopping aisle. Along the shelves are rows of cans decked in brightly colored labels, clear plastic bags burgeoning with curly macaroni, boxes and cartons that boast, "just add water." The bounties of the harvest fill the produce section, and the cooler boasts meats, eggs, and cheese.

What do you do now?

Shopping well—picking the best produce, determining the best buys, avoiding potential food poisoning, getting the most for your money—requires a real skill. By following these guidelines, you can succeed in getting good food for bargain prices.

SHOPPING: MAKING YOUR MONEY WORK FOR YOU

Getting the most for your food dollar involves a little time and effort—not only in the aisles of the grocery store, but at home, before and after you shop.

Before You Go Shopping

• Take a couple of hours to find out what kinds of grocery stores are available in your community. Prices really *can* vary from store to store. Generally, food co-ops and food warehouses feature the lowest prices; many require you to do some of the work, such as mark prices on your purchases and bag your own groceries. In some food warehouses, you can get good buys on non-perishables (food that doesn't require refrigeration), but many food warehouses don't carry items such as meat, eggs, cheese, milk, and fresh produce. You can save significantly by picking up staples at a food warehouse and shopping for perishables at another store.

Check to see whether your community has a "farmer's market"—usually an open arena where area farmers market their own produce. You can usually get a good price on fresh produce

13

from farmers who are competing with one another. The same is not true of produce stands, however: generally, the produce stand owner buys produce from farmers, marks up the price, and passes it along to the customer.

Some communities have thrift stores where day-old bread and other baked goods are sold; while they may not be quite as fresh, they are still good and provide the same nutritional value for a real bargain.

- Sit down and plan your week's menu *before* you go shopping. Carefully plan out all three meals each day, and plan your menu around leftovers. If you're eating baked chicken one night, for instance, you can plan to put the leftover chicken in an omelet the next morning, in a salad the next day for lunch, or in a casserole the next night for dinner. Consult your recipes and make a shopping list, including every item you'll need for the week's menus.
- Keep a shopping list taped to the inside door of your cupboard; when you get close to running out of a staple—such as flour, baking powder, or cooking oil—write it on the list. Before you go shopping for the week, include those items on your shopping list.

As You Shop

- Learn to accurately calculate how much food you'll need. It's no bargain if you buy a large quantity to save money—and then end up letting the leftovers go to waste because you forget about them or are bored with them.
- Learn to read labels so you'll be well-informed about price, amount, ingredients, and other important information. Consult the information later in this chapter for help in deciphering labels.
- Compare the various forms in which you can buy a certain food— for example, you can buy fresh peas, frozen peas, or canned peas. While you need to consider personal likes and dislikes, you can often save by purchasing a less expensive form of the food. Fresh peas in the pod, for example, are usually much more expensive than the same amount of frozen or canned peas.
- Consider buying less expensive cuts of meat, especially if you'll be using the meat in a dish that cooks for an extended time, such as a stew. Even inexpensive cuts of meat will be tender and delectable when simmered in stew or soup.

- Whole chicken fryers cost significantly less per pound than chicken parts; you can cook them at one time, and use the leftovers in soups, stews, casseroles, salads, and tacos.
- *Always* eat just before you go shopping—you'll have a much easier time sticking to what you've written on your shopping list.
- Plan a time to shop when you can be unhurried; allow yourself time in the store to do some comparison shopping for the best buys.
- Compare brands of the same kind of packaged foods. Many large grocery store chains have their own "house brands" that are less expensive than the national brands of the same products—and don't completely pass up generic ("no-name") products. Many generic products are just as good as brand names, but they lack the fancy packaging that adds cost. Nutritional quality is the same by law.
- Resist the temptation to grab "extras." Grocery stores are specifically designed to tempt you to buy on impulse: in order to get to the milk, you have to walk down a long aisle packed with delicious-looking foods. While you're standing in line at the cash register, you'll notice that lots of items are placed near the register: candy bars, magazines, gum, and trinkets such as plastic soap

For Every Thing, There is a Season

You can realize significant savings on your food bill if you plan your menus around the fresh produce that is in season. While seasons do vary in some parts of the world, the following can serve as a general guide:

Winter

apples	onions
artichokes	oranges
cabbage	pears
cauliflower	potatoes
celery	squash

Spring

apricots	oranges
artichokes	peas
asparagus	radishes
carrots	strawberries
cherries	spinach
new potatoes	lettuce
onions	

Summer

apples	nectarines
cucumbers	peaches
grapes	peas
green beans	radishes
melons	tomatoes
lettuce	

Fall

apples	lettuce
chestnuts	spinach
cucumbers	sweet potatoes
figs	zucchini
grapes	pears

15

dishes. Merchants are betting that you'll be standing around, bored, and that you'll reach for one or more of these items. Resist the urge: stick with your shopping list religiously.

- While you should stick to your list, you should be willing to make a change in one circumstance: if you spot a bargain at the store, see if you can substitute. For example, if you had planned to eat corn with your supper and you find that green beans are on sale, make the switch: use green beans instead of corn
- Buy milk in one-gallon containers—it's less expensive that way, and you can get more milk for the money. Skim milk or milk with 2% fat content costs less and is better for you.

Choosing a Good Egg

In a society where we're conditioned to think that bigger is better, you may have to realign your thinking when it comes to the humble egg.

Eggs are one of your best sources of protein—and they're a real bargain when compared to the cost of meat. But the size and quality have nothing to do with each

other—nor does the color of the shell affect the quality of the egg inside.

So just how are eggs graded? The quality of an egg depends on four factors:

1. The condition of the yolk
2. The thickness of the white
3. The size of the air sac
4. The condition and texture of the shell

In the United States, eggs are usually sized—jumbo, extra large, large, medium, and small—and graded, generally from AA to C. If you're buying an egg to poach, scramble, fry, or hard-boil, buy A or AA eggs; if you're buying eggs to use as ingredients in cooking, you can safely use Grade B eggs.

Remember: buy only eggs that have been refrigerated in the store, and check the eggs for cracked shells *before* you buy. A crack in the shell can let in dangerous bacteria and lead to food poisoning. Shells should be dull, not shiny; never wash the shells before you use the eggs.

To get the best bargain, buy only the size and grade you really need; if there is less than 8¢ difference between sizes, always buy the larger size.

- In general, avoid foods that are already prepared. You can buy boxes of "mix," for instance, that call for nothing but hamburger and water to make a casserole. You can save considerably by purchasing your own fresh produce and taking the extra effort to make it from scratch.
- As you buy fresh produce, pay attention to amounts: it's a temptation to grab the largest bunch of grapes, but don't buy more than you will eat. Food that goes to waste is a waste of money.
- Learn to check for weights instead of making your purchases based on size. A large loaf of bread, for instance, may weigh several ounces less than a smaller—and tastier—loaf of bread on the next shelf.
- When you can, buy foods labeled "enriched," "fortified," or "vitamin C added."
- Buy cereals that you fix yourself—such as oatmeal and farina—instead of prepackaged cereals in instant or ready-to-serve form. Steer away from pre-sweetened cereals, drink mixes, and other pre-sweetened foods.
- When buying breads and cereals, buy whole-grain products.
- Buy cheese in solid bricks. Pre-sliced or pre-grated cheese is considerably more expensive than the same amount of solid cheese.
- Keep an eagle eye at the checkout counter: mistakes can easily be made. Monitor the price of each item as it is rung up on the cash

---

A Fish By Any Other Name . . .

You stand before the fish counter and examine the bounties of the sea. You recognize the names of the fish, all right, but how do you know exactly what you're getting?

Fish are generally sold in three different ways. Look for the following, and make your choice based on personal taste:

Fillets. Fish fillets are boneless, as far as possible, and some are also skinless. Some tiny bones may remain in fillets because they are virtually impossible to remove, but the fish shouldn't contain any bones large enough to cause problems during eating.

Steaks. While most of the bones have been removed from fish steaks, the backbone usually remains. Some steaks have had the skin removed, but many still have skin around the edge.

Whole. A whole fish is just that: whole, with the head and tail still attached. Some whole fish have had the organs removed, but some are sold complete with internal organs; ask the butcher or store owner if you can't tell from the label.

register, and point out any errors to the clerk. Likewise, be honest enough to point out errors in your favor and to return excess change.

HOW TO CHOOSE THE BEST QUALITY FOODS

How can you tell whether that musky-smelling cantaloupe is really ripe? Which apples are the best for eating? Which mushrooms should you pick out of a crowded bin? What's your best cheese bet?

Use the following chart to determine the best quality of fresh produce, meat, and dairy products.

FOOD ITEM	WHAT TO LOOK FOR	HOW TO STORE IT
Apples	Rich, deep, uniform color; avoid bruised, soft, or blemished fruit	Store at room temperature 1–3 weeks; if cut, sprinkle with lemon juice and store, covered, in refrigerator
Apricots	Deep color with rosy blush, firm; avoid bruised, soft, or shriveled fruit	Store, covered or uncovered, in the refrigerator
Artichokes	Small with tightly closed leaves of uniform color; avoid fruit that is discolored or that has spreading leaves; watch out for insect infestation	Store, covered or uncovered, in the refrigerator
Asparagus	Tender, firm stalks; tips compact; 6–8 inches in length; avoid stalks that are whitish or that are too large or long	Store covered in the refrigerator; use within 1–3 days to avoid toughening

18

Avocado	Dark, with either smooth or pebbled skin; when held in palm, yields to gentle pressure; will ripen during storage; avoid fruit that is too dark and soft	Store covered or uncovered in the refrigerator; to ripen, store at room temperature
Bananas	Firm, uniform in color, pale yellow to rosy red; will ripen during storage; avoid fruit that is soft, bruised, or spotted	Store at room temperature in a paper bag; if ripens too much during storage, mash and freeze for use in breads and cakes
Beans, Snap	Young, tender, small; avoid large, dry-looking beans	Store covered in refrigerator
Beets	Small (3 inches in diameter maximum), with uniform deep red color	Store at room temperature; remove tops before storing
Berries	Medium sized, uniform color, firm and solid, and plump; avoid berries that have started to "juice" or that have mold on them	Store unwashed, spread out in the refrigerator, covered; check frequently for mold
Broccoli	Tight, close buds of uniform green color; avoid broccoli with yellow flowers or yellow buds or with smudgy spots	Store covered in the refrigerator

Brussels Sprouts	Firm, deep green; tight heads; avoid those that have started to wilt	Store covered in the refrigerator
Cabbage	Pick small heads heavy for their size, light to bright green; avoid those with holes (indicates worm infestation)	Store covered in the refrigerator
Cantaloupe	Webbed skin with yellowish coloring underneath, smoothly rounded depression at ends, stem end yields to slight pressure; has fragrant aroma; avoid fruit that is sunken or that has a calloused scar on the end	Ripens during storage; store at room temperature to ripen; in refrigerator after ripens; once cut, store tightly covered in refrigerator
Carrots	Uniform bright orange color, no longer than 6 inches long, 1-inch maximum diameter at widest point; avoid carrots that are too big or that look "woody"	Store either in the refrigerator or at room temperature; cut off tops before storing
Casaba Melon	Large, round, heavy for size, slightly softened tips, deep yellow ridged skin; avoid fruit that is misshapen, sunken, or rigid at tips	Store either at room temperature or in refrigerator

20

Cauliflower	Flower clusters tight, head firm, flowers well-formed and white; avoid those with smudgy or dirty spots (indicates insect infestation)	Store covered in the refrigerator
Celery	Light, pale green; avoid celery that is too dark	Store in the refrigerator in a paper bag (do not store in plastic bag)
Coconut	Well-rounded, heavy for size, sloshing sound when shaken; avoid softened or those with greenish color	Store at room temperature; when cut, cover tightly and store in the refrigerator; store milk covered in refrigerator
Corn	Tip of ear blunt, not tapered; silk darkened and dry; when kernal pierced with fingernail, juice spurts out; avoid corn that has tapered end, moist silk, or dried-out kernals; watch for worms	Stays fresh longer if not husked; store in the refrigerator either covered (husked) or uncovered (in husks)
Crenshaw Melon	Bright yellowish-green or yellow; firm pear shape that yields to pressure on ends; pleasant aroma; avoid fruit that is misshapen, mostly green, or sunken	Store either at room temperature or in the refrigerator

Cucumbers	Medium to dark green; long and slender; firm; avoid cucumbers that are yellowed or soft with wrinkled skin	Store covered in the refrigerator
Eggplant	Glossy shine, deep purple color, firm; avoid fruit that lacks glossy shine or that has green spots	Store covered in the refrigerator
Grapefruit	Heavy for size, with smooth, thin skin; avoid fruit that is light for size, has puffy skin, or has sunken, withered, or soft areas	Store either at room temperature or in refrigerator; when cut, store tightly covered in refrigerator
Grapes	Plump, deep uniform color, tight clusters, on dark green stems; avoid those with brown stems or grapes that are soft and discolored	Store covered or uncovered in refrigerator
Green Pepper	Firm; thick-walled; deep green color; avoid peppers that are wrinkled, soft, or have uneven color	Store covered in the refrigerator
Honeydew Melon	Large (5–7 pounds), firm, pale yellow or creamy white; avoid soft, small, or greenish fruit	Store at room temperature until cut, and then tightly covered in refrigerator

Lemons	Heavy for size, deep yellow with uniform color and smooth, thin skins; avoid fruit with greenish tinge or thick skins	Store at room temperature; will yield more juice if warmed in oven or hot water for 15 minutes before juicing; when cut, store covered in refrigerator
Lettuce	Heavy for size, firm head, deep green leaves; scratch core and sniff, avoid those with bitter smell; avoid soggy or wilted heads	Store in paper bag in refrigerator (do not store in plastic bag)
Lima Beans	Well-filled, firm pods; green color; avoid tan or yellowed pods, pods that are bulging, or pods that are dry or flabby	If shelled, store covered in refrigerator
Limes	Heavy for size, dark green uniform color; avoid those with pale color or those that are soft and wrinkled	Store at room temperature; when cut, store tightly covered in refrigerator
Mushrooms	Light color, tightly closed around stem, well-rounded; avoid mushrooms that are spotted, discolored, woody, or showing signs of decay; *do not forage for wild mushrooms*	Store covered in the refrigerator

Nectarines	Smooth, shiny skin; deep uniform color with rosy blush; firm, but not hard; avoid fruit with brown spots or bruises	Store covered or uncovered in refrigerator
Okra	Pods 2–3 inches long, uniform green color; avoid soft, shriveled, discolored okra	Store covered in the refrigerator
Onions	Full, firm, and slightly flat; tops brown and shriveled; avoid those with wet necks or signs of mold	Store at room temperature
Oranges	Heavy for size, smooth thin skins; may be deep orange or tinged with green; firm, but yield to pressure; avoid oranges with sunken, withered, or discolored areas and oranges that are light for their size with thick, puffy skin	Store at room temperature or in refrigerator; when cut, store covered in the refrigerator
Parsnips	Small, uniform tannish–yellow color; avoid those that are large, "woody," or split	Store either at room temperature or in refrigerator
Peaches	Firm, deep uniform color with rosy blush; avoid those with a green tint or those with soft, brown, or bruised areas	Store covered or uncovered in refrigerator

24

Pears	Choose slightly underripe, just turning yellow; firm; slightly soft at stem end; ripen during storage; avoid discolored, those with brown spots or bruises	Store at room temperature until yellow and slightly soft at stem end; store covered in refrigerator when cut

Savoring Some Tasty Bacteria

We're usually looking for ways to get rid of bacteria—but in the case of yogurt, the more the merrier!

Yogurt, simply stated, is milk that has been "contaminated" with bacteria. The sugars in the milk are transformed into lactic acid, which cause the milk to curdle and develop the characteristic yogurt taste.

If you've never tried yogurt, start now! Yogurt is relatively low in calories, and it gives you a big boost of protein, phosphorus, vitamin B-12, calcium, and riboflavin. It's extremely easy to digest, so it's soothing to even the queasiest stomachs.

Yogurt can be used in cooking in a variety of ways: use it as a substitute for sour cream, and it makes a wonderful topping for some kinds of meats. If you do decide to use it in cooking, heat it gently—never boil!—to preserve the nutrients, and don't stir too much (yogurt gets thin when stirred).

Besides its versatility and good taste, yogurt packs some health benefits, too. When you take antibiotics, the "friendly" bacteria in your intestinal tract, essential for proper digestion, can be destroyed; eating yogurt while you take antibiotics can help preserve them. Yogurt, when eaten regularly, also helps lower your blood cholesterol. So scan your supermarket dairy section. You'll find yogurt in several different varieties:

French-style yogurt. The French-style yogurt, which can be purchased either plain or flavored with fruit, is slightly sweeter and a little thinner than conventional types. The fruit is blended throughout, and the yogurt is creamy and smooth.

Plain yogurt. This is the kind of yogurt you use as a substitute for sour cream and in cooking: it has no flavorings and no fruit added. Plain yogurt is more tart and tangy than other kinds of yogurt; if you decide to try it, buy the kind made from skim—not whole—milk for a significant calorie savings.

Flavored yogurt. Flavored yogurt is a little sweeter than plain yogurt, and has a flavoring added—usually lemon, vanilla, or coffee. Some brands also add sweeteners, but there is no fruit in flavored yogurt.

Fruit yogurt. There are two different kinds of fruit yogurt: in one, the fruit is in a thick syrupy base and is in the bottom of the carton, with plain yogurt on top. To blend the two, you stir with a spoon—or, if you want to, you can eat the unflavored yogurt and enjoy the fruit last. The other kind comes with the fruit already blended throughout the yogurt; because stabilizers are added to keep the fruit from settling, this kind of yogurt is slightly thicker than the others—almost like gelatin.

25

Peas	Small pods, well-filled, deep green; avoid pods that are bulging, withered, yellow, dry, or discolored	Store in refrigerator, covered when hulled
Plums	Uniform color (purple, blue, red, yellow, or pale green, depending on variety), firm, and slightly soft; avoid fruit that is spotted, too soft, or wrinkled	Store uncovered in refrigerator or, to ripen, at room temperature
Pineapple	Small, tight crown; sweet fragrance; bulging eyes; center leaves come out easily when tugged gently; makes dull, solid sound when thumped; avoid those that are greenish, those whose stems don't pull out, or those with fermented odor	Store at room temperature; when cut, store tightly covered in refrigerator
Potatoes	Firm, net-like texture on skin; shallow eyes; even color; avoid those with rot (unpleasant odor), green color (indicates poison), or sprouted eyes (sprouts are poisonous)	Store in dark, cool, well-ventilated place away from light; do *not* store whole potatoes in refrigerator; cover cut potatoes with water and a few drops of vinegar, store in refrigerator for three days
Pomegranates	Round, full, firm; uniform color; avoid those with spots, dents, or bruises	Store at room temperature; when cut, cover tightly and store in refrigerator

Rhubarb	Deep red color, tender young shoots; avoid those stalks that are large, thick, and stringy	Store in paper sack in refrigerator
Squash	Small, tender; summer squash skin should pierce easily with fingernail; winter squash has hard rinds; avoid squash with blackened or dried-up stems, watery spots, or soft spots	Store covered in refrigerator when cut, at room temperature when uncut; use only flesh if skins and seeds are tough
Sweet Potatoes	Small, firm; uniform rose to bronze color; avoid those that are soft, shriveled, or blackened	Store at room temperature
Tomatoes	Firm, but yields to pressure; heavy for size; deep uniform red color; ripen during storage; avoid mushy, light for size, or those that are extremely hard	Store at room temperature to ripen; when ripe or cut, store covered in refrigerator
Watermelon	Rounded; ends filled out; smooth surface; creamy color on underside; when scraped with fingernail, skin should yield thin green shaving; avoid those with shiny surface or creamy color on more than half of melon	Store in refrigerator or at room temperature; store tightly covered in refrigerator if cut

Canned Produce		Store at room temperature in a dry, cool place; when opened, store covered in refrigerator
Frozen Produce	Choose those that are frozen hard; avoid those that are mushy or thawed	Keep frozen hard for 6–12 months in freezer; once thawing begins, don't refreeze; use within 2–3 days once thawing begins

Dairy and Egg Products

Butter or Margarine		Store covered in refrigerator
Shortening		Store at room temperature
Eggs	Dull shells; avoid eggs with shiny shells, eggs that have been cracked, or eggs with an odor; use large (Grade A) eggs for eating, medium (Grade B) for baking; buy only eggs that have been refrigerated	Store in own carton in refrigerator, pointed end down, for four weeks; never wash eggs before storing them (film protects against bacteria); store whites covered in the refrigerator no longer than 3 days; store yolks covered with water in refrigerator no longer than 3 days
Instant Nonfat Milk	Choose instant milk; if in United States, choose U.S. Extra Grade	Store powdered milk in cool, dry place; refrigerate after mixing; *never* freeze

28

| Cheese | In United States, choose U.S. Grade A or AA | Leave cheese in original wrapper, refrigerated, until ready for use; after opening original wrapper, wrap cheese snugly in foil or plastic wrap; scrape off mold; to freeze, wrap tightly in moisture-proof paper |

Meat and Poultry Products

| | | *General Freezing Tips:* Wrap in airtight moisture-proof wrapping; press out extra air before sealing; do not freeze meat on the plastic tray it comes on; double-wrap smoked meat before freezing |

| Poultry | Choose young poultry (broiler, fryer, roaster, capon, Rock Cornish, or young turkey); full, meaty flesh; smooth, tender skin; flexible breast-bone; well-distributed fat; avoid poultry that is blemished, has too many pinfeathers, has flabby discolored skin, or is in a torn or damaged packaged | If purchased frozen, keep frozen until ready for use; thaw in original wrapping in refrigerator for 24 hours or submerged in cold water; after cooking, store loosely covered in refrigerator, use within 2–3 days; remove stuffing from bird and store separately in airtight container in refrigerator |

Fish	Bright, clear, bulging eyes; tight, bright, shiny scales; firm, elastic flesh; fresh odor; reddish-pink gills without slime; avoid fish with slimy gills, dull sunken eyes, loose dull scales, sagging flesh, flesh that is separating from the bones, or fish with offensive odor	Store in refrigerator, loosely covered; use within 2–3 days; freeze for 3–6 months; thaw in milk, or cook frozen

Rice: The Nice Grain

Rice can be nice in a number of ways: it's extremely nutritional, it goes with many different dishes, and it is inexpensive. Thrown in a casserole or Oriental meal, rice can make two servings of meat and vegetables magically stretch into four or even six.

Rice comes in three basic "grain" types—and the type you choose will depend on what you're using the rice for.

Long-grain rice. Long-grain rice is the most common rice in the United States, and for good reason—as the rice cooks, the grains stay separate, and the rice is usually very fluffy. Long-grain rice is good as an ingredient in casseroles, soups, and stews, and can be used as a base for creamed meat or vegetables. You should choose long-grain rice if you're planning on eating the rice plain, as a side dish.

Medium-grain rice. The shorter grains in medium-grain rice cause it to be slightly less fluffy—and its higher stickiness makes it ideal for rice desserts and molded rice dishes, such as molded salads or rice rings.

Short-grain rice. Most common in the Orient and least common in the United States, short-grain rice is sticky and difficult to separate when cooked. It's the best rice to use in pudding!

You can also get rice that has been processed by removing the hull and bran; called *parboiled rice,* it is most popular because it cooks up firm and fluffy. Regular white rice is the most economical—and you might choose brown rice (rice with most of the bran layers intact) for its superb nutritional value. Brown rice takes longer to cook, and you'll need to use more water, but you'll enjoy its slightly nutty flavor.

The fastest rice to cook is the kind that has been pre-cooked—usually called "instant" rice, it is more expensive than the other kinds of rice.

Beef	Flecks of fat throughout lean part of meat; dark purplish-red to bright red color; firm, fine-textured muscle; little extra fat; avoid meat that is discolored (greenish or dark brown), has offensive odor, or has large amounts of extra fat	Wipe with paper towel, wrap loosely, and store in refrigerator; wrap in airtight moisture-proof wrapping to freeze; beef keeps in freezer for 6–12 months; ground beef keeps in freezer for 1–3 months; thaw beef until it separates easily
Pork	Lean, bright pink to grayish pink in color; choose pork with little "cover" fat; avoid pork that is discolored or fatty or that has a foul odor	Wipe with paper towel and store, loosely covered, in refrigerator; pork can be frozen for 3–6 months in an airtight moisture-proof wrapping; sausage can be frozen for 1–3 months
Hot Dogs	Check labels on hot dogs; meat should be listed as first ingredient; avoid those that list "variety meats" as ingredients	Store, loosely covered, in refrigerator; do not freeze

Storage for Miscellaneous Food Items

Bread	Store in airtight plastic bag; can be frozen for up to three months in an airtight, moisture-proof wrapping
Brown Sugar	Store at room temperature in a tightly closed plastic bag or an airtight jar with a screw-on lid

Cottage Cheese	Turn carton upside-down and store on a saucer in the refrigerator
Crackers	Keep wrapped at room temperature; in areas of high humidity, store in a jar with a screw-on lid
Cream	Store covered in the refrigerator for up to one week; can be frozen in a glass jar with a screw-on lid for up to six months
Flour	Keep in a dry, airtight container; metal containers are best, since they prevent insect and rodent infestation
Garlic Cloves	Keep in the freezer or in a jar of cooking oil with a screw-on lid at room temperature
Honey	Store in a small, covered, airtight container at room temperature; if honey begins to turn to sugar, put the honey container in a pan of boiling water until honey liquefies again. Shake well before using after heating
Ice Cream	Store in freezer in original carton; enclose original carton with a plastic bag, and seal closed
Jam and Jelly	Store in refrigerator after opening; store in a jar with a screw-on lid
Jello	Store in a dry, cool place in original container; if only part of the box is used at a time, store the remainder in an airtight container at room temperature
Marshmallows	Store in the freezer in an airtight, moisture-proof bag
Milk	Store in a carton or bottle in the refrigerator for up to five days
Mixes	Store in cool, dry, airtight containers for up to six months
Peanut Butter	Store in a jar with screw-on lid for up to six months in a dry, cool place; do not refrigerate
Popcorn	Store in a jar with a screw-on lid in the freezer

Sandwiches	Store in the freezer in airtight, moisture-proof containers; sandwiches can be frozen for up to two weeks, and will thaw at room temperature in about three hours
Soup	Store in the refrigerator in an airtight container; store for up to three months in the freezer in a jar with a screw-on lid
Spices	Store in airtight containers in a dry, cool place
Sugar	Store at room temperature in a metal airtight container
Syrup	Store at room temperature in an airtight container

HOW TO AVOID FOOD POISONING

As good as most food is, it can make you extremely ill or even kill you under certain conditions. Food poisoning is a condition that occurs when bottled or canned food, dairy products, or meat is invaded with bacteria or fungus; when ingested, the bacteria or fungus multiplies and results in illness or death.

Unfortunately, food poisoning doesn't always affect the appearance, taste, or odor of food—so it can be difficult, if not impossible, to detect ahead of time. In many cases, though, you can suspect contamination and food poisoning from certain signs.

To protect yourself against food poisoning, avoid as many processed foods as possible: foods you prepare yourself from fresh produce, dairy products, and meat are less likely to become tainted if you prepare and store them properly. Avoid eating rare or raw meat, and avoid eating too much shellfish. Keep your freezer set at 8° F, and your refrigerator no higher than 40° F. If food begins to thaw, eat it immediately or discard it. Don't let your leftovers sit around for longer than two hours before you put them in the freezer or refrigerator.

Never thaw frozen foods at room temperature; thaw them instead in the refrigerator, or submerge them in *cold* water.

Suspect contamination or food poisoning in the following cases:

- Fruits or vegetables have started to decay (look for brown spots, soft spots, or discoloration)
- There is visible mold on fruits or vegetables
- Eggs have been cracked in the carton
- Cans are dented
- Cans are bulging at the ends
- The contents of a can forcefully spray when you open the can
- The food inside a can is bubbly or frothy
- Meat feels slimy to the touch
- Meat, produce, or any other food has a foul odor
- Food has discolored
- Food has a strong unusual flavor

You'll know before too long whether you have contracted food poisoning: in most cases the symptoms are violent, and the onset is rapid. The type of food poisoning you get depends on its source. If you suffer any of the following symptoms after eating the indicated foods, seek medical help immediately.

Seafood

Within five to 30 minutes, your lips and fingertips start to tingle, you lose strength in your muscles, and you have difficulty breathing. This type of food poisoning is often fatal.

Undercooked Meat

Twenty-four to 72 hours after eating raw or undercooked meat, you experience abdominal pain, nausea, vomiting, and diarrhea; you develop a flu-like illness, with muscle pain, stiffness in the muscles and joints, and fever. You are unable to sleep. This type of food poisoning is also usually fatal.

Food That is Cooked and Then Kept Warm in Warming Trays for Extended Periods

Within four to 24 hours after eating in a restaurant, you develop abdominal pain and severe diarrhea. This type of food poisoning can make you extremely ill, but is rarely fatal.

Contaminated Eggs, Milk, Meat, Poultry, and Fish

Within eight to 72 hours after eating any of the above products, you develop chills and a fever, nausea and vomiting, severe diarrhea, and intense abdominal pain. This type of food poisoning is rarely fatal.

Rice: Brown is Nice

You probably never considered color before, but you should now: if you replace your white rice with brown, you'll get a big nutrition boost!

Color isn't the only difference, either. White rice has been stripped to the grain; brown rice has had only the outer hull removed. The bran layer still covers the grain—which provides you with greater energy for the amount you eat plus more protein, vitamin E, calcium, phosphorus, potassium, and niacin than white rice.

Brown rice is a pale tan color; it tastes nutty, and is slightly crunchy because of the bran layer. It's a delightful difference we think you'll love!

Ready to dig in?

There are a few more important differences if you're considering brown rice. Follow these guidelines for cooking and storing your brown rice:

Storing it right. Brown rice can't be stored as long as white rice can—the bran layer starts to deteriorate, especially in climates with high humidity. If you'll be storing a package of brown rice for an extended period, put it in the fridge.

Cooking it right. Brown rice takes longer to cook than white rice does. Why? The bran layer adds fiber and oil, which increase the length of cooking time needed. Remember— when it's finished, brown rice will have a slightly different texture. The inside grain will be tender when cooked; the outside bran layer,

which explodes during cooking, will cling to the grain and will provide a slightly crunchy texture.

Adding enough liquid. Because of the bran layer and the extra cooking time required, you'll need to cook brown rice in more water than you do white rice. Follow package directions closely—but if your package doesn't give precise cooking directions, here's a standard formula.

    ½ C. brown rice
    1¼ C. water
    ½ t. salt
    2 t. butter

Combine all ingredients in a medium saucepan with a tight-fitting lid. Bring to a boil; reduce heat and simmer, 45–55 minutes, or until all liquid is absorbed and rice is tender.

Canned Goods

This is the most highly fatal form of food poisoning: called *botulism*, it strikes within eight to 72 hours after you eat the contaminated food. You will develop dizziness, weakness, difficulty in breathing, severe abdominal pain and bloating, nausea and vomiting, and blurred vision. Paralysis begins in the facial muscles and progresses downward to involve the muscles of the chest, abdomen, arms, and legs. Coma and death follow.

Improper or Inadequate Cooking or Refrigeration

This type of food poisoning, which is rarely fatal, usually involves products that contain mayonnaise, cream, or eggs (potato salad is a common culprit). Two to three hours after eating the food, you develop cramps, nausea, and vomiting; symptoms usually disappear on their own after about 24 hours.

HOW TO READ LABELS

You can select good quality food intelligently if you learn to read labels. The name of the product is just the beginning on product labels: you can find plenty of other information there, too.

1 The product brand name—in this case, Campbell's.

2 The name of the product—in this case, cream of mushroom soup. In some cases—such as the one illustrated here—there may also be a description of the product, such as "condensed." Other typical product descriptions include "cream-style," "evaporated," or "crinkled."

3 By law, labels must contain information about the weight of the product, listed in pounds and ounces. This information is critical when you're using a recipe that calls for a certain size can or package of an ingredient. For example, you'd ruin your food if you used a 15-ounce can of tomato paste when the recipe called for a 6-ounce can.

4 Nutrition information is required on all labels. Nutrition information is listed per *serving*, not for the entire amount of food in the container. For example, the nutrition information on the sample label is for 4 ounces of condensed soup—which means that the can would contain 2¾ servings. Typical nutrition information includes the number of calories in a serving as well as the amount of nutrients, usually expressed as percentages of the U.S. Recommended Daily Allowance.

5 Ingredients are listed in descending order: in other words, the ingredient with the most volume is listed first, and the ingredient with the least volume is listed last. For the sample label, the Campbell's Cream of Mushroom Soup contains more water than anything else. On some labels, additives such as flavoring or coloring are listed by their chemical names; on other labels, they are listed simply as "added color" or "added flavor."

6 Labels give directions for use; most directions also include valuable storage information (such as, in this case, "Promptly refrigerate unused portions").

7 Some labels contain guarantee information if the manufacturer decides to guarantee satisfaction. This information is valuable if you are dissatisfied and need to file a claim—in the case that you might find a contaminant in a canned product, for example.

8 Labels also contain the place of origin of the product. This can of Campbell's soup, for instance, originated in Camden, New Jersey.

9 Some labels provide extra information on product use, such as ways you can use the product. This label contains a recipe for perfect tuna that can be made using the soup; some cereal boxes, for example, contain information about how you can send the cereal boxtop with a small amount of money for products such as flashlights or camping gear. Still other labels list ideas for creative ways to serve the product—"for variety, serve topped with bacon bits and chopped peppers," for example.

If you're in doubt about a certain product, check the label—you can determine what's in the product, what kind of freshness guarantee you'll have if you purchase it, and what kind of nutritional benefits you'll be getting.

Pay extra attention to the labels of products that contain meat, such as stew, or meat products, such as corned beef. By law in the United States, a product that contains *meat* can also contain natural amounts of fat. Products that are labeled *All Meat* cannot contain any type of extender, such as cereal. A product that is labeled *All Beef* can contain only beef—no other type of meat. Keep your eye out for the word "flavored," too—"Chicken-flavored soup" is soup that has been flavored to taste like chicken, while "chicken soup" contains actual chicken pieces or broth.

Y ou've retrieved the frying pan from the kitchen cupboard, you have the bounties of the grocery store spread out in front of you, and you're ready to start whipping up something delicious.

Hold on!

Between now and then, there are plenty of things you'll need to do; and measuring and mixing are just the beginning.

Measurements: Key to Success

Maybe you've seen a practiced cook at work, pinching a bit of salt, tossing in a handful of raisins, spooning in a little cream, dumping in a bunch of flour.

But that system doesn't work for most of us. One of the time-honored secrets to good cooking is accurate measuring—and, while it seems simple, measuring requires a real skill.

You'll need three basic tools: 1) a set of measuring spoons, 2) a set of nested measuring cups, and 3) a liquid measuring cup (the kind with a small spout for pouring). Use the following methods for measuring:

Salt, spices, baking powder, or baking soda. Fill the measuring spoon to overflowing, and then level the spoon off using the edge of a knife.

Flour or powdered sugar. Spoon the flour lightly into the measuring cup until it's overflowing; use the edge of a knife to carefully level the cup (make sure you don't pack the flour in or shake the cup as you level it off). As you empty the cup, tap it lightly to get all the flour out. If the recipe calls for *sifted* flour, sift the flour onto a plate or a square of waxed paper before you spoon it into the measuring cup.

Brown sugar. Spoon the brown sugar into the measuring cup, and pack it down tightly with the back of the spoon. Keep packing the sugar into the cup until the sugar is level with the top of the cup.

Granulated sugar. Spoon the sugar into the measuring cup to overflowing, and level with the edge of a knife. If the sugar is lumpy, sift it before you measure it.

Milk, water, or other liquids. Set the liquid measuring cup on a level surface (your counter top works well), lower your head so you're at eye level with the cup, and slowly pour the liquid into the measuring cup until it reaches the appropriate level.

Shortening. Measuring shortening can leave you with a sticky mess if you don't do it properly! Try one of these methods for easy measuring and quick cleanup:

1. Pack the shortening into the appropriate-sized measuring cup, and scrape off the excess with a spatula or the edge of a knife. Submerge the bottom of the measuring cup in hot water for a minute—the shortening will slide right out!

2. If the recipe calls for less than a cup of shortening, use the liquid measuring cup. Subtract the amount of shortening called for,

---

A Chicken in Every Pot

Want to put a chicken in *your* pot?

Then you'd better have a pot on hand—not to mention a few other basics!

Use the following checklist to guarantee that you're ready for that chicken—and anything else that might come along!

Food Staples

baking powder	ginger
baking soda	mayonnaise or
basil	salad dressing
bay leaves	nutmeg
bouillon cubes	oregano
brown sugar	paprika
butter or	pepper
margarine	powdered sugar
catsup	salt
cinnamon	sugar
cloves	shortening
cooking oil	vanilla
corn syrup	yeast
cornstarch	
flour	

Cooking Equipment

can opener	mixing/serving
frying pan	spoon
with lid	pancake turner
measuring cups	paring knife
measuring	saucepan with lid
spoons	baking/casserole
mixing/serving	dish
bowl	

and fill the rest of the cup with cold water; for example, if you need ¼ cup of shortening, fill the one-cup measuring cup with ¾ cup of cold water. Then drop in small spoonfuls of shortening until the water level reaches the 1-cup mark; the shortening will simply float, and you can easily spoon it back out!

But measuring isn't always that simple. You might run across a recipe that calls for a "pound" of flour—do you break out the bathroom scale? Or how do you figure out how much cheese to buy if a recipe calls for 3 cups grated? Even worse, how many eggs make 1 cup?

Use the following chart to determine measurements:

The Recipe Calls For:	You'll Need:
½ cup butter	1 stick, or ¼ pound
1 ounce butter	2 tablespoons
1 pound butter	4 sticks
1 ounce baking chocolate	1 square or 3½ tablespoons
1 pound brown sugar	2¼ cups, packed
1 pound powdered sugar	3½ cups, sifted
1 pound granulated sugar	2 cups
1 pound white flour	4 cups
1 pound whole wheat flour	4½ cups
3 cups cooked rice	1 cup uncooked
2 cups cooked spaghetti	1 cup uncooked, or 4 ounces
2 cups cooked noodles or macaroni	1 cup uncooked, or 4 ounces
1 cup bread crumbs	2 slices of bread
1 cup of cracker crumbs	12 graham crackers, 20 saltine crackers, 23 vanilla wafers
2 cups grated cheese	½ pound
1 cup chopped nuts	¼ pound
1 cup chopped celery	2 medium stalks
1 cup chopped onion	2 medium onions

1 cup chopped apple	1 medium apple
3 tablespoons lemon juice	1 lemon
8 tablespoons orange juice	1 orange
1 teaspoon grated lemon peel	1 lemon
2 teaspoons grated orange peel	1 orange
1 cup egg yolks	14 eggs
1 cup egg whites	10 eggs
1 pound hamburger or ground meat	2 cups

Substitutions

After rifling frantically through your kitchen cupboards, you're ready to wave the white flag of surrender: you just don't have all the ingredients you need to make that batch of cookies!

Don't give up! Countless simple ingredients can work double-time, giving you great versatility. Next time you can't scare up any cornstarch or baking chocolate, scan this chart for a handy substitute.

When the Recipe Calls For:	You Can Use This Instead:
Dairy Products	
½ cup butter	½ cup shortening plus ¼ teaspoon salt
1 cup whipping cream	⅓ cup butter plus ¾ cup milk
½ cup buttermilk	½ cup milk plus 1½ teaspoons vinegar
½ cup sour milk	½ cup milk plus 1½ teaspoons lemon juice
1 cup whipped cream	1 egg white whipped with 1 sliced banana (the banana dissolves)
1 cup whole milk	1 cup water, 4 tablespoons nonfat instant milk, and 2 teaspoons melted butter; or ½ cup water and ½ cup evaporated milk

1 cup skim milk	1 cup water with 4 tablespoons nonfat instant milk
½ cup honey butter	2 tablespoons butter or margarine with ¼ cup honey
½ cup sour cream	½ cup plain (unflavored) yogurt

Baking Ingredients

1 teaspoon baking powder	½ teaspoon cream of tartar with ¼ teaspoon baking soda
1 tablespoon flour (for thickening)	2 egg yolks; ½ tablespoon cornstarch; or 2 teaspoons tapioca (quick-cooking)
1 teaspoon double-acting baking powder	1½ teaspoons regular baking powder
1 cup cake flour	1 cup regular flour, sifted twice, minus 2 tablespoons
1 cup flour, for baking bread	½ cup flour plus ½ cup cornmeal, bran, or whole wheat flour

Add a Little Spice

That pungent pinch of cinnamon in the corner of your cupboard has an impressive past: spices were once considered as valuable as gold and precious jewels. Wars were fought—and kingdoms conquered—over the likes of your nutmeg and paprika.

Spices make the difference between bland boredom and exciting eating. There's virtually no limit to the way you can use them (ever tried cinnamon on your ham? paprika in a hamburger?), so follow these tips on buying, storing, and using a variety of fragrant spices.

- Save money by purchasing spices in plain containers—you usually pay more for fancy packaging.

- Buy spices in small containers and replace them frequently—the aromatic oils evaporate, and they lose their flavor.

- Store spices in airtight jars or cans; if you buy them in cardboard containers, switch.

- Store spices in a cool, dark, dry place.

- Go easy on using spices: the flavor should be extremely subtle.

- Timing is essential! Add whole spices as you begin soups and stews; mix spices in early when fixing uncooked foods, such as juices, salad dressings, and salads. Add ground herbs, spices, and seeds just before you finish cooking—prolonged heat destroys their flavor and aroma.

1 package dry yeast	2 teaspoons dry yeast or 1 cake compressed yeast
1 square unsweetened chocolate	3 tablespoons cocoa with 1 tablespoon butter or margarine
½ cup molasses	½ cup honey
1 cup tomato juice	½ cup tomato sauce with ½ cup water
1 cup wine	1 cup apple juice
1 cup beer	1 cup water
1 cup orange liquer	1 cup orange juice
1 large marshmallow	10 miniature marshmallows
½ cup honey	⅝ cup sugar with ⅛ cup water
1 cup canned bouillon	1 cup boiling water with 1 bouillon cube
½ cup graham cracker crumbs	½ cup saltine cracker crumbs
1 can cream of celery soup	1 can cream of mushroom or cream of chicken soup

Seasonings

½ cup catsup for cooking	½ cup tomato sauce, 1 tablespoon vinegar, and ¼ cup sugar
1 teaspoon dry mustard	1 teaspoon prepared mustard
1 cup chopped onion	⅓ cup dehydrated onions
1 teaspoon instant onion	4 tablespoons chopped fresh onion
1 tablespoon fresh parsley	1 tablespoon parsley flakes

Eggs

1 egg	2 egg yolks with 1 tablespoon water
2 egg whites	1 egg white with 1 tablespoon ice water

1 egg	1 teaspoon unflavored gelatin mixed with 3 tablespoons cold water and 2 tablespoons plus 1 teaspoon boiling water

Fruits

mandarin oranges	pineapple tidbits
8 ounces of canned grapefruit sections	1 medium fresh grapefruit

Vegetables

½ pound fresh mushrooms	1 4-ounce can mushrooms
10-ounce package frozen peas	8-ounce can peas
8-ounce can whole tomatoes	8-ounce can stewed tomatoes

When Even Your Water is Dirty

If you're in an underdeveloped country, or have been the victim of a natural disaster, you may have reason to doubt the purity of your water. You can use one of three easy methods listed below to make sure your water is safe for drinking and cooking:

Boiling. Boil the water vigorously for a full three minutes; boiling will destroy bacteria, but will not remove radioactivity.

Iodine. Use 3 drops of household iodine (2% tincture) in each quart of water, and 12 drops in each gallon; double the amount of iodine if the water is cloudy.

Bleach. Use chlorine bleach that contains 5.25% sodium hypochlorite; use 2 drops per quart, 8 drops per gallon, and ½ teaspoon per five gallons of water. Double the amount of bleach you use if the water is cloudy. Thoroughly mix in the bleach and let the water stand for five minutes; check to see if you can taste or smell the chlorine—a sign of safety. If you can't, mix in another dose, and let the water stand for fifteen minutes. Don't use the water until you can taste or smell the chlorine.

45

Miscellaneous

1 can chow mein noodles	1 can potato shoestrings; or 3 cups cooked rice
1 cup hominy	1 cup cooked rice
1 cup cooked rice	1 cup cooked macaroni or noodles
1 cup seasoned bread crumbs	1 cup regular bread crumbs with 1 teaspoon pepper; or 3 slices of bread (cubed) with 1 teaspoon pepper
½ cup pecans, chopped	½ cup walnuts or almonds, chopped
1 pound ground pork	1 pound ground beef
½ cup cubed ham	½ cup chopped luncheon meat
8-ounce can chili beans	8-ounce can kidney beans with 2 teaspoons chili powder

Cooking Terms

Every recipe has one thing in common: following the list of necessary ingredients are the instructions—brief, sometimes abbreviated, orders on how to put the ingredients together and emerge with a steamy pot of soup, a crusty loaf of bread, a chewy batch of cookies.

Most terms are self-explanatory. Many others are quite simple—once you're used to hearing them. The science of cooking has a jargon all its own, and the following definitions should help you wade through almost any recipe.

Bake. To cook, either covered or uncovered, in an oven.

Baste. To keep foods moist during cooking by pouring a liquid over them; you can use the meat drippings, melted fat, or any other liquid.

Beat. To make a mixture creamy, smooth, or filled with air b' whipping it in a brisk motion.

Blanch. To precook a food briefly in boiling liquid, usually to loosen the skin; for example, you can drop tomatoes in boiling liquid for less than a minute, and the skin comes off easily.

Blend. To stir two or more ingredients together until they are smooth and uniform throughout.

Boil. To cook at a boiling temperature—212° F at sea level. When boiling a liquid, you will see bubbles forming rapidly, rising continually and breaking when they reach the surface of the liquid. You can either boil liquid, or can boil some other food in a liquid.

Braise. To first brown meat quickly in fat and then cook it in a covered pan on top of the stove or in the oven; liquid may or may not be added.

Bread. To coat a raw food with bread crumbs; the bread crumbs are often mixed with a beaten egg, or the food is first dipped in the beaten egg and then coated with bread crumbs.

Broil. To cook a food by placing it on a rack that is placed directly under the source of heat or directly over an open fire. To *pan-broil* is to cook the food in a heavy pan on top of the stove; the pan is usually ungreased, and any grease from the food is poured off as it accumulates so the food won't start to fry.

Chill. To put food in the refrigerator until it is cold throughout.

Chop. To cut food in pieces about the size of small peas.

Cool. To remove a food from the source of heat and let it stand at room temperature until it reaches room temperature; food should not be put in the refrigerator to bring the temperature down more quickly.

Cream. To mix one or more foods together until they are creamy and soft.

Cut in. To use a knife or pastry blender to add shortening to dry ingredients; the shortening is actually cut into tiny pieces during the blending process.

Deciphering the Codes

It doesn't have to be Greek to you: the abbreviations used in most recipes are simple, once you learn the basics. The following abbreviations are used for the recipes in this book—and for most of the other recipes you'll use, too:

t., tsp.	teaspoon
T., Tbl.	tablespoon
C., c.	cup
pt.	pint
qt.	quart
spk.	speck
oz.	ounce
lb.	pound
min.	minute
hr.	hour

Dice. To cut food in small cubes all of the same size and shape.

Dredge. To coat raw meat with a dry mixture, usually flour or cornmeal and usually prior to frying.

Fold in. To gently add a new ingredient to an already-beaten mixture. The new ingredient is dumped on top of the mixture; with a large spoon, the new ingredient is brought down through the middle of the mixture, and the mixture is scraped off the bottom of the bowl and brought to the top. The procedure is often used to add blueberries or other fruit to biscuit or muffin batter.

Fricassee. To braise small, individual serving pieces of meat or poultry in a little broth, sauce, or water.

Fry. To cook food in hot fat; no water is added, and no cover is used. To *pan-fry*, food is cooked in a small amount of fat (a few tablespoons to half an inch) in a frying pan; to *deep-fry*, food is cooked in a large kettle that contains enough hot fat to cover the food or allow it to float.

Glaze. To cover a food with "glaze"—a mixture that hardens, adds flavor, and makes the food look glossy or shiny.

Grate. To cut food into fine particles, usually with the use of a grater.

Grill. To cook food on a rack directly under or over the source of heat.

Knead. To make a dough or dough-like substance smooth and elastic by folding, stretching, and pressing it continuously until it reaches the desired texture. (When fondant for candies is kneaded, it gets satiny instead of elastic.)

Marinate. To make foods more flavorful or tender by allowing them to stand in a liquid for several hours or overnight; the food is generally completely covered. Most marinades are a mixture of cooking oil and vinegar or lemon juice with a variety of spices added for flavor.

Mince. To chop food in very fine pieces.

Mix. To stir ingredients until they are very well blended.

Parboil. To cook a food in boiling liquid only until it is partly cooked.

Poach. To simmer in hot liquid slowly; poaching is a gentle process, and food should hold its shape.

Pot-roast. To brown a roast or other large piece of meat in fat quickly, and then cook it in a covered pan in the oven or on top of the stove; liquid is usually added to make the roast more tender.

Puree. To blend a cooked fruit or vegetable until it is smooth and uniform throughout.

Roast. To make a food in the oven, uncovered, without added liquid.

Saute. To cook a food quickly in melted butter until tender; onions are cooked until they are transparent.

One Box You Won't Want to be Without

That humble box of baking soda in your kitchen cupboard can become your best friend . . . well, almost!

Baking soda is the key to all kinds of baked goods—cakes, breads, cookies, biscuits—but did you know it can do all kinds of other things, too? Try using baking soda in some of these ways:

- Sprinkle it in your shoes to kill odor
- Mix a teaspoon of it in a glass of water when you take aspirin—and the aspirin won't upset your stomach
- Sprinkle it on your carpet and let it stand for half an hour before vacuuming to freshen your room
- Mix into a paste with water and use it to soothe bee stings, insect bites, and skin irritations
- Tuck a small bowl of baking soda in the corner of your refrigerator or freezer to eliminate odors
- Get your combs and brushes sparkling clean by soaking them in a mixture of warm water, a few drops of shampoo, and a dash of baking soda
- Mix it with water and use the paste to scrub your fingernails
- Use it to extinguish kitchen fires (especially those involving grease)
- Swirl it through warm water and soak your feet at the end of the day
- Half a cup of baking soda dissolved in a quart of water will clean your car's battery cables; use the leftovers to polish your windshield, headlights, and chrome
- Dump a handful in the washing machine to keep whites sparkling
- Combine it with salt and use as a toothpaste
- Use it in water to clean and deodorize dish drainers, silverware, Teflon-coated pans, tile surfaces, Thermos jugs, lunch boxes, plastic dishes, enamel surfaces, and plastic tablecloths or place mats

Scald. To heat liquid to just below the boiling point.

Scallop. To cook a food in a sauce; many scalloped foods are cooked in a cheese or a cream sauce and topped with browned crumbs.

Sear. To brown meat rapidly by using extremely high heat.

Shred. To cut food in narrow, long, small pieces, usually with a grater.

Simmer. To cook a food in hot liquid just below the boiling point (usually above 185° F but below 210° F); bubbles form slowly, but they break before they reach the liquid's surface.

Soft peaks. To beat egg whites or cream until the peaks hold their shape, but droop slightly.

Steam. To cook a food in steam; food is usually put on a rack or in a perforated pan, and placed in a covered container that has a small amount of boiling water in the bottom. In some cases, the food is cooked in a container that creates pressure (called a "pressure cooker").

Steep. To simmer a food in liquid just below the boiling point over an extended period of time so that the flavor or other element is extracted into the water.

Stew. To simmer slowly in a small amount of liquid, usually for several hours.

Stiff peaks. To beat egg whites or cream until it is moist and glossy and the peaks stand up straight without drooping.

Stir. To use a spoon to thoroughly combine two or more ingredients.

Toss. To mix lightly and gently, usually with a slight lifting motion.

Whip. To beat a food rapidly so you add air to it.

RECIPES FOR THINGS YOU CAN'T EAT

Think of recipes and cooking, and you think of delectable delights: creamy cheesecakes, nutty brownies, cheesy casseroles. But there's an exciting way to use some unusual recipes that can save you money, too: you can brew up your own furniture polish, window cleaner, and drain cleaner, to name a few!

Try some of these:

Window Cleaner
Mix in a quart bottle:
½ C. rubbing alcohol
1½ t. ammonia
1½ t. liquid dish soap

Fill the quart bottle to the top with water and shake vigorously. Pour the mixture into a squirt bottle; use it to clean windows, mirrors, and porcelain.

Ant Killer
1 C. molasses
2 packages dry yeast
½ C. sugar

Mix into a paste. Coat one side of small squares of cardboard, and put them where the ants are. When the paste gets dry, replace it with fresh paste; continue until the ants are gone.

Furniture Polish
2 C. mineral oil
6 drops lemon extract, if desired

Put the mineral oil in a spray bottle; if you want a scented polish, add the lemon extract and shake well. Spray a small amount of furniture, and polish with a soft, clean cloth.

Outdoor Window Cleaner
½ gal. warm water
2-3 T. laundry or dishwasher detergent
1 T. liquid "Jet Dry" or other dishwasher wetting agent

Mix ingredients. Brush or sponge on window. Immediately hose off. Water will sheet off, no drying necessary. Caution: Be sure windows are tightly closed.

General Household Cleaner
1 T. ammonia
1 T. liquid detergent
2 C. water

Mix together and use for general cleaning. Put in a spray bottle for touch-ups, if desired.

Wall Cleaner

1 gal. hot water
1 C. ammonia
½ C. vinegar
¼ C. washing soda

Mix ingredients. Wash small area at a time. Wipe each area with a second cloth wrung out of clean warm water. This mixture cleans badly soiled painted surfaces. Moisture can be drying to the skin, so wear rubber gloves.

Carpet Cleaner

1 t. mild detergent
1 t. white vinegar
1 quart warm water

Mix ingredients. Apply with a clean cloth, using only amount of cleaning solution you need. Be careful not to soak the carpet through and always absorb excess liquid with a clean rag.

Dusting Cloths

1 T. mild soap powder
1 quart warm water
1 T. ammonia
2 T. boiled linseed oil or a good furniture polish

Mix ingredients well. Dip soft, cotton cloth into solution. After a few minutes squeeze out, dry and store in covered glass, plastic or tin container. Treat cloths after each washing.

Furniture Beauty Treatment

3 T. boiled linseed oil (buy it as such)
1 T. turpentine
1 quart hot water

Mix ingredients in two-quart pan or top of old double boiler. Place over hot water until mixture is as warm as a gloved hand can stand. (For best results, keep solution hot while it is being used.)

Dip a soft, clean cloth into the solution. Lift out and squeeze until it does not drip. Go over area about 1 to 2 feet at a time, redipping cloth as needed until area is clean.

Follow immediately with a clean, dry, absorbent cloth until all oil is removed. Linseed oil allowed to remain on wood will become tacky. Continue until piece is done.

This solution is excellent to clean the wood and to protect the finish.

Septic Tank Recharger

If you're in a rural area, chances are you have a septic tank—and septic tanks depend on the action of bacteria to break down solids and purify the resulting liquids. You can prevent sludge buildup and keep the bacteria working right by using this formula once a month.

2 C. brown sugar, packed
1 package dry yeast
1 quart water

Mix thoroughly, pour into the toilet bowl, and flush.

We'd Like to Propose a Roast!

On a tight grocery budget, roast—beef, lamb, veal, and pork—may be overlooked entirely. But we're asking you to look again!

A roast represents a big initial expense—but it's economical when you consider the number of meals it can play a starring role in. Use it the first time to accompany potatoes and vegetables—and use the leftovers in soup, stew, tacos, casseroles, sandwiches, or a crispy chef's salad.

To figure out cooking time, set your oven at 325° and use the following chart:

Meat	Weight	Minutes per Pound
Beef	3–6 lbs.	30–35
boned or rolled	3–6 lbs.	40–45
Pork loin	3–6 lbs.	30–35
Pork shoulder	5–8 lbs.	35
Pork shoulder, butt	3–6 lbs.	40–50
Ham	10 lbs. or less	20–22
Half hams	all weights	22–25
Shoulder or picnic ham	5–8 lbs.	30–35
Veal loin	4–6 lbs.	35
Lamb shoulder	4–6 lbs.	35
Leg of lamb	5–8 lbs.	35

Drain Cleaner

½ C. salt
½ C. baking soda
2 T. cream of tartar

Mix dry ingredients in a bowl, and store, covered. To use, spoon ¼ C. of the mixture into a drain, and slowly pour 1 C. cool water in the drain; the mixture will bubble. When bubbling has stopped, run water down the drain. Use the mixture once a month to keep your drains clear and clean.

MAKING LIFE EASIER

Learning how to cook is only one way of saving time and energy—once you do it the right way, cooking can be fast and simple. There are plenty of other things you can do, too, to simplify those necessary tasks so you'll have time for the more important things in life!

Kitchen Hints

• Keep a box of baking soda or a carton of salt near the stove; both can be used to extinguish kitchen fires.
• If you don't have hot water to rinse your dishes with, dip the dishes in a solution of a gallon of cold water and ¼ cup of liquid bleach; wipe the dishes thoroughly with a clean towel, and store in a clean, dry place.
• To make defrosting the freezer a breeze, wipe the inside with a clean towel; put a small amount of shortening on a paper napkin, and wipe the metal with it. Next time the ice builds up, it will fall off with ease!

Cleaning Hints

• To clean the glass of an oven door, sprinkle baking soda on a damp cloth; use circular motions to wipe over the entire door, dissolving baked-on stains.
• If food boils over in the oven, sprinkle the spill generously with salt while the oven is still hot; once the oven has cooled, scrape up the spill with a pancake turner.
• Sprinkle newspaper with water before you empty your vacuum cleaner bag onto it; the dust won't scatter.

- To get mildew off paper, sprinkle cornstarch over the mildew, let it stand for at least 48 hours, and remove it with a soft brush.
- To keep newspaper clippings from turning yellow, spray them lightly with hairspray; use two or three coats, waiting for each coat to dry between applications.

Removing Odors

- To prevent fish from smelling while you cook it, squeeze lemon juice on all surfaces and let stand in the refrigerator for an hour before cooking.
- To eliminate bathroom odors, strike a match.
- Wipe fresh lemon juice on your hands to take away the smell of onions.
- To get rid of onion or fish smell on your hands, rub your hands with a stalk of celery.
- When cooking cabbage or sauerkraut, put half a cup of vinegar on the stove near the pot or add a small chunk of red pepper to the pot—it will absorb odor, but won't affect flavor.
- Keep a small bowl of baking soda in the refrigerator and the freezer to eliminate strong odors.
- To get musty odors out of your suitcases, wipe the inside with a mixture of baking soda and water and let the suitcase dry in the sun; put a few drops of cinnamon oil on a cotton ball and tuck it inside.
- To remove food odor from a lunch box, wipe the inside out with baking soda and water, and let the box dry in the sun.
- To get rid of onion odor on utensils and knives, rub them with either raw potato or celery.
- To freshen the air, try one of the following:

  1. Sprinkle a few tablespoons of cinnamon or nutmeg in an old aluminum TV dinner tray or pie plate, and heat it on the stove until the spice is completely burned up.

  2. Put a few whole cloves on a piece of orange peel in a tin or aluminum pan; burn until it is ashy.

  3. Dab your vacuum cleaner bag with cologne; as you vacuum, the scent will subtly fill the house.

- To get rid of body odor that didn't disappear during laundering, soak the clothing in a mixture of one cup of salt in a gallon of water for at least an hour; repeat the laundering.

Cooking Hints

- When you use flour to thicken food, sprinkle the flour with salt first, and it won't turn lumpy.
- If you find out your roast isn't done all the way through, slice it, arrange the pieces on an oven-proof plate, and return the pieces to the oven for ten to fifteen minutes.
- Lighten and sweeten your leftover pancake batter with a half teaspoon of baking soda and enough ginger ale to make the batter the right consistency.
- Use instant mashed potato flakes to thicken soup or stew.
- To dissolve Jello in boiling water, shake it in a jar—it's quicker, and there's no mess.
- To double the volume of whipped cream, add one egg white to one cup of whipping cream; whip as usual.
- To absorb the grease in soup or stew, stir in a little baking soda, or drop in a clean leaf of lettuce; remove the lettuce when the cooking is finished.
- If you're going to use raisins in baking, toss them in a paper bag with some flour and shake to coat: they won't sink to the bottom of the dough or batter during baking.
- You'll like cheese better if you let it stand at room temperature for an hour before you eat it.
- If your soup or stew is too salty, add equal amounts of sugar and vinegar, or add chunks of raw potato; remove the potato before you serve the soup or stew, since it will have absorbed the salt.
- As soon as you take your cake out of the oven, put the pan on a wet towel—the cake won't stick to the pan.
- When you melt chocolate, grease the pan you're melting it in first.
- If you bake bread, put a small dish of water in the oven while the bread is baking: it keeps the crust soft.
- If you need pieces of marshmallows, rub a little butter on a pair of scissors and cut the marshmallows into the desired shapes or sizes.
- When you wash spinach, beet greens, lettuce, or other greens, put a small handful of salt in the water to remove grit; be sure you rinse the greens thoroughly and well with clear water afterward.
- To cut down baking time for meatloaf, bake it in muffin tins.
- Add a teaspoon of sugar to the water when you cook vegetables—it brings out their natural flavors.

- To salvage soggy potato chips, crackers, or cereal, spread them on a cookie sheet and bake in a 250° oven for three to five minutes.
- To cook spaghetti or other noodles a day ahead of time, undercook it slightly, drain it, and rinse it in cold water; cover it with cold water and keep it in the refrigerator. At serving time, drain it and cover it with salted boiling water; when it's heated through, drain and serve.
- Cheese grates more easily when it's chilled.
- Meat slices more easily when it's partially frozen.
- When you cook cauliflower, add a little milk to the water—it keeps the vegetable sparkling white.
- To rebake a leftover baked potato, dip it in water and bake in a 350° oven for 15 to 20 minutes.
- To speed up baking time, soak potatoes in salt water for 30 minutes before baking them.

To Whip Cream

Whipping cream expands to twice its volume when air is beaten into it. Before beating the cream the beaters, bowl, and cream should be chilled in order to obtain the best results.

Beat the cream on medium speed with an electric mixer or you can use a hand mixer that is commonly known as an "egg beater." Watch very carefully and whip only to the point where it is in soft peaks and will fall easily from a spoon. If beaten too long it will gather and turn into butter.

To sweeten the cream, add 1 to 2 teaspoons confectioner's sugar (or granulated sugar). Powdered sugar makes the cream smooth and helps it to thicken and hold its shape. If desired, ½ to 1 teaspoon vanilla may be added.

A couple of substitutes for whipping cream are:

- Use 1 can evaporated milk (any size; if you use a 13 oz. can of milk, add 3 tablespoons lemon juice). Canned milk must be thoroughly chilled, even to being partially frozen before whipping. This will whip to about 3 times its volume.

- Or use ½ cup powdered non-fat dry milk with ⅓ cup water. Mix and chill, then whip until mixture stands in soft peaks. Then add 1 tablespoon lemon juice. Whip again, then carefully beat in 2 to 4 tablespoons sugar.

- To make your broiled chicken crispy, rub mayonnaise over the skin before broiling.
- To get whipping cream to whip better, chill the bowl and beaters, and add a dash of unflavored gelatin or three drops of lemon juice to the cream before whipping.
- To reheat biscuits, put them in a brown paper sack; twist it closed; sprinkle it generously with water; and put it in a 300° oven for five minutes.
- To keep hard-boiled eggs from cracking while you cook them, wet the shells with cold water first; submerge them in the cold water and let them heat slowly; and put a spoonful of salt in the water. If the shell does crack, add vinegar to the water as the egg cooks—it helps seal the crack.
- To store egg yolks, cover them with cold water and a spoonful of salad oil; store in the refrigerator.
- Place a roll of paper towels in the front of a drawer. To use, open the drawer slightly and let the towel hang out so it can be torn off.
- To bake potatoes in half the time, cut in half and place cut side down on lightly-greased baking sheet. Bake 35 minutes at 425° F.
- Nut bread is easier to slice when it's partially frozen.
- Meat loaf is easier to slice if you wait ten minutes after taking it out of the oven.
- To make juicy hamburgers, put a chip of ice in the middle of the hamburger patty as you start to grill it.
- To keep roast beef from drying out when you reheat it, simmer it in broth in a saucepan instead of heating it in the oven.

CUTTING ENERGY COSTS

Utility bills really add up in a hurry—especially during hot and cold weather. You can cut costs—and conserve energy, too—by following some simple guidelines.

Laundry

- Wait to do laundry until you have a full load.
- Try to buy clothing that is permanent-pressed or wrinkle-free; remove it from the dryer promptly and hang it up.
- When you can, hang things to dry.
- Avoid over-drying your clothes.

Cooking

- Choose a burner that's the right size for your pan, and use a lid when cooking.
- Avoid the temptation to keep opening the oven door during baking.
- If you can, bake more than one item in the oven at the same time.
- Make sure foods are completely thawed before you try to cook them.

Air Conditioning

- Keep curtains or window shades pulled during the part of the day when the sun shines directly in the windows.
- Dress in light-colored clothing when you can.
- Keep your thermostat set as high as you possibly can—78° to 80° is a good guideline.

Heating

- Open curtains and window shades during the part of the day when the sun shines directly in the windows.
- Wear warmer clothing, and layer your clothing if you can—several layers of light clothing are warmer than one layer of heavy clothing.
- Check to make sure nothing is blocking your heat registers—move furniture and other objects away so the registers are free and clear.
- Lower your thermostat to 60° while you are out during the day.
- Keep your thermostat low at night—60° or lower will help save significantly on your heat bill.
- If you have a fireplace, make sure the damper is closed when not in use.
- Close off any rooms you may not be using.

Water Heater

- Check and repair any leaking faucets.
- When shaving or washing your face, fill the basin with hot water instead of letting the hot water run.

- Learn to take shorter showers; you might even turn the water off while you lather, and turn it on again to rinse off—you can save more than half the hot water that way!
- When taking a bath, don't fill the tub all the way.
- If you do laundry at home, rinse all loads in cold water.

Refrigerator/Freezer

- Avoid overloading your refrigerator and freezer.
- Let hot foods cool down partially before putting them in the refrigerator.
- Avoid holding the door open unnecessarily: decide what you want to get *before* you open the door.
- Keep your refrigerator and freezer clean and organized so food will be easy to find and leftovers won't be overlooked and spoiled.
- Keep the freezer defrosted.

RECOVERING STOLEN GOODS

- Write your name, address, telephone number and bicycle serial number on a card or paper and roll into a tight roll. Take off the seat and drop roll into the frame of your bike. If bicycle is stolen, you can easily identify it.

A Liter by Any Other Name . . .

. . . is still the same! Confused by the switchover to metrics? Take heart: just as it took you a little bit of time to learn numbers and equations as a child, it will take you a little bit of time to learn the metric system—but, eventually, you'll be just as good at it!

Until that time, use this simple chart for your basic cooking needs. For cooking weights and measures, all you'll need to remember are *milliliters* (ml) and *liters:*

Weight or Measure	Metric Equivalent
8 ounces	240 ml
4 ounces	120 ml
2 ounces	60 ml
1 ounce	30 ml
1 gallon	3.8 liters
1 quart	.95 liters
1 pint	480 ml
1 cup	240 ml
¾ cup	180 ml
⅔ cup	160 ml
½ cup	120 ml
⅓ cup	80 ml
¼ cup	60 ml
1 tablespoon	15 ml
1 teaspoon	5 ml

All recipes yield 2-4 servings.

BREAKFASTS

Moist Oatmeal Pancakes

2 C. quick-cooking oatmeal	2 eggs, well beaten
1½ C. milk	dash of salt
½ C. granulated sugar	¼ t. cinnamon
1 t. baking powder	

Mix all ingredients; beat into thin batter. Cook on greased griddle until done. If batter is not thin enough to pour, add a little more milk.

Applesauce Roll Pancakes

2 eggs, well beaten	½ t. salt
½ C. milk	1 T. sugar
½ C. flour	1 C. applesauce

Heat applesauce in small saucepan; keep warm over low heat. Mix eggs and milk; add flour, salt, and sugar, and beat until smooth. Grease a small frying pan and heat until very hot. Pour a fourth of the batter into the pan; tip pan quickly until batter covers bottom of pan. Turn and brown slightly on other side. Remove from pan, spread with ¼ C. warm applesauce, and roll. Sprinkle with powdered sugar if desired.

Delicious Whole Wheat Pancakes

⅔ C. whole wheat flour	1 egg, well beaten
1½ t. baking powder	⅔ C. milk
4 t. granulated sugar	4 t. cooking oil
¼ t. salt	

Stir flour, baking powder, sugar, and salt together. Combine egg, milk, and oil, and stir into flour mixture. Pour batter onto hot ungreased griddle; turn when slightly browned.

Potato Pancakes

Ty these for a delicious dinner, too!

2 eggs
1 T. flour
½ t. salt
2 t. minced onion

dash nutmeg
2 potatoes, grated
4 slices bacon, cooked and crumbled
1 C. warm applesauce

Combine eggs, flour, salt, onion, nutmeg, and potatoes. Spoon ¼ C. of batter into hot greased griddle at a time; flatten and cook on both sides until lightly browned. Sprinkle with crumbled bacon and spoon warm applesauce over tops.

Norwegian Pancakes

⅓ C. sour cream
⅓ C. small-curd cottage cheese
2 eggs, well beaten
¼ C. sifted flour

1 t. granulated sugar
¼ t. salt
1 can sliced peaches, warmed

Combine sour cream and cottage cheese until well blended; stir in eggs, flour, sugar and salt. Pour batter onto hot, greased griddle; brown on both sides. Top each pancake with a spoonful of warm peaches. Serve immediately.

Deluxe Pancakes

¾ C. whole wheat flour
1½ t. baking powder
¼ t. salt
1 T. brown sugar
1 egg yolk

¾ C. milk
4 t. cooking oil
¼ C. chopped nuts
1 egg white, beaten until stiff

Combine ingredients in order listed, folding in egg white last.

Pour onto lightly greased hot griddle; brown on both sides. Serve with syrup or cream cheese.

German Pancake

You'll love this old favorite!

6 eggs   ¼ t. salt
1 C. milk   4 T. butter or margarine
1 C. flour

In a bowl, combine eggs, milk, flour, and salt; beat until fluffy and smooth. Put 2 T. butter in each of two pie pans; melt as oven preheats. Pour half of batter in each pan. Bake at 450°F for 20 minutes. Pancakes will puff up. Serve with syrup, warm jam, or warm fruit.

Classic Pancakes

2 eggs, well beaten   2 t. baking powder
½ C. milk   ½ t. salt
2 T. cooking oil   ½ t. sugar
¾ C. flour

Beat together eggs, milk, and oil. Sift together flour, baking powder, salt, and sugar. Stir into egg mixture until all ingredients are well blended. Cook on hot greased griddle. Serve with choice of toppings.

Swedish Pancakes

3 eggs   1 T. sugar
1¼ C. milk   ½ t. salt
¾ C. sifted flour

Combine ingredients, beat with wire whip or mixer on medium speed until thoroughly mixed. Cook as thin pancakes on a medium heat setting. Brown on both sides, roll or fold in quarters and serve with favorite topping.

Quick Waffles

½ C. butter or margarine

1 T. sugar

4 egg yolks

2 C. milk

2 C. flour

4 egg whites, stiffly beaten

4 t. baking powder

Melt butter; stir in the sugar and egg yolks. Beat well. Beat in milk and sifted flour; fold in egg whites and baking powder. Bake in a greased waffle iron. Store leftover waffles, wrapped in plastic wrap or foil, in refrigerator; reheat in toaster or in frying pan.

Cheese and Bacon Waffles

1 egg

1 C. milk

2 t. lemon juice

½ t. baking soda

1 C. sifted flour

1 t. baking powder

¼ t. salt

3 T. butter or margarine, softened

½ C. grated cheese

6 strips bacon, fried and crumbled

Beat egg well; beat in milk and lemon juice. Sift together baking soda, flour, baking powder, and salt; stir into egg-milk mixture. Fold in softened butter, grated cheese, and crumbled bacon. Bake in greased waffle iron.

Nutty Whole Wheat Waffles

1 C. whole wheat flour

1½ t. baking powder

½ t. salt

3 egg yolks

1 C. milk

3 T. butter or margarine, melted

3 egg whites, stiffly beaten

½ C. chopped nuts

Sift together flour, baking powder, and salt. In separate bowl, beat together egg yolks, milk, and melted butter. Pour into dry ingredients. Fold in egg whites and nuts, stirring just enough to combine ingredients. Cook on greased waffle iron.

Best-Ever Easy Waffles

1 C. flour	1 C. milk
1 t. baking powder	2 t. lemon juice or vinegar
¼ t. salt	1 egg, beaten
¼ t. baking soda	2 T. butter or margarine, melted

Sift together flour, baking powder, salt, and baking soda; stir in milk, lemon juice or vinegar, and melted butter. Stir in beaten egg. Cook on greased waffle iron.

Southern Cornmeal Waffles

¾ C. yellow cornmeal	1 t. granulated sugar
⅛ C. flour	1 egg, beaten
¼ t. salt	1 C. milk
¼ t. baking soda	2 t. lemon juice
½ t. baking powder	¼ C. cooking oil

Sift together cornmeal, flour, salt, baking soda, baking powder, and sugar; stir in egg, milk, lemon juice, and cooking oil. Cook on greased waffle iron.

Gingerbread Waffles

¼ C. butter or margarine	1½ t. cinnamon
½ C. brown sugar, packed	1 t. ginger
½ C. light molasses	¼ t. allspice
2 eggs, well beaten	½ t. salt
1 C. milk	2 bananas, sliced
2 C. sifted flour	½ C. whipping cream, whipped
1½ t. baking powder	

Cream butter, brown sugar, molasses, eggs, and milk. Sift together flour, baking powder, ginger, allspice, and salt; add to molasses mixture. Bake on greased waffle iron. Top with sliced bananas and whipped cream.

Peachy Rice Waffles

A delicious way to use leftover rice!

3 eggs

2 C. milk

4 t. lemon juice

6 T. cooking oil

2 C. sifted flour

½ t. salt

1 T. baking powder

1 T. sugar

½ t. baking soda

1 C. cooked rice

½ C. butter, softened

½ C. peach jam

Beat together eggs, milk, lemon juice, cooking oil; set aside. Sift together flour, salt, baking powder, sugar, baking soda; stir into egg mixture until well blended. Fold in cooked rice. Bake on greased waffle iron. Beat together softened butter and peach jam until smooth; spread on waffles.

Breakfast Apple Pie

1 egg, well beaten

4 T. cooking oil

1 C. milk

1½ C. biscuit mix

½ C. sugar

½ C. chopped nuts

2 large apples, cut into wedges

2 T. sugar

½ t. cinnamon

¼ t. nutmeg

2 T. butter or margarine

Beat together egg, oil, and milk; add biscuit mix, sugar, and nuts, beating well. Pour into greased 9-inch pie plate. Arrange apple wedges on top of pie; sprinkle with sugar, cinnamon, and nutmeg. Dot with butter. Bake at 375°F for 30 minutes. Serve hot.

Quick Cinnamon Toast

¼ C. butter or margarine,
softened

¼ C. brown sugar, packed

¼ t. nutmeg

1 t. cinnamon

Beat all ingredients until fluffy. Refrigerate in a covered jar. Spread on hot toast or muffins.

Waffles with Creamed Chicken

2 eggs, well beaten
2 C. flour
4 t. baking powder
½ t. salt
2 C. milk
½ C. butter or margarine, melted
¼ C. butter or margarine
¼ C. flour

½ t. salt
¼ t. pepper
½ C. mushrooms
2 C. milk
2 C. cooked cubed chicken
½ C. green peppers
¼ C. minced onion
1 12-oz. can whole-kernel corn

Combine eggs, 2 C. flour, baking powder, milk, salt, and ½ C. melted butter; beat well. Bake on greased waffle iron. To make creamed chicken sauce, melt butter; stir in flour, salt, and pepper. Add mushrooms; beat in milk, and cook until thickened. Stir in chicken, green peppers, onion, and corn; simmer until vegetables are tender. Spoon over waffles.

Cinnamon Breakfast Cake

You can make this the night before.

1¼ C. flour
¼ C. granulated sugar
1 T. baking powder
¼ C. shortening
⅔ C. milk
1 egg

⅔ C. chopped nuts
4 T. flour
6 T. granulated sugar
3 T. butter or margarine, softened
1 t. cinnamon

Sift together flour, sugar, and baking powder; cut in shortening. Add milk and egg; mix only until ingredients are moistened. Fold in nuts. Pour into greased 8×8 square pan. Combine flour, sugar, butter, and cinnamon; sprinkle over batter. Cover with foil or plastic wrap and refrigerate until ready to serve. Bake at 400°F for 25 minutes.

Nutty Granola

4 C. quick-cooking oatmeal 1 C. cooking oil
1½ C. shredded coconut ½ C. water
1 C. sunflower seeds 2 t. vanilla
2 C. chopped walnuts

Combine all ingredients; bake on cookie sheets at 275°F for 2 hours, stirring often.

Apple Granola Crunch

1½ C. quick-cooking cereal 1 C. dried apples, chopped
1 C. coarsely chopped walnuts ½ C. brown sugar, packed
1 C. Grape Nuts cereal

Combine all ingredients; spread on a cookie sheet. Bake at 350°F for 10 minutes, stirring several times. Store in tightly covered container and serve as a cereal with milk.

Simple Granola

3½ C. quick-cooking oatmeal 1 T. vanilla
¼ C. cooking oil ½ C. raisins
¼ C. honey ½ C. chopped nuts

Combine all ingredients; spread on a cookie sheet and bake at 300°F for 10 minutes. Serve with milk and shredded coconut, if desired. Store in tightly covered container.

Fruited Grits

1¼ C. boiling water ½ t. cinnamon
1½ oz. instant-cooking grits ¼ t. nutmeg
½ C. raisins ¼ C. chopped nuts
1 T. sugar

Stir together grits, raisins, sugar, cinnamon, nutmeg, and nuts; pour boiling water over mixture. Serve warm with milk.

Four-Fruit Breakfast Cocktail

2 C. orange juice

2 bananas, sliced

1 flat can pineapple tidbits

1 orange, sectioned and diced

Pour orange juice over bananas, pineapple tidbits, and orange pieces. Stir to combine well. Serve in two bowls. Top with shredded coconut if desired.

Breakfast Cookies

⅓ C. butter or margarine

½ C. granulated sugar

1 egg, beaten

½ t. vanilla

½ C. flour

¼ t. baking soda

¼ t. salt

1½ C. quick-cooking oatmeal

½ C. cheese, grated

5 slices bacon, cooked and crumbled

Cream butter, sugar, egg, and vanilla. Sift together flour, baking soda, salt; stir into creamed mixture. Beat in oatmeal, cheese, and crumbled bacon. Bake on greased cookie sheet at 350°F for 7–10 minutes or until lightly browned.

Breakfast Sandwiches

A delicious way to use leftover waffles—and a quick breakfast idea!

8 cooked waffles, heated

¼ C. peanut butter

¼ C. strawberry jam

2 bananas, sliced

Spread 4 waffles with peanut butter; spread other 4 waffles with strawberry jam. Layer sliced bananas between each peanut butter and strawberry waffle. These sandwiches can be frozen—wrap in foil and heat before eating.

TOPPINGS FOR WAFFLES AND PANCAKES

Easy Maple Syrup

2 C. granulated sugar

1 C. water

½ t. mapeline

Combine sugar and water, and bring to a boil; remove from heat and stir in mapeline. Serve hot.

Rich Maple Syrup

1½ C. granulated sugar   ¼ t. mapeline

½ C. brown sugar, packed   ¼ t. vanilla extract

1 C. water

Combine sugars and water; bring to a boil. Remove from heat and stir in mapeline and vanilla. Serve hot.

Bubbly Apple Topping

¼ C. butter or margarine   ¼ C. chopped nuts

2 small apples, cored and sliced   ⅛ C. water

¼ C. brown sugar, packed

In small frying pan, melt butter. Add apples and cook, stirring occasionally, until tender. Stir in brown sugar, nuts, and water; heat through. Serve hot.

Banana-Orange Sauce

½ C. orange juice   1 large banana, sliced

¼ C. sugar   1 large orange, sectioned and

1½ t. cornstarch   chopped

Combine cold orange juice, sugar, and cornstarch; stir until cornstarch is completely dissolved. In small saucepan, bring mixture to a boil and simmer until thickened, stirring constantly. Stir in bananas and oranges; heat through. Serve hot.

Brown Sugar Syrup

1 C. brown sugar, packed   1 T. butter or margarine
½ C. water   ½ t. vanilla

Combine sugar and water; bring to a boil and boil for 2 minutes. Remove from heat and stir in butter and vanilla. Serve hot.

Cinnamon Syrup

½ C. light corn syrup   1 t. cinnamon
1 C. granulated sugar   ½ C. evaporated milk
¼ C. water

Combine corn syrup, sugar, water, and cinnamon; bring to a boil, stirring constantly. Cook for 2–3 minutes. Remove from heat and allow to cool for 5 minutes. Stir in milk. (Make sure you allow syrup to cool, or milk will curdle.) Serve warm.

Fruit and Whipped Cream Topping

Serve pancakes or waffles with sweetened whipped cream. Top with jam or sweetened fresh fruit or thawed frozen fruit.

Honey Maple Syrup

¾ C. granulated sugar   ¼ t. maple flavoring
½ C. light corn syrup   ⅛ C. honey
½ C. water   1 t. butter or margarine

Combine all ingredients in saucepan; cook, stirring occasionally, until butter is melted and sugar has dissolved. Serve warm or cold.

Pancake and Waffle Variations

Bored with the same old pancakes? Try some of these delicious variations:

1. Blend 3 T. peanut butter into the batter; top with sliced bananas.

2. Slice bananas on the uncooked side of the pancakes before you turn them over. Serve with whipped cream.

3. Sprinkle the pancakes with cinnamon and spoon applesauce over each cake.

4. Core and chop an apple; stir it into the pancake or waffle batter. Add ½ t. cinnamon to the batter, and top the pancakes with cinnamon syrup.

5. Wash and drain ½ C. blueberries; gently fold them into the batter.

6. Instead of using all flour, use half the amount of flour and half cornmeal. Fold in ½ C. whole-kernel corn and ½ C. grated potato.

New-Twist Apple Rings

1 C. biscuit mix	½ C. milk
1 egg	2 apples

Mix baking mix, egg and milk together until smooth. Grease griddle. Cut apples crosswise into ⅛-inch slices. Dip slices into batter and cook on hot griddle until golden brown. Turn once. Serve hot with syrup, jelly or powdered sugar.

Carmelized French Toast

4 slices bread	2 T. butter or margarine
3 eggs	½ C. brown sugar
¼ C. milk	¼ C. water
dash salt	

Melt 2 T. butter in fry pan. Beat eggs, milk, and salt together. Dip bread into egg mixture and fry until light brown and egg is cooked. Remove from pan. Add brown sugar. Stir until melted and sticky. Add water and stir. Place french toast in carmel sauce. Turn to coat, then remove from pan. Enjoy!

MOM'S OLD Standbys

_____

_____

_____

_____

_____

_____

_____

_____

_____

_____

_____

_____

_____

_____

_____

_____

_____

_____

_____

_____

_____

_____

_____

_____

EGGS

The Basics

Fried Eggs

To keep a fried egg tender, you must cook it quickly at moderate heat. In a skillet, melt 1–3 T. butter or margarine (more for a large skillet). Break the eggs, one at a time, onto a saucer and slip each egg into the skillet. Reduce the heat to low, and spoon the melted butter or margarine over the eggs periodically as they cook. Season with salt and pepper. A firmly cooked fried egg takes about 10 minutes.

Scrambled Eggs

Scrambled eggs should be cooked at a low heat with a minimum of stirring. For each serving, break two eggs into a bowl. Beat the eggs slightly with 3 T. milk and a dash of salt and pepper. Melt 2 T. butter or margarine over medium heat; pour in egg mixture. As egg begins to set in skillet, lift cooked portion with a spatula so that uncooked portion flows to the bottom. Continue process for three to five minutes, or until eggs are completely cooked. Stir slightly to break up eggs.

Soft-Cooked Eggs

Place desired number of eggs in a saucepan; cover with cold water. (Water should be at least 2 inches above eggs.) Bring the water rapidly to boiling. Cover pan and remove it from heat; let stand for 2 minutes. Fill pan with cold water and cool eggs for several seconds. To serve, break shell with a knife and scoop out egg.

Hard-Cooked Eggs

Place desired number of eggs in a saucepan; cover with water. (Water should be at least 2 inches above eggs.) Bring water rapidly to boiling; cover pan and remove it from heat. Let stand for 20 minutes. Cool eggs quickly by filling pan with cold water. To remove shells, drain water off eggs; shake eggs briskly back and forth in saucepan until shells are shattered. Remove shells under cold running water.

Poached Eggs

Fill a shallow pan or frying pan with about two inches of water. Heat water to boiling and reduce heat to low. One at a time, break eggs onto a saucer and slip each one gently into the simmering water. Cook eggs until firm, about 4–5 minutes. Remove with a spatula or slotted spoon; drain each egg on paper towels before serving. Serve on toast or a biscuit.

Baked Eggs

Lightly grease a small baking dish with butter or margarine. Heat oven to 325°F. Gently break eggs into the dish; sprinkle with salt and pepper. Bake for 15–20 minutes, or until of desired firmness.

Quick Quiche

3 slices bacon, cooked and crumbled	2 C. milk
1 C. grated cheese	½ C. biscuit baking mix
½ C. chopped onions	½ t. salt
4 eggs	dash pepper

Grease a pie plate or pan; sprinkle bacon, cheese, and onions over bottom. Beat eggs and milk together; add remaining ingredients, and beat until well mixed. Pour into pie plate and bake at 350°F for 50–55 minutes. (A knife inserted in the center of the quiche will come out clean when quiche is done.) Let stand 5–10 minutes before cutting and serving.

Corned Beef Eggs

½ of 12-oz. can corned beef	3 T. chili sauce
2 T. butter or margarine	4 slices toast
4 eggs	parmesan cheese

Flake corned beef and heat slowly in melted butter. Beat eggs with chili sauce; stir slowly into corned beef, cooking until soft but done. Spoon onto hot buttered toast; sprinkle with parmesan cheese.

Camel's Eye

1 slice bread   salt
½ T. butter or margarine   pepper
1 egg

Cut a round circle from the center of the bread; set aside. In small frying pan, melt butter; place bread in pan. Crack egg gently into center of bread; sprinkle with salt and pepper to taste. Cook over medium heat, turning over after five minutes, to desired doneness.

Classic Quiche Lorraine

1 9-inch pie shell, baked   1 C. milk
6 eggs, beaten   ½ t. salt
6 slices bacon, cooked and   dash pepper
   crumbled   dash nutmeg
1 C. shredded Swiss cheese

Sprinkle bacon and cheese in bottom of pie shell. Combine remaining ingredients and pour over bacon and cheese. Bake at 350°F for 35–40 minutes; knife inserted in center comes out clean. Let stand for 5–10 minutes before cutting and serving.

Chicken Quiche

1 9-inch pie shell   1½ C. milk
1 C. grated cheese   1 t. salt
1 C. chopped cooked chicken   dash pepper
6 eggs, beaten

Sprinkle cheese and chicken over bottom of pie shell. Combine remaining ingredients and pour over chicken. Bake at 350°F for 35–40 minutes. Let stand for 10 minutes before cutting and serving.

Vegetable Quiche

This is a fabulous way to use leftover veggies!

1 C. cooked vegetables
(any combination)

1 C. grated cheese

1 C. milk

6 eggs, beaten

3 T. minced onion

½ t. salt

dash pepper

Grease a pie plate or pan; sprinkle vegetables and cheese over bottom. Beat together remaining ingredients and pour over vegetables. Bake at 350°F for 35 minutes; knife inserted in center should come out clean. Let sit for 5 minutes before cutting and serving.

Poached Eggs in Mushroom Sauce

2 T. butter or margarine

1 can cream of mushroom
soup

¼ C. milk

2 T. unsweetened
apple juice

4 eggs

2 English muffins, split   and
buttered and toasted,   or 2
slices buttered toast

Melt butter in small skillet; add soup, milk, and apple juice, and heat to simmering. Break eggs, one at a time, onto saucer, and slide each one gently into simmering mushroom mixture. Cook 3–5 minutes, or until done. Spoon eggs onto muffins or toast and cover with sauce. Serve immediately.

Chicken Omelet

This makes an entire meal!

6 eggs

½ C. milk

½ t. salt

dash pepper

2 T. butter or margarine

1 can cream of chicken soup

2 T. chopped green pepper

2 T. minced onion

2 T. chopped ripe olives

Beat eggs with milk, salt, and pepper. Melt butter in large skillet; pour in egg mixture and cook over low heat. Lift edges of egg as it cooks to allow uncooked egg to flow underneath. When egg is cooked but still glossy, fold over half and serve with sauce. To make sauce, combine soup, green pepper, onion, and olives; heat through and pour over omelet.

South-of-the-Border Scrambled Eggs

2 T. butter or margarine	2 T. water
1 T. minced onion	½ t. salt
¼ t. garlic salt	dash pepper
½ C. chopped green pepper	4 eggs, beaten
1 small tomato, chopped and seeded	

Melt butter in frying pan; cook onion, garlic salt, green pepper, and tomato until vegetables are tender. Beat together eggs, water, salt and pepper; pour into frying pan with vegetables and cook over low heat, stirring occasionally. Serve with hot sauce if desired.

Creamed Ham and Eggs

Good any time of day!

2 T. butter or margarine	⅛ t. dry mustard
2 t. minced onion	1 C. milk
3 T. flour	3 hard-cooked eggs, sliced
1 t. salt	1 C. cooked ham, cubed
dash pepper	

Melt butter in frying pan; cook onion until golden. Stir in flour, salt, pepper, and mustard until a thick paste. Whip in milk; cook, stirring constantly, until thickened. Stir in eggs and ham; heat through. Serve over rice, noodles, or toast.

Spanish Omelet

2 t. cooking oil	12 green olives, chopped
2 t. butter or margarine	2 t. chopped parsley
¼ C. minced onion	¼ t. salt
½ C. chopped green pepper	4 eggs, beaten
1 medium tomato, chopped	

Heat oil and butter in skillet; add onions and cook until tender. Add green pepper and tomatoes and cook until green pepper is tender. Remove from pan and drain. Stir into eggs along with parsley, salt, and olives. If necessary, melt a little more butter in skillet; pour egg mixture into skillet and cook until firm, lifting edges to allow uncooked egg to flow underneath. When firm but still glossy, lift edges and fold over omelet.

Cheese Omelet

1 T. butter or margarine	dash pepper
3 eggs	1 T. milk
¼ t. salt	1½ C. grated cheese

Melt butter in skillet. Beat together eggs, salt, pepper, and milk until fluffy; pour into skillet and cook over medium heat. When eggs are done but still glossy, sprinkle cheese over omelet and fold in half. Serve immediately.

Oven Omelet

4 eggs	½ C. milk
½ C. grated cheese	1½ t. grated onion
¼ t. seasoned salt	½ pkg. thinly sliced corned beef
1 T. water	(3 oz.)

Beat eggs, milk and seasoned salt together. Tear corned beef into small pieces. Add to egg mixture. Stir in cheese and onion. Pour into greased baking dish. Bake at 325°F for 20 to 30 minutes or until eggs are set.

MOM'S OLD STANDBYS

_____

_____

_____

_____

_____

_____

_____

_____

_____

_____

_____

_____

_____

_____

_____

_____

_____

_____

_____

_____

_____

_____

_____

_____

_____

_____

SANDWICHES

Toasty Chicken Salad Sandwiches

½ C. cooked cubed chicken   ⅓ C. mayonnaise
½ C. celery slices   ¼ t. paprika
2 t. minced onion   2 slices bread
2 t. lemon juice   butter or margarine

Combine chicken, celery, onion, lemon juice, mayonnaise, and paprika. Spread butter on bread; top bread with a scoop of chicken salad and spread to cover bread. Bake on cookie sheet at 400°F for 12–15 minutes or until bubbly. Makes 2.

Pizza Sandwich

½ lb. ground beef   dash pepper
½ C. grated cheese   ⅓ C. tomato paste
3 T. minced onion   1 tomato, sliced thinly
3 T. chopped ripe olives   4 slices cheese
½ t. salt   4 slices French bread

Brown ground beef; add cheese, onion, olives, salt, and pepper, and cook until onion is tender and cheese is melted. Stir in tomato paste and heat through. Put a fourth of the meat mixture on each slice of bread; top with a slice of cheese and a slice of tomato. Bake on a cookie sheet at 425°F until cheese melts.

Creamed Tuna Sandwich

1 can cream of chicken soup   1 T. finely minced green pepper
1 6½-oz. can tuna, drained   4 slices toast
2 T. minced onion

Heat soup, tuna, onion, and green pepper; simmer for 7–10 minutes, or until onion and pepper are tender. Spoon over toast.

Western Egg Sandwich

¼ C. diced green pepper

¼ C. diced onion

2 T. butter or margarine

4 eggs, well beaten

2 T. milk

¼ t. salt

dash pepper

¼ C. diced cooked beef

4 large rolls, split and toasted

4 slices tomato

Saute green pepper and onion in butter until tender. Beat eggs with milk, salt, and pepper; add to peppers and onions and scramble until done. Stir in beef. Spread on rolls and top each with a slice of tomato.

Hoagie Sandwich

2 hoagie buns

¼ C. Thousand Island dressing

2 T. mustard

4 slices cheese

4 slices luncheon meat

1 small tomato, sliced thinly

1 small onion, sliced and separated into rings

1 dill pickle, sliced thinly

¼ head lettuce, torn into leaves

Split hoagie buns and spread with dressing and mustard. On each, layer cheese, meat, tomato, onion, pickle, and lettuce.

Cheese Puff Sandwich

2 slices bread

2 slices cheese

2 slices tomato

1 egg white, beaten until stiff

¼ C. mayonnaise

½ t. salt

dash pepper

Trim the crusts from the bread and toast on one side. On untoasted side, layer a slice of cheese and a slice of tomato. Fold mayonnaise, salt, and pepper into egg white; spoon a dollop on each tomato. Bake in a 350°F oven until puffy and brown. Serve hot.

Peanut Butter–Raisin Sandwiches

¼ C. raisins, finely chopped

½ C. peanut butter

Mix raisins and peanut butter well, until creamy. Spread on sandwiches.

French Hamwiches

2 T. butter or margarine, softened

2 t. mustard

4 slices bread

4 slices Swiss cheese

2 slices cooked ham

1 egg, well beaten

2 T. milk

½ C. applesauce, warmed

Spread each slice of bread with butter and mustard; place a slice of Swiss cheese on each. Use the bread to make two sandwiches; place a slice of ham between each two slices. Beat the egg and milk together; dip the sandwiches in the egg mixture. Brown sandwiches on both sides in a lightly buttered frying pan. Top each with a spoonful of warm applesauce.

Cheesy Devil Sandwich

2 slices French bread

1 4½-oz. can deviled ham

1 small tomato, sliced thinly

4 slices cheese

Spread each slice of French bread with deviled ham; top with sliced tomatoes and cheese. Put sandwiches under the broiler until cheese is bubbly. Serve hot.

Corned Beef and Coleslaw Sandwiches

4 T. mayonnaise

1 T. horseradish

2 t. mustard

½ t. salt

2 C. shredded cabbage

8 slices rye bread

8-oz. can corned beef, sliced thin

mayonnaise

Combine mayonnaise, horseradish, mustard, salt, and cabbage; mix well. Spread on 4 slices of bread. Spread other 4 slices with mayonnaise and top with sliced corned beef; pair with coleslaw slice to make 4 sandwiches.

Make-Ahead Cheese Sandwiches

You can whip these up in the morning for an easy lunch.

8 slices bread	1¼ C. milk
2 T. butter or margarine, softened	¼ t. salt
	dash pepper
4 slices cheese	
3 eggs	

Butter bread; place a slice of cheese on four slices of bread, and top with four slices to make sandwiches. Place sandwiches in a lightly buttered square pan. Beat together eggs, milk, salt, and pepper; pour over sandwiches, making sure each one is moistened. Cover and refrigerate for 2–4 hours. Bake, uncovered, at 350°F for 10–15 minutes or until golden.

Hot Salmon Sandwiches

½ C. mayonnaise	½ C. diced celery
¼ t. salt	1 C. cream of celery soup
dash pepper	¼ C. canned milk
½ C. canned milk	3 T. water
1½ C. salmon, drained and flaked	
3 T. chopped pickle	

In a bowl, combine mayonnaise, salt, pepper, canned milk, salmon, pickle, and celery. Spread on buns. Combine soup, milk, and water in a small saucepan; heat until bubbly. Pour over sandwiches.

Cheesy Tuna Burgers

1 6½-oz. can tuna	1 t. minced onion
3 T. mayonnaise	8 strips cheese
2 T. chopped pickle	4 hot dog buns

Combine tuna, mayonnaise, pickle, and onion; spread on hot dog buns. Top each bun with 2 strips cheese. Broil until bubbly.

Western Beans 'n' Franks Sandwich

4 hamburger buns	½ C. cubed cheese
4 frankfurters	2 T. barbecue sauce
2 T. butter or margarine	4 slices tomato
1 C. baked beans	4 slices onion

Cut frankfurters into pieces and fry in butter until curled. Layer on bun bottoms. Combine beans, cheese, and sauce; spoon over frankfurters. Heat in 350°F oven for 10–12 minutes, or until cheese melts. Top each with a slice of tomato and a slice of onion. Serve hot.

Egg Salad Sandwich Fillings

4 hard-cooked eggs, chopped
¼ cup chopped sweet pickles
¼ cup mayonnaise or salad dressing

*Variations that can be added to the above recipe include: chopped crisp bacon or ham, diced cooked chicken, meat, or fish; chopped pickle, minced onion or celery, diced green pepper, or sliced tomato.

Quick Toaster Cheese Sandwich

Take 1 slice of bread and lay on cutting board or cupboard. Cut the bread horizontally into 2 thinner slices. Place slices of favorite cheese between the 2 thinner slices and pop into toaster. Toast lightly and watch carefully that the cheese does not melt to the insides of the toaster. Easy and delicious.

Best-Ever Hamburgers

½ lb. ground beef	1½ t. soy sauce
1 T. minced onion	1 T. minced green pepper
2 T. mustard	

Combine all ingredients and form into patties. Fry until cooked all the way through on both sides. Garnish with tomato, onion, and relish.

Tuna Boats

½ C. cheese, grated
2 hard-cooked eggs, chopped
2 T. chopped celery
2 T. chopped green pepper

2 T. chopped pickle
⅓ C. mayonnaise
1 6½-oz. can tuna
4 hot dog buns

Combine cheese, eggs, celery, green pepper, pickle, mayonnaise, and tuna until well blended. Fill hot dog buns. Wrap each bun in foil. Bake at 300°F for 20 minutes.

Picnic Sandwiches

¼ lb. bologna, diced
1 hard-cooked egg, diced
2 t. diced pimento (optional)
¼ C. pickle relish

1 T. canned milk
2 T. mayonnaise
dash salt
dash pepper

Combine all ingredients; mix well and chill. Spread on crusty buns and garnish with lettuce if desired.

Barbecued Cheese Buns

1 C. grated cheese
2 hard-cooked eggs, chopped
¼ C. diced green pepper
¼ C. diced tomato
1 T. grated onion

¼ C. canned milk
2 T. catsup
½ t. salt
dash pepper

Combine all ingredients and spread on buns. Place on cookie sheets and bake at 400°F for 7 minutes or until hot and bubbly.

The Classic Tuna

1 6½-oz. can tuna, drained and flaked
¼ C. diced celery
1 T. minced onion
¼ C. mayonnaise
2 t. lemon juice

⅛ t. salt
dash paprika
dash pepper

84

Combine all ingredients and mix well. Makes enough for 4 sandwiches.

Carrying Lunch with You

Want to carry lunch with you? There are all kinds of things you can do to make lunchbox meals as delicious as the ones you eat at home:

- Make sure your lunchbox is well-balanced nutritionally. You should have a protein, vegetable (hail the carrot stick!), fruit, and dairy product along with your grain—good old bread.
- To keep your lunch cool, try including a small can of frozen apple juice. By the time you're ready to eat, the juice will be thawed.
- If you tote along a hard-cooked egg, leave the shell on—it will preserve freshness and retard spoilage.
- Don't limit yourself to carrot and celery sticks. Try the unusual: opt for raw cauliflower, broccoli, turnip, zucchini squash, or other crunchy veggies.
- Your protein doesn't always have to come from meat. Try using peanut butter, eggs, or cheese in your lunch.
- Stock up on fresh fruits. Oranges are common fare; more unusual (and delicious, as well!) are grapes, plums, pears, peaches, and other fruit in season.
- Include foods with cream in them only if the lunch can be refrigerated until it's eaten.
- You'll find sandwiches easier to pack if you cut them in quarters first.
- Sandwiches in a lunchbox won't get soggy if you wrap tomatoes and lettuce separately in foil; put them on the sandwich just before you're ready to eat.
- You can keep many foods fresh by packing them in a small jar with a tight-fitting screw-top lid. Prevents spillage, too!
- Don't get stuck in the sandwich rut. With a small Thermos, you can pack stews, soups, and other hot dishes. And don't forget salads: try cottage cheese, yogurt, or take along the fixings for a delicious tossed salad.

Pizza in a Roll

1 1-lb. loaf of frozen white
   bread dough
½ C. tomato paste or pizza
   sauce
4 oz. pepperoni chopped (1 C.)
   or ¼ lb. ground beef (browned)

1 t. oregano
¼ t. garlic powder
¼ C. onion chopped
1 C. shredded cheese

Thaw bread for 2 hours. Roll out to 12x9 rectangle. Spread with sauce. Top with remaining ingredients. Roll up jelly-roll fashion from long side. Seal the edges well. Place on greased baking sheet, seam side down. Brush with water, sprinkle with a little salt. Let rise until almost double in size—about 1 hour. Make 3 slashes across the top. Bake at 375°F for 30 minutes. Slice to serve.

The Great Sandwich

Be daring and also try your favorite sandwich combination.

1 loaf French bread, small narrow
   size
Equal parts of mayonnaise and sour cream
Seasoned salt to taste

Slice loaf of bread in half lengthwise—with spoon scoop out some of the soft bread in each piece. Keep bread covered so it won't dry out. Prepare fillings and spoon each one into the bottom crust for about 4 to 6 inches. Place top crust over fillings. Slice with sharp knife.

Filling suggestions:

Tuna Salad
Chicken Salad or Chicken slices
Egg Salad
Canned Corned Beef shredded and mixed with Pickles, chopped
   Onion and Dressing
Cheese and Ham or Lunch Meat—layered
Tomatoes, Bacon and Cucumbers with Lettuce

MOM'S OLD Standbys

SOUP

Soup in a Hurry

1 envelope dry onion soup mix
4 C. water
3 C. frozen vegetables
   (any combination)

½ t. salt
¼ t. pepper
grated cheese

Cook soup and water according to package directions. Heat to boiling and add vegetables. Bring to a boil and reduce heat; simmer until all vegetables are tender. Stir in salt and pepper. Sprinkle grated cheese over individual servings.

Easy Minestrone

3 cubes beef bouillon
2 C. boiling water
1 12-oz. can corn
1 16-oz. can undrained
   tomatoes
1 18-oz. can undrained
   lima beans

2 T. chopped onion
½ t. salt
¼ t. pepper
¼ t. basil
½ C. uncooked elbow macaroni

Dissolve bouillon cube in water in large saucepan. Add remaining ingredients. Cover and simmer about 30 minutes.

10-Minute Carrot Soup

6 medium-sized carrots, grated
1 medium-sized onion, grated
2½ C. water

1 C. milk
2 chicken bouillon cubes
½ t. sugar

Simmer carrots and onions in water and milk for 8 minutes; add bouillon cubes and sugar and simmer 2 more minutes, stirring to dissolve bouillon cubes. Garnish with croutons if desired.

Quick French Onion Soup

2 large onions, sliced thinly
   and separated into rings
¼ C. butter or margarine
2 t. flour
3 C. hot water

4 beef bouillon cubes
4 slices French bread
1 C. Swiss cheese, grated

Brown onions in butter or margarine; sprinkle with flour, add hot water and bouillon cubes, and simmer for 20 minutes or until onions are tender. Season with salt and pepper. Sprinkle French bread with cheese, and melt under broiler. Place a piece of bread in the bottom of each soup bowl, and pour soup over the bread.

Easy Corn Chowder

3 slices cubed bacon
2 hot dogs, sliced
½ C. onion, chopped
2 medium potatoes, peeled
   and diced
1 small can corn, drained

1 t. salt
¼ t. pepper
1 C. water
1 C. canned milk

Fry bacon in large skillet until crispy; add hot dogs, and brown slightly. Add onion, potatoes, corn, salt, pepper, and water; bring to a boil. Cover and cook over low heat until potatoes are tender, about 10 minutes. Add milk and heat just to serve (do *not* boil).

10-Minute Corn Chowder

2 T. butter or margarine
¼ C. flour
1 C. water
1 chicken bouillon cube

2½ C. milk
1 10-oz. pkg. frozen corn,
   thawed, or a can of corn,
   drained

Melt butter over low heat in medium saucepan; stir in flour. Stirring constantly, add water, bouillon cube, and milk; cook until thick. Add corn and heat through. Add salt and pepper if needed.

Easy Clam Chowder

2 large potatoes, peeled and diced
2 stalks celery, diced
¼ C. butter or margarine

2 T. flour
1 C. milk
1 can diced clams, drained

Cook potatoes and celery in salted boiling water until tender, about 8–10 minutes. Drain and mash. In separate saucepan, melt butter or margarine; stir in flour. Add milk gradually, stirring constantly, until thickened. Stir in mashed potatoes and onions and clams; heat through.

Creamy Clam Chowder

2 medium potatoes, peeled and diced
1 carrot, grated
1 can minced clams, drained
1 C. canned milk

2 t. sugar
1 T. vinegar
2 T. flour
¼ C. butter or margarine

Cook the potatoes and carrot in salted boiling water until tender, about 8 minutes. Drain. Stir in minced clams. In separate saucepan, melt butter or margarine; stir in flour. Add milk, stirring constantly; cook until thickened. Stir in sugar and vinegar. Stir in vegetables and heat through.

Cream of Tomato Soup

1 large can stewed tomatoes
½ C. finely diced onions
1 t. sugar
1 t. salt

¼ t. pepper
2 T. butter or margarine
2 T. flour
1½ C. milk

Combine tomatoes, onions, sugar, salt, and pepper in a large saucepan. Simmer for 10 minutes over low heat. In a small saucepan, melt butter or margarine; add flour and stir in milk, stirring constantly, until thickened. Slowly add hot tomatoes, stirring constantly. Heat through.

Potato Chowder

2 large potatoes, peeled and diced
1 T. butter
¼ C. diced onions
¼ C. chopped green pepper
1 C. water
½ t. salt
⅛ t. pepper
¼ t. paprika
2 T. flour
1 C. milk
1 C. diced cooked ham

Melt butter in a large saucepan; add onion and green pepper, and saute until tender. Add potatoes, water, salt, pepper, and paprika; cover and simmer about 10 minutes, or until potatoes are tender. Combine flour and small amount of water into a paste; add to the potato soup. Add milk and cook until thickened, stirring constantly. Stir in ham and heat through. Sprinkle with croutons or chopped parsley if desired.

Dieter's Tomato Soup

1 C. water
1 beef bouillon cube
1 C. shredded cabbage
½ C. thinly sliced celery
½ C. thinly sliced carrots
1 C. tomato juice
¼ t. pepper

Dissolve bouillon cube in water; bring to a boil, and add cabbage, celery, and carrots. Cook over low heat until tender, about 5 minutes. Stir in tomato juice and pepper; bring to a boil. Serve immediately.

Hearty Tomato-Rice Soup

1 T. butter or margarine
1 C. chopped onion
½ C. chopped celery
1 large can tomatoes
2 beef bouillon cubes
½ C. uncooked rice
1 t. salt
½ t. chili powder
3 C. water

Saute onion and celery in butter; add rest of ingredients and bring to a boil. Reduce heat and simmer for 20 minutes or until rice is tender. Serve immediately.

Hamburger Vegetable Soup

1 envelope dry onion soup mix

1 lb. ground beef

1 46-oz. can tomato juice

1 t. salt

½ t. pepper

4 cups of sliced or cubed vegetables (green pepper, celery, carrots, potatoes, cabbage, red cabbage, parsnips, or turnips)

Brown ground beef in a large heavy saucepan. Drain most of fat. Add remaining ingredients and simmer over low heat until done (about 15 minutes). May be served with croutons or parmesan cheese if desired.

Jiffy Vegetable Soup

2 small carrots, cubed

2 small potatoes, cubed

1 onion, finely diced

1 t. salt

6 C. hot water

1 C. instant nonfat dry milk

Cook carrots, potatoes, onion in salted water over low heat until tender, about 10–15 minutes. Stir in dry milk and serve immediately.

Cream of Celery Soup

½ C. chopped celery

½ C. chopped onion

1 medium potato, peeled and diced

1 C. hot water

1 chicken bouillon cube

½ t. salt

¼ t. pepper

1 T. butter or margarine

2 T. flour

1 C. milk

Dissolve bouillon cube in water; simmer celery, onion, and potatoes in water until done, about 10 minutes. Season with salt and pepper. In small saucepan, melt butter or margarine; stir in flour and, stirring constantly, add milk and cook until thickened. Stir sauce into soup and heat through. Garnish with croutons.

Spicy Tomato Soup

2 C. water	¼ t. pepper
2 t. granulated sugar	4 C. cooked tomatoes
3 bay leaves	2 T. butter or margarine
5 whole cloves	3 T. flour
1½ t. salt	

Mix water, sugar, bay leaves, cloves, salt, and pepper in a pan; simmer for 15 minutes and strain. Add tomatoes. In separate saucepan, melt butter and stir in flour. Gradually stir in tomato soup, stirring constantly, until thickened. Cook over low heat 10 minutes.

Easy Chili

1 lb. ground beef	1 t. salt
1 C. chopped onion	2 T. sugar
2 1-lb. cans stewed tomatoes	2 T. vinegar
2 1-lb. cans kidney beans	2 t. garlic powder
2 T. chili powder	

In a large heavy saucepan, brown ground beef and onions until beef is done and onions are transparent. Drain grease. Add remaining ingredients and simmer for 20 minutes.

Western Chili

You can also use this for Sloppy Joes.

1½ lbs. ground beef with ½ lb. sausage or 2 lbs. ground beef	2 T. brown sugar
	1 T. mustard
	1 t. salt
1 C. chopped onion	1 t. paprika
1 C. chopped celery	½ t. pepper
1 small green pepper, chopped	2 C. water
1 t. chili powder	¼ C. cider vinegar
1 16-oz. can kidney beans	1 T. Worcestershire sauce
¾ C. catsup	

Brown ground beef and sausage in a skillet; drain grease. In 1 T. of grease, saute onion, celery, green pepper, and chili powder until vegetables are soft. Return meat to the skillet. Add beans, catsup, mustard, salt, paprika, pepper, water, cider vinegar, and Worcestershire sauce. Simmer, stirring frequently, 1 hour, or until thick.

Creamy Cheese Soup

2 T. butter or margarine	dash pepper
2 T. celery, finely chopped	3 T. cornstarch
2 T. carrot, grated	2 C. cold milk
1 T. onion, finely chopped	2 C. grated cheese
½ t. salt	

Saute celery, carrot, and onion in butter until tender; add salt and pepper. Stir cornstarch into cold milk until well blended; stir slowly and constantly into vegetables. Heat until thickened and bubbly. Add cheese and stir until melted. Serve with croutons.

Speedy Potato Soup

Eat a slice of cheese with this soup and you have a complete meal.

4 potatoes, cubed in chunks

4 carrots, sliced

4 stalks celery, cut up

1 onion, chopped

Cover with water and cook until tender, about 20 minutes. Mash.

1 square margarine or butter

½ C. flour

1½ C. water

In separate pan melt butter or margarine. Stir in flour until smooth. Add water and bring to a boil, stirring constantly. Fold into potato mixture. Season to taste with salt and pepper.

New Potato Soup

10 new potatoes
1 can evaporated milk
2 C. milk

¼ C. butter or margarine
½ t. salt
¼ t. pepper

Boil potatoes until tender; don't drain off water. Add remaining ingredients and simmer for 10 minutes. Serve immediately.

Rich Potato Soup

2 C. diced potatoes
1 C. celery, cut up
1 C. onions, chopped

Cover with enough water to just cover and cook until tender. Mix in blender or quart jar:

1 large can evaporated milk
¾ C. flour
1 t. salt

½ t. salt
pepper to taste

Blend and pour over hot potatoes, stir and add 1 cube of butter or margarine. Heat and stir until soup thickens. If too thick, add a small amount of milk until desired consistency.

Gourmet Potato Soup

4 potatoes, peeled and diced
½ C. diced onion
½ C. diced celery
½ C. hot water
2 chicken bouillon cubes

2 C. milk
1 8-oz. carton sour cream dip with chives
1 T. flour

Dissolve bouillon cube in hot water; add potatoes, onion, celery, and milk. Cover and cook until vegetables are tender, about 15 minutes. Do *not* boil. Blend in sour cream dip and flour; heat until thickened and bubbly. Garnish with parsley or chives.

Hot Dog Soup

1 T. butter or margarine
¼ C. chopped onion
¼ C. chopped celery
1 8-oz. can whole-kernal corn
1 8-oz. can whole
  peeled tomatoes

3 hot dogs, sliced
¼ C. water
¼ t. salt
½ t. sugar
⅛ t. pepper

Saute onion and celery in butter until tender; add remaining ingredients, bring to a boil, and simmer for 8–10 minutes.

Country Hamburger Soup

1 lb. ground beef
1 envelope Lipton Country
  Vegetable Soup Mix
3 C. water
1 16-oz. can tomatoes

1 C. uncooked elbow macaroni
1 T. sugar
¼ t. pepper

Brown meat in a large kettle; drain. Add remaining ingredients and bring to a boil. Reduce heat; cover and simmer for 30 minutes or until macaroni is tender. Serve with bread sticks.

Quick Sausage Soup

½ C. chopped onion
½ C. chopped green pepper
1 T. butter or margarine
1 T. cooking oil
4 C. water
2 C. cooked tomatoes

1 8-oz. can pork and beans
1 t. salt
¼ t. pepper
1 4-oz. can Vienna sausages,
  sliced

Saute onion and green pepper in butter and oil; add water, tomatoes, pork and beans, salt, and pepper. Simmer, covered, 15 minutes. Add sliced sausage and heat through. Serve immediately.

Meatball Soup

½ lb. ground beef	1 C. hot water
4 T. bread crumbs	1 beef bouillon cube
4 T. tomato juice	1 10½-oz. can vegetable soup
1 T. onion, finely minced	1 16-oz. can tomatoes
1 t. chili powder	¼ C. instant rice
1 T. soy sauce	¼ C. chopped onions
2 T. soft butter or margarine	1 t. salt

Combine ground beef, bread crumbs, tomato juice, 1 T. minced onion, chili powder, soy sauce, and soft butter in a large bowl; work with hands until well mixed. Form into small meatballs. Brown over low heat for 10–15 minutes, or until cooked. Drain. In large saucepan, combine remaining ingredients; simmer for 15 minutes. Add meatballs and heat through.

Chicken Soup and Dumplings

If you want an inexpensive meal-in-one, try this delicious easy-to-fix cold-weather dish.

Dumplings:

1 C. sifted flour	2 T. shortening
1½ t. baking powder	⅔ C. milk
½ t. salt	1 egg, beaten

Sift together dry ingredients. Cut in shortening with pastry blender or use 2 knives, until mixture is crumbly. Mix together egg and milk and add to flour mixture. Stir only until flour is dampened. Dough will be lumpy. Drop by spoonfuls on top of boiling soup. Cover tightly and steam 15 minutes without removing cover.

Now to make the chicken soup:

1 3–4 lb. chicken, cut up

8 cups water

½ bay leaf (if desired)

1 onion, chopped

Salt and pepper to taste

Place cut up chicken in a large cooking pan. Add water, onion and seasonings, cover and bring to boil. Cook until chicken is tender and will come off from bones easily, about 2 hours. Remove chicken from broth—remove skin and meat from bones. Discard bones and skin. Strain broth.

Add to broth:

1 C. celery, cut into pieces	½ t. seasoning salt
2 or 3 carrots, peeled and sliced or cut into chunks	½ t. poultry seasoning (optional)
Meat of the chicken	Salt and pepper to taste
1 small onion, chopped	

Add prepared vegetables to chicken broth, adding more water if needed. Bring to boil and cook about 15 minutes. Top with dumpling dough and cook as directed.

Variations: Instead of the dumplings you may add ½ cup rice or 1 cup noodles. Bring to boil and cook 20 minutes.

Cream of Turkey Soup

Great way to use leftover turkey!

1 T. butter or margarine	1 10-oz. pkg. frozen peas, thawed
½ C. chopped onion	
2 C. hot water	1 t. salt
2 chicken bouillon cubes	½ t. pepper
2 C. diced potatoes	1 C. evaporated milk
1 C. cooked turkey, cubed	
1 10-oz. pkg. frozen carrots, thawed	

Saute onion in butter; dissolve bouillon cubes in hot water. Add remaining ingredients except milk, and simmer for 10 minutes. Stir in milk and heat through.

Cream of Corn Soup

1 17-oz. can whole-kernal corn   1 t. salt
1 medium onion, chopped   ¼ t. pepper
1 T. cooking oil   3 C. milk
3 T. flour

Drain corn and chop it coarsely; set aside. In saucepan, saute onion in oil until transparent. Stir in flour and salt and pepper; gradually add milk, stirring constantly, until thickened and bubbly. Add corn and heat through.

Extra Good Chili

1 lb. 14 oz. can chili beans   1 lb. ground beef
1 can tomato soup   1 medium onion

Fry meat to brown, add onion to saute—drain. Add beans and soup. Add chili powder, salt and pepper to taste. Simmer 30 minutes. Serve.

Hamburger Soup

2 lb. ground beef, browned   2 envelopes Lipton's Country
6 C. water   Vegetable Mix
1 #2½ can tomatoes (or 1 qt.)   1 #2½ can pork and beans
1 or 2 handfuls of dry noodles   1 t. seasoned salt

Combine all ingredients and bring to a boil. Simmer 30-45 minutes.

MOM'S OLD Standbys

BREADS

Universal Dough

Use this for rolls, cinnamon rolls, or scones.

½ C. cooking oil   1 pkg. yeast
2 t. salt   2 eggs, beaten
½ C. granulated sugar   5 C. flour
1 C. canned milk

In a large bowl, combine oil, salt, and sugar; add milk. Add yeast and let sit 15–20 minutes. Add eggs and flour; stir until mixed well. Let sit 2–3 hours, or until more than doubled in size. Dough should be light. Bake at 425°F for 10–15 minutes.

90-Minute Bread

2 pkgs. yeast   2 T. cooking oil
½ C. warm water   2 T. granulated sugar
1½ C. warm water   2½ t. salt
                                4–4½ C. flour

Dissolve yeast in warm water; let stand for 10–15 minutes. Set aside. In large bowl, combine hot water, oil, sugar, salt, and enough flour to make a sticky dough. Mix well. Add yeast and let stand for 15 minutes. Turn dough out onto floured surface and knead until firm and elastic. Shape into two loaves, put in greased loaf pans, and let rise for 30 minutes. Bake at 375°F for 30 minutes.

One-Hour Whole Wheat Bread

2 T. yeast (2 pkgs.)   2 t. salt
2 C. warm water   4 C. whole wheat flour
¼ C. granulated sugar

Dissolve yeast in warm water; let stand for 10 minutes, or until bubbly. Stir in sugar, salt, and flour, and mix well. Spoon into two well-greased loaf pans and lightly oil tops of loaves. Let rise until loaves reach top of pans. Bake in 400°F oven for 30 minutes. Let cool in pans for 5 minutes; finish cooling on wire racks.

Quick and Delicious Bread

¾ C. granulated sugar   1 egg, beaten

3 C. warm water   3 t. salt

2 pkgs. yeast   8 C. flour

⅓ C. cooking oil

Combine sugar, warm water, and yeast in large mixing bowl; let stand 10 minutes. Combine cooking oil and egg and add to yeast mixture. Stir in salt and 3 C. of flour; mix well. Stir in additional 3 C. of flour; mix well. Add enough of the remaining flour to make a soft, sticky dough. Cover bowl and allow dough to rise until double in bulk; punch down, turn dough over in bowl, and allow to rise, covered, until double in bulk again—about 45 minutes. Shape dough into three loaves and put in greased loaf pans; cover and allow to rise until doubled, about 30 minutes. Bake at 400°F for 25 minutes, or until loaves are lightly browned. Brush crusts with melted butter to soften.

English Muffin Bread

2 pkg. yeast   ¼ t. baking soda

¼ C. lukewarm water   1 T. warm water

1 T. sugar   1 C. raisins

2 t. salt   5 C. flour

2½ C. milk, scalded and cooled

Dissolve yeast in warm water; allow to sit for 10 minutes. Add sugar, salt, milk, raisins, and 2½ C. of flour; beat until well blended. Add remaining flour, mix well, and cover; let rise about 1½ hours, or until double in bulk. Dissolve baking soda in 1 T. warm water; stir down dough and blend in soda water. Divide dough into two loaves and place in well-greased loaf pans; cover and let rise until doubled, about 1 hour. Bake at 375°F for 45 minutes, or until golden in color. Remove from pan to cool.

Simple Cinnamon Rolls

2¼ C. biscuit mix   6 t. melted butter or margarine

⅔ C. milk   ½ C. chopped nuts

¼ C. sugar   ½ C. raisins

1½ t. cinnamon

Beat biscuit mix and milk together with a fork until dough is stiff; knead on floured surface about 12 times, or until dough is smooth. Roll out into rectangle. Spread with half the melted butter; sprinkle with sugar, cinnamon, nuts, and raisins. Roll the dough up tightly and press to seal. Cut into 10 slices. Place rolls close together on a greased cookie sheet and brush with rest of melted butter. Bake at 425°F for 10–12 minutes, or until lightly golden.

Cinnamon Puffs

1 pkg. yeast   2 C. flour

¼ C. warm water   1½ t. vanilla

½ C. milk, scalded and cooled   ¼ C. butter or margarine,

⅛ C. granulated sugar   melted

¼ t. salt   ½ C. granulated sugar

¼ C. cooking oil   2 t. cinnamon

1 egg, beaten

Dissolve yeast in warm water; set aside for 10 minutes. Stir in milk, sugar, salt, oil, egg, and 1 C. flour; mix well. Beat in additional flour and vanilla until dough is sticky. Spoon dough into greased muffin tins. Let raise until doubled, about 45 minutes. Bake at 375°F for 15–18 minutes. Dip tops in melted butter and then in cinnamon-sugar combination. Let cool.

101

Caramel Rolls

1 loaf frozen bread dough	2 T. light corn syrup
¼ C. butter or margarine	4 T. melted butter
½ C. brown sugar, packed	¼ C. granulated sugar
¾ C. pecan halves	2 t. cinnamon

Brush frozen loaf with a little cooking oil; cover and let thaw completely (about 3 hours). Melt ¼ C. butter; stir in brown sugar, nuts, and corn syrup, and spread in the bottom of a 13×9 pan. Spread dough into a rectangle; spread with 4 T. melted butter. Sprinkle with sugar and cinnamon. Roll tightly and pinch to seal. Cut into 12 slices, and place slightly apart in pan. Let rise until doubled, about 1 hour. Bake at 375°F for 15–20 minutes. Turn pan immediately over on a large tray; leave pan on top of rolls for a few minutes so caramel will drizzle down over rolls. Cool and serve.

Basic Rolls

1 pkg. yeast	2 eggs, beaten
¼ C. warm water	1 t. salt
1 C. milk, scalded	⅓ C. sugar
¼ C. shortening	4½ C. flour

Dissolve yeast in water; set aside until bubbly. Pour warm milk over sugar, salt, and shortening; stir until well blended. Add yeast mixture, stir to blend. Add eggs, mix well. Cool. Stir in flour and place dough in a greased bowl; cover and let rise until doubled in bulk (about 1 hour). Punch dough down and form into rolls of desired shape. Place rolls on greased cookie sheet or in greased muffin tins; cover and let rise until doubled again, about 1 hour. Bake at 375°F for 15–18 minutes.

Baking Soda Biscuits

2 C. flour	½ C. shortening
¾ t. baking soda	¼ C. vinegar
½ t. salt	½ C. milk

Sift together flour, baking soda, and salt. Cut in shortening. Stir in vinegar and milk until dough is sticky. Spoon onto greased cookie sheet. Bake at 450°F for 12–15 minutes, or until lightly golden brown.

Simple Corn Bread

1 C. yellow cornmeal	½ t. salt
1 C. flour	1 egg, beaten
¼ C. granulated sugar	1 C. milk
4 t. baking powder	¼ C. cooking oil

Mix all ingredients until well blended. Pour into greased 8×8 square pan. Bake at 425°F for 20 minutes or until light golden color. Knife inserted in center will come out clean.

Rich Buttermilk Biscuits

1 C. sifted flour	⅛ C. shortening
½ t. salt	½ C. milk
2 t. baking powder	1 t. lemon juice or vinegar
⅛ t. baking soda	

Sift together flour, salt, baking powder, and baking soda; cut in shortening. Combine milk and lemon juice or vinegar; stir into flour mixture to make a soft dough. Turn dough onto a floured surface and knead until soft and elastic. Roll into a rectangle, about ½" thick; cut into biscuits. Place on ungreased cookie sheet and bake at 450°F for 8–10 minutes.

Fast and Easy Cheese Twist

1 can refrigerated buttermilk biscuits

1 egg, beaten

1 C. grated cheese

Separate biscuits; roll each into a 10" strip and twist. Bring around in a circle and seal ends by pinching dough. Brush with beaten egg and sprinkle with cheese. Bake at temperature and time indicated on can of biscuits. Cool slightly before serving.

Garlic Bread

1 loaf French bread, sliced	½ t. oregano
½ C. butter or margarine, softened	4 t. chopped parsley flakes
	3 T. parmesan cheese
½ t. garlic salt	

Combine butter, garlic salt, oregano, parsley flakes, and parmesan cheese until well mixed. Spread both sides of bread with mixture; wrap bread in foil and bake at 400°F for 12–15 minutes or until butter is melted and bread is crusty.

Spicy Pumpkin Bread

1½ C. sugar	¼ t. salt
1 C. cooked pumpkin	1 t. baking soda
2 eggs, beaten	½ t. cinnamon
½ C. cooking oil	½ t. nutmeg
⅓ C. water	½ C. chopped nuts
1¾ C. flour	1 C. raisins

Combine sugar, pumpkin, eggs, oil, and water; mix well. Sift together flour, salt, baking soda, cinnamon, and nutmeg; beat into flour mixture. Stir in nuts and raisins. Pour batter into greased loaf pan; bake at 350°F for 1 hour. Cool.

Soft Zucchini Bread

3 eggs, beaten	1 t. salt
1 C. cooking oil	3 t. cinnamon
2 C. granulated sugar	¼ t. baking powder
2 C. grated zucchini squash	1 t. baking soda
1 t. vanilla	1 C. chopped nuts
3 C. flour	

Combine eggs, oil, and sugar until well blended. Stir in zucchini and vanilla. Sift together flour, salt, cinnamon, baking powder, baking soda; stir into zucchini mixture. Stir in chopped nuts. Bake in well-greased loaf pan at 350°F for 1 hour.

Easy Pretzels

1 loaf frozen bread dough	1 T. salt
1 slightly beaten egg white	coarse salt

Thaw bread completely; on floured surface, roll into a square. Cut dough into 30 strips; roll each strip between your palms into a long rope. Shape into pretzels by tying in a loose knot and looping ends through; pinch to seal. Let stand for 30 minutes. Mix egg white and water; brush mixture on pretzels and sprinkle with coarse salt. Bake on greased cookie sheet at 350°F for 15–18 minutes, or until pretzels are golden brown.

Early American Brown Bread

You can make this bread without any eggs.

2 C. whole wheat flour	½ t. salt
¾ C. white flour	2 C. milk
1 C. brown sugar, packed	4 t. lemon juice or vinegar
2 t. baking soda	

Mix whole wheat flour, white flour, brown sugar, baking soda, and salt in large bowl. Combine milk and lemon juice or vinegar; let stand 10 minutes. Stir milk gradually into flour mixture until well blended. Spoon batter into greased loaf pan. Bake at 350°F for 1 hour.

Easy Cherry-Filled Rolls

1 loaf frozen bread dough	1 C. powdered sugar, sifted
2 C. cherry pie filling	2 T. milk

Thaw bread dough completely and roll into rectangle. Cut into 15 strips. Roll between palms into long ropes, twist, and bring ends around into a circle; pinch to seal. Place on greased cookie sheet. Press center of each roll and spoon 1½ T. cherry pie filling in each. Let rise until double in size. Bake at 375°F for 15–20 minutes. Beat powdered sugar and milk together to form a glaze; drizzle over warm rolls.

Crunchy Banana Bread

⅓ C. shortening
¾ C. granulated sugar
1 egg, beaten
2 C. bran flakes cereal
1½ C. flour
2 t. baking powder

½ t. salt
½ t. baking soda
¾ C. chopped nuts
2 C. mashed bananas
2 T. water
1 t. vanilla

Cream shortening and sugar; beat in egg. Stir in bran flakes. Sift together flour, baking powder, salt, and baking soda; stir into bran flake mixture. Combine bananas and water; stir in vanilla. Stir into flour mixture. Stir in nuts. Bake in greased loaf pan at 350°F for 1 hour.

Simple Orange Nut Bread

¾ C. granulated sugar
1 egg, beaten
1¼ C. orange juice

3 C. biscuit mix
1 C. chopped nuts

Beat together sugar, egg, orange juice, and biscuit mix. Stir in nuts. Pour into greased loaf pan. Bake at 350°F for 1 hour. (Top of bread will split.)

Basic Muffin Mix

2 C. sifted flour
1 T. baking powder
½ t. salt
3 T. sugar

1 egg, beaten
1 C. milk
3 T. oil or melted shortening

Sift together flour, baking powder, salt and sugar. Combine in bowl egg, milk, and oil and pour into dry ingredients all at once. Stir *only* until dry ingredients are moist. Do not overmix. Spoon batter into greased muffin pans, filling only about two-thirds full. Bake at 450°F for 20–25 minutes.

Muffin Variations:

Apple–Nutmeg: Peel and dice 1 medium-sized apple. Sprinkle with 1 t. nutmeg and 2 T. sugar. Stir into batter.

Apricot–Nut: Thoroughly drain ½ C. cooked, finely chopped apricots. Combine with ½ C. chopped walnuts. Stir into batter.

Cheese–Garlic: Combine 1 C. grated processed cheese with ⅛ t. garlic salt. Stir into dry ingredients. Bake 20–25 minutes.

Cherry: Thoroughly drain ¾ C. canned or freshly cooked red sour cherries. Add ¼ C. sugar and ⅛ t. cinnamon. (Do not let stand—more juice will form.) Gently fold into batter after mixing liquid and dry ingredients.

Jam: Fill pans half-full of batter. Put 1 t. jam in each; top with batter so pans are two-thirds full. Strawberry jam is especially good.

Grape Nuts: Stir ½ C. Grape Nuts cereal into batter after liquid and dry ingredients have been partially mixed.

Lemon–Sugar: Combine ½ C. sugar with 2 T. grated lemon rind (or use ½ C. chopped nuts with 2 T. brown sugar). Put enough batter in pans to fill one-fourth full. Sprinkle with sugar mixture, then top with another layer of batter; fill the pans only one-half to two-thirds full (otherwise sugar will melt out and make muffins stick).

Orange: In the basic muffin recipe, use only ¾ C. milk, and combine with ¼ C. orange juice. Grate 1 T. orange rind, and stir into liquid ingredients.

Pineapple: Thoroughly drain 1 C. crushed pineapple. Stir into batter after liquid and dry ingredients have been partially mixed. Or substitute 1 C. well-drained, sweetened, stewed rhubarb for the pineapple and add 1 T. grated orange rind.

Oatmeal Raisin Muffins

2½ C. quick-cooking oatmeal   ⅔ C. water
1 egg, beaten   ½ C. raisins

Combine all ingredients and stir with a fork just enough to moisten ingredients. Spoon into greased muffin tins. Bake at 425°F for 20 minutes.

107

Buttermilk Oatmeal Muffins

1 C. quick-cooking oatmeal	1 C. flour
1 C. milk	1 t. baking powder
2 t. lemon juice or vinegar	½ t. baking soda
⅓ C. butter or margarine, softened	1 t. salt
	¾ C. raisins
½ C. brown sugar, packed	½ C. chopped nuts
1 egg, beaten	

Combine milk and lemon juice or vinegar; soak oatmeal in milk for 30 minutes. Cream shortening, sugar, and egg; sift together flour, baking powder, baking soda, and salt. Stir into shortening mixture. Stir in raisins and nuts just until all ingredients are moistened. Stir in oatmeal. Spoon into greased muffin tins and bake at 400°F for 20 minutes.

Nutty Whole Wheat Muffins

1 C. white flour	1 C. milk
1 C. whole wheat flour	2 eggs, beaten
½ t. salt	⅓ C. cooking oil
3 t. baking powder	1 C. chopped nuts
½ C. brown sugar, packed	

Combine all ingredients, stirring just enough to moisten. Spoon into greased muffin tins. Bake at 400°F for 12–15 minutes.

Spicy Muffins

2 C. flour	½ t. nutmeg
1 egg, well beaten	¼ t. ginger
¾ C. sugar	¼ t. ground cloves
1 C. milk	3 t. baking powder
¼ C. cooking oil	1 t. salt
1 T. cinnamon	½ C. chopped nuts

Combine all ingredients, stirring with a fork just to moisten ingredients. Spoon into greased muffin tins; bake at 425°F for 15–20 minutes.

Six-Week Muffin Mix

Make up this batter and keep it in the fridge—for up to six weeks!

2 C. boiling water

5 t. baking soda

1 C. shortening

1½ C. granulated sugar

4 eggs, slightly beaten

4 C. bran cereal

2 C. bran flakes

4 C. milk

3 T. lemon juice

5 C. flour

1 t. salt

1 C. chopped nuts

1½ C. raisins or chopped dates

Combine boiling water and baking soda; cream shortening and sugar, and add to boiling water mixture. Stir in remaining ingredients until well mixed in a sticky batter. Store, tightly covered, in refrigerator until ready to use (up to six weeks). *Do not stir batter after it has initially been made.* When ready to use, spoon into greased muffin tins and bake at 400°F for 12–15 minutes.

Hush Puppies

¾ C. yellow cornmeal

¼ t. salt

⅛ t. baking soda

3 T. minced onion

⅛ C. milk

¼ t. lemon juice

¼ C. water

Combine all ingredients and stir to moisten. Drop by teaspoonfuls into hot fat; fry until golden brown. Drain briefly on paper towels and serve hot as a side dish.

Cheese Puffs

½ C. flour

¼ C. butter or margarine, softened

¼ lb. cheese, grated

Mix all ingredients well. Roll into small balls about the size of large marbles. Bake on an ungreased cookie sheet at 350°F for 15–20 minutes. Serve immediately.

Quick and Easy Doughnuts

2 C. biscuit mix

⅓ C. granulated sugar

⅓ C. milk

1 t. vanilla

1 egg, beaten

½ t. cinnamon

¼ t. nutmeg

Mix all ingredients until well blended. Turn onto lightly floured surface and knead until smooth and elastic. Roll out into a rectangle, ½ thick. Cut into doughnuts. Drop into hot fat and fry, 1 minute on each side, until golden. Remove from fat immediately and drain on paper towels. Roll doughnuts in powdered or granulated sugar or frost if desired.

Hamburger Buns

1¾ C. warm water

¼ C. honey

½ C. cooking oil

3 pkgs. yeast

1½ t. salt

5 C. flour

2 eggs, beaten

Combine water, honey, oil, and yeast; let sit 10–15 minutes, or until bubbly. Stir in salt, flour, and eggs. Shape into the size of a hamburger patty. Place on greased cookie sheets and let rise for 10 minutes. Bake at 425°F for 10 minutes. Let cool, and split with knife.

Quick Jam Turnovers

1 8-oz. pkg. refrigerated biscuits

jam

milk

granulated sugar

Separate biscuits and flatten with a fork to twice their original size. Place a heaping spoonful of jam in the center of each; fold over and seal edges with fork. Brush with milk and sprinkle with sugar. Bake on ungreased cookie sheet at 375°F for 12–15 minutes, or until lightly browned.

Easy Bread Sticks

stale hot dog buns
melted butter or margarine
parmesan cheese

Cut each hot dog bun lengthwise into four sticks; brush with melted butter and sprinkle with parmesan cheese. Bake on a lightly greased cookie sheet at 350°F for 10 minutes or until sticks begin to turn golden brown. Serve immediately.

Refrigerator Rolls

1 C. shortening
2 t. salt
2 cakes yeast
4 eggs
1 C. cold water

¾ C. sugar
1 C. boiling water
½ C. lukewarm water
7½ C. flour

Cream shortening, sugar and salt. Add boiling water and stir to melt shortening. Add yeast to lukewarm water—then add to cooled shortening mixture. Add eggs and beat. Add flour alternately with cold water and stir until dough is well combined and smooth. Cover and refrigerate for several hours or overnight. Make rolls about 2 hours before baking so they can rise until double in bulk. Bake at 450°F for 12—15 minutes. This dough makes delicious sweet rolls. It will keep for up to a week in the refrigerator.

Cheese Balls

1 C. biscuit mix
¼ C. milk
2 T. mayonnaise
½ C. parsley, snipped fine

½ C. grated cheese
dash salt
1 T. grated onion

Blend together biscuit mix, cheese, milk, mayonnaise and salt with a fork. Shape into balls. Combine parsley and onion. Bake on greased baking sheet for 7—10 minutes at 450°F.

Zesty Lemon Bread

1/3 C. melted butter or margarine

2 eggs

1½ C. sifted flour

1 t. salt

1 T. grated lemon peel

3 T. fresh lemon juice

1¼ C. sugar

¼ t. almond extract

1½ t. baking powder

½ C. milk

½ C. chopped nuts

Cream butter and 1 cup sugar. Beat in eggs and add extract. Sift dry ingredients and add to egg mixture alternately with milk. Blend just enough to mix. Fold in lemon peel and nuts. Pour into loaf pan (8½x4½x2¾ inches). Bake 325°F for 70 minutes or until done. Mix lemon juice and ¼ cup sugar, spoon over hot bread. Cool for 10 minutes. Remove from pan and cool on rack. Slice to serve. Freezes well.

MOM'S OLD Standbys

BEVERAGES

Instant Cocoa

2 C. instant nonfat dry milk   4 t. cocoa

3 T. granulated sugar   dash salt

Mix all ingredients well; store in a covered container. For a quick cup of cocoa, stir ⅓ C. mixture into 1 C. steaming hot water; stir until well dissolved.

Jiffy Hot Chocolate

2 t. cocoa   ¾ C. boiling water

1 T. corn syrup   milk or light cream

dash salt

Mix cocoa, corn syrup, and salt in a mug or cup; add boiling water and stir to completely dissolve. Dilute to taste with milk or light cream.

Morning Nog

1 C. orange juice

1 C. milk

2 eggs, well beaten

Combine ingredients in a jar with a tight-fitting lid; shake well until blended.

Sweet Banana Shake

1 C. instant nonfat dry milk   3 T. honey

2 C. cold water   3 ripe bananas, mashed

Stir dry milk into water in a jar with a tight-fitting lid. Stir in honey and bananas; cover and shake vigorously until well-blended.

Minute Milk Shake

1 C. milk

1 envelope strawberry instant breakfast drink

¼ C. crushed pineapple

Combine ingredients in a jar with a tight-fitting lid; shake well until blended. For variety, use chocolate instant breakfast with mashed bananas or vanilla instant breakfast with mashed peaches.

Bubbly Grapefruit Ice

1 can grapefruit sections	2 C. water
1 C. granulated sugar	4–6 C. ginger ale
juice from 1 lemon	

Drain the grapefruit; beat the grapefruit with the sugar. Add the drained grapefruit juice, water, and lemon juice; mix until well-blended. Freeze. When ready to serve, scoop out into a glass and fill the glass with ginger ale.

Pineapple Floats

2 C. pineapple juice

2 C. ginger ale

4 scoops pineapple sherbet

Fill two glasses each halfway with pineapple juice; drop two scoops of sherbet into each one. Fill to the top with ginger ale, and stir until slightly mixed. Serve immediately.

Wassail

Make this traditional Christmas drink for the holidays!

1 gallon apple cider	½ t. salt
2 quarts orange juice	3 cinnamon sticks
1 C. granulated sugar	½ t. whole cloves

Mix all ingredients in a large pan; simmer over low heat for 3 hours. Strain and serve, piping hot.

Tangy Almond Punch

1 6-oz. can frozen lemonade

1 6-oz. can frozen orange juice

2 quarts water

1 C. granulated sugar

½ t. vanilla

½ t. almond extract

Mix all ingredients until juices are thawed; serve over ice, and add ginger ale if desired.

Orange Slush

1 6-oz. can frozen orange juice

2 C. cold water

2 C. granulated sugar

ginger ale

Combine water and sugar in a saucepan; heat to boiling and boil for two minutes. Remove from heat and stir in orange juice concentrate. Freeze. When ready to serve, spoon into glasses and fill with ginger ale.

Triple Fruit Punch

2 quarts unsweetened apple juice

2 C. cranberry juice

2 C. orange juice

1 16-oz. bottle ginger ale

Mix all ingredients well; serve chilled over ice. Garnish with orange or lemon slices, if desired.

Easy Fruit Punch

2 pkgs. unsweetened cherry fruit drink mix

2 6-oz. cans frozen orange juice concentrate

2 C. sugar

Stir drink mix and sugar together until mixed well; stir in water and thawed orange juice concentrate. Add enough water to make 1½ gallons of punch. (Reduce amount of water if you are adding ice cubes to the punch.)

Sweet Cherry-Apple Punch

1 pkg. unsweetened cherry fruit drink mix

1 6-oz. can frozen lemonade concentrate

2 C. unsweetened apple juice

1 quart ice water

¼ C. granulated sugar

Combine all ingredients and stir until sugar is well dissolved.

Easy Banana Shake

1 fully ripe banana

1 C. cold milk

Mash the banana well with a fork until creamy. Mix with milk in a jar with a tight-fitting lid. Shake vigorously until well blended. Serve immediately.

Lemonade

¼ C. granulated sugar

½ C. hot water

rind of 1 lemon, grated

juice of 2 lemons

2 C. cold water

Dissolve sugar in the hot water; add the grated lemon rind, and let cool. Add the lemon juice and the cold water, and stir until well mixed. Strain and serve over ice. Garnish with a slice of lemon if desired.

Creamy Berry Floats

2 scoops vanilla ice cream

1 C. berries

12 oz. ginger ale

Put a scoop of ice cream in each of two glasses; spoon half the berries over each. Fill the glasses with ginger ale, and stir gently.

Cherry Soda

1 pkg. unsweetened cherry
   drink mix

1 C. granulated sugar

2 C. cold milk

vanilla ice cream

ginger gale

Mix the drink mix, sugar, and milk until well-blended; pour into 6 glasses. Add a scoop of vanilla ice cream to each glass, and fill with ginger ale.

Tangy Citrus Punch

1 pkg. instant lemon-lime soft drink mix

1 C. granulated sugar

1 6-oz. can frozen orange juice concentrate

6 C. cold water

1 16-oz. bottle ginger ale

Mix soft drink mix, sugar, frozen orange juice, and water, stirring until sugar is dissolved and juice is thawed. Store in refrigerator. Just before serving, stir in ginger ale. Serve immediately.

Tutti-Frutti Sparkle

1 pkg. unsweetened orange drink mix

1 pkg. unsweetened lime drink mix

1 pkg. unsweetened lemonade mix

1½ C. granulated sugar

9 C. water

ginger ale

Mix each of the drink mixes separately with ½ C. of sugar and 3 C. water until sugar is dissolved; pour each into a separate ice cube tray and freeze. When ready to serve, put a cube of each flavor into a glass and fill with ginger ale. Garnish with a lemon or lime slice if desired.

117

Easy Strawberry Soda

1 T. strawberry jam
½ C. vanilla ice cream
ginger ale

Spoon strawberry jam into the bottom of a tall glass; drop in the scoop of ice cream. Fill the glass with a ginger ale and stir gently.

Traditional Eggnog

5 eggs, well beaten
½ C. canned milk
1 3¾-oz. pkg. instant
  vanilla pudding
¾ C. granulated sugar

7 C. milk
½ t. vanilla extract
dash nutmeg

Beat eggs with canned milk and instant pudding mix. Stir in sugar until well dissolved. Add milk and vanilla extract and stir well. Sprinkle a dash of nutmeg in each glass at serving time.

Christmas Eggnog

3 eggs, slightly beaten
½ C. granulated sugar
¼ t. salt
3 C. milk

1½ C. canned milk
½ t. vanilla extract
dash nutmeg

Combine eggs, sugar, and salt; stir in milk and canned milk, and cook over boiling water until the mixture coats a spoon (about 10 minutes). Stir constantly to prevent scorching. Remove from heat. When cool, stir in vanilla extract; chill. Strain. Beat until frothy, and add a dash of nutmeg to each serving.

Orange Eggnog

2 C. milk
½ C. frozen orange juice
  concentrate
2 eggs, well beaten

2 T. granulated sugar
2 t. vanilla extract

Combine all ingredients and place in a jar with a tight-fitting lid. Shake vigorously until well blended. Serve immediately.

Sweet Eggnog

2 eggs, well beaten

1 15-oz. can sweetened condensed milk

¼ t. salt

½ t. vanilla extract

4 C. milk

½ C. heavy cream, whipped

dash nutmeg

Combine eggs, condensed milk, salt, and vanilla; stir until well blended. Beat in milk until well blended. Gently fold in whipped cream. Top each serving with a dash of nutmeg if desired.

Red Tangy Punch

1 pkg. strawberry drink powder

1 pkg. cherry drink powder

1 cup sugar

8 cups cold water

2 12-oz. cans (3 cups) apricot juice

1 6-oz. can frozen limeade

1 6-oz. can frozen lemonade

1 32-oz. bottle lemon-lime carbonated beverage

Combine ingredients and chill. Place ice cubes in glass and fill ¾ full of the fruit juice. Fill the rest of the glass with carbonated beverage.

Individual Summer Cooler

For each soda, place 2 to 3 tablespoons of chocolate syrup in tall glass. Fill glass half-full with a chilled carbonated lemon-lime beverage. Add 2 scoops vanilla ice cream, stirring after each addition. Fill glass with beverage.

Chocolate-Peppermint Soda: Substitute peppermint ice cream for the vanilla.

Orange Soda: In each glass, place 2 scoops of orange sherbet. Pour in chilled carbonated orange beverage to fill glass.

A Most Refreshing Drink

1 can (6 oz.) frozen limeade (diluted)

8 C. water

3 C. sugar

2 qts. 7Up, Sprite, etc.

Combine sugar and water, stir until dissolved (may be heated to dissolve sugar). Add diluted limeade—freeze until solid. Two hours before serving remove from freezer and allow to thaw in punch bowl. One hour before serving pour carbonated beverage over it. Also, can be made by the glass—Put about 1/3 glass of frozen slush, 2 ice cubes and fill up with carbonated beverage.

Party Punch with Zing

½ gallon apple juice

1 quart cranberry juice

1-16 oz. bottle 7Up, Sprite, etc.

Mix together. Pour over ice cubes. Add lemon, lime or orange slice.

Spiced Grape Juice

4 C. water

2 sticks cinnamon

4 C. grape juice

2 C. orange juice

¾ C. sugar

8 whole cloves

lemon slices (optional)

Combine water, sugar and spices. Boil mixture for 10 minutes—strain. Add fruit juices to spiced water and heat. Serve hot with lemon slices.

MOM'S OLD Standbys

Cherry Waldorf Salad

1 3-oz. pkg. cherry gelatin   ½ C. diced banana

dash salt   ¼ C. chopped celery

1 C. boiling water   ½ C. chopped nuts

½ C. cold water

½ C. diced apples

Dissolve gelatin and salt in boiling water; add cold water and chill until partially set. Fold in remaining ingredients, spoon into an 8×8 pan, and set until firm. Top with whipped cream.

Fruity Emerald Salad

1 3-oz. pkg. lemon gelatin   1 C. cottage cheese

1 3-oz. pkg. lime gelatin   1 C. canned milk

1½ C. pineapple juice   1 C. chopped nuts

1 C. drained pineapple,   1 C. fruit cocktail, drained
    crushed

1 C. mayonnaise

Heat pineapple juice; dissolve gelatin in it. Chill until partially set. Whip gelatin briskly; fold in remaining ingredients and chill until firm.

Raspberry Cooler

1 C. applesauce

1 3-oz. pkg. raspberry gelatin

1 C. fresh or frozen raspberries

½ C. chopped nuts

Heat applesauce until it boils; dissolve gelatin in it. Stir in raspberries, and fold in nuts. Chill until firm.

Cherry-Applesauce Salad

2 3-oz. pkg. cherry gelatin
2 C. boiling water
1 6-oz. can frozen orange juice concentrate, partially thawed
1 C. cold water
1 can applesauce
1 C. diced apple

Dissolve gelatin in boiling water. Stir in orange juice, water, applesauce; pour into 9×13 pan. Top with diced apples. Set until firm.

Vegetable Bounce

1 3-oz. pkg. lemon gelatin
½ C. hot water
2 T. lemon juice
½ C. chopped celery
½ C. shredded carrots
½ C. chopped nuts
1 small green pepper, chopped
3 green onions, chopped
1 C. crushed pineapple (undrained)
1 C. small-curd cottage cheese, drained
½ C. mayonnaise

Dissolve gelatin in hot water and lemon juice; add remaining ingredients and chill until set. Will keep up to a week in the fridge.

Cool Summer Salad

2 C. watermelon, cubed
1 C. cantaloupe, cubed
1 C. seedless green grapes
1 C. strawberries, halved

Mix and serve.

Apple-Pecan Salad

½ C. unpeeled, diced apples
½ C. diced bananas
2 t. lemon juice
¼ C. drained pineapple tidbits
½ C. raisins
½ C. chopped pecans
¼ C. mayonnaise

Toss apples and bananas in a bowl with lemon juice until the fruit is coated. Stir in pineapple tidbits, raisins, and pecans. Toss. Add mayonnaise and toss just until mixed throughout. Serve on lettuce.

Marshmallow Fruit Salad

½ C. strawberries, quartered   ½ C. whipping cream

8 large marshmallows   ¼ C. mayonnaise

2 bananas, mashed   ½ C. cubed peaches

½ C. crushed pineapple

Melt marshmallows over boiling water; let cool. Add strawberries, mashed bananas, pineapple, and peaches. Stir in mayonnaise and whipping cream until well blended. Pour into a freezing tray and freeze. To serve, cut into quarters and top with sliced marshmallows.

Easy Fruit Salad

1 can drained fruit cocktail

1 or 2 sliced bananas

1 can drained mandarin oranges (optional)

1 cup crushed pineapple

½ cup whipping cream, whipped and sweetened

Mix drained fruit and fold in whipped cream. (If desired, it can be served without cream and substituted with approximately ⅓ cup carbonated soda water, such as 7-Up or Sprite.)

Diced Apple Salad

2 C. diced apples   ½ C. raisins

½ C. diced celery   ½ C. mayonnaise

½ C. chopped nuts   2 t. sugar

Combine apples, celery, nuts, and raisins in a salad bowl. In a small bowl, stir mayonnaise and sugar together; beat until creamy. If needed, stir in a teaspoon of milk to thin. Pour dressing over salad and stir to coat.

Fruit Whip Delight

1 10-oz. carton frozen whipped topping, thawed
1 6-oz. pkg. cherry gelatin
1 can fruit cocktail, drained
1 pint small-curd cottage cheese, drained well

Combine all ingredients and chill.

Fruit Cups with Banana Dressing

1 small head lettuce	1 small ripe banana
½ C. pineapple tidbits	2 T. powdered sugar
½ C. pitted cherries	½ C. mayonnaise
1 orange, peeled and sectioned	½ t. vinegar
¼ C. nuts, chopped	

Arrange three lettuce leaves in a cupped shape on each salad plate. On each plate, fill one lettuce leaf with pineapple bits, one leaf with cherries, and one leaf with orange sections. In a small bowl, mash the banana with a fork; beat in the powdered sugar, vinegar, and mayonnaise. Sprinkle the fruit with nuts and top with a dollop of banana dressing.

Sour Cream Fruit Salad

1 C. sour cream	1 C. miniature marshmallows
1 C. flaked coconut	2 C. cubed fresh fruit

Mix together; chill for several hours before serving.

Stuffed Tomatoes

2 medium tomatoes	¼ C. chopped green pepper
1 C. small-curd cottage cheese	2 radishes, grated
¼ C. grated carrot	¼ t. salt
¼ C. peeled, pared, diced cucumber	

124

Cut tomatoes in half and scoop out pulp and seeds; drain on paper towels. In a small bowl, mix remaining ingredients with tomato pulp until well blended. Spoon cottage cheese mixture into tomato halves and serve on crisp lettuce leaves.

Fruit Dip

1 C. fruit-flavored yogurt

½ C. frozen whipped topping, partially thawed

Cut-up fruit

Fold yogurt into whipped topping and use as a dip for fruit (strawberries, melon balls, grapes, and so on).

Creamy Carrot Salad

½ C. mayonnaise	½ C. crushed pineapple
2 t. milk	¼ C. chopped nuts
½ C. miniature marshmallows	1½ C. grated carrot

Mix mayonnaise and milk until creamy. Fold in remaining ingredients and chill for several hours before serving.

Vegetable Garden Dip

1 C. sour cream

¼ C. parmesan cheese

1 envelope dry soup mix

Combine all ingredients and beat until fluffy. Use as a dip for cut-up vegetables, such as cauliflower, broccoli, carrots, celery, and cucumbers.

Sweet Cole Slaw

¼ C. cream	½ t. salt
¼ C. granulated sugar	2 C. shredded cabbage
¼ C. vinegar	

Beat cream, sugar, vinegar, and salt together until fluffy. Stir in shredded cabbage until cabbage is completely coated. Chill.

Crunchy Bean Salad

1 8-oz. can kidney beans, drained

¼ C. diced celery

¼ C. diced green pepper

2 T. minced onion

3 T. salad dressing

¼ t. salt

dash pepper

Rinse kidney beans well in cold water and drain. Combine all remaining ingredients and mix well. Chill before serving on crisp lettuce leaves.

Seven-Layer Salad

You can munch on this for several days if you keep it in the fridge!

Make the following layers in a large salad bowl:

1. 1 head lettuce, torn or chopped
2. 1 bunch celery, chopped
3. 1 small white onion, chopped
4. 1 large green pepper, chopped
5. 1 large cucumber, chopped
6. 1 10-oz. package frozen peas, thawed
7. 2 C. mayonnaise, spread over the top

Sprinkle the top with a mixture of:

2 T. granulated sugar

1 C. parmesan cheese

½ C. crisply cooked, crumbled bacon

Keep covered in the refrigerator.

Apple Slaw

¼ head of cabbage, shredded

¼ C. mayonnaise

3 t. granulated sugar

2 t. lemon juice

2 t. milk

½ t. salt

dash pepper

1 apple, cored and chopped

In large bowl, mix mayonnaise, sugar, lemon juice, milk, salt, and pepper until creamy. Toss with cabbage and chill for several hours. Just before serving, toss in apples and fold until well distributed.

Easy Cabbage Salad

½ head cabbage, chopped

3 T. vinegar

3 T. granulated sugar

½ C. chopped onion

1 cucumber, chopped
and seeded

Sprinkle vinegar and sugar over chopped cabbage; refrigerate for 5–6 hours or overnight. Drain. Stir in onion and cucumber; serve with choice of salad dressing.

Quick Cole Slaw

½ head cabbage, shredded

1 carrot, grated

1 green onion, minced

¼ C. mayonnaise

2 T. granulated sugar

2 T. milk

2 t. vinegar

Combine cabbage, carrot, and green onion. In a small bowl, stir together the mayonnaise, milk, sugar, and vinegar until well blended. Stir into cabbage mixture until vegetables are well coated. Chill and serve.

Hot Dutch Potato Salad

2 slices bacon

½ C. chopped onion

3 T. cider vinegar

1 T. water

2 T. granulated sugar

½ t. salt

dash pepper

2 potatoes, cooked and diced

Dice bacon into fine pieces and fry until crispy and brown. Add onion and cook until browned. Add vinegar, water, sugar, salt, and pepper. Bring to a boil. Add potatoes; heat through and serve hot.

Wilted Lettuce Salad

½ head lettuce, torn
into large pieces

4 slices bacon, cooked
and crumbled

3 T. vinegar

½ t. salt

2 t. granulated sugar

¼ C. sliced green onion

1 T. cold water

dash pepper

Put lettuce pieces in a large serving bowl. In a skillet, cook bacon until crisp; drain off all but 1 T. bacon fat. Add the vinegar, salt, sugar, onion, water, and pepper; heat until mixture simmers. Immediately pour dressing over lettuce; toss until all lettuce is well coated. Garnish with crumbled bacon.

Classic Waldorf Salad

1 C. diced apple

1 t. lemon juice

1 C. diced celery

½ C. raisins

½ C. chopped nuts

½ C. mayonnaise

1–2 T. milk

1 t. granulated sugar

Toss apple pieces with lemon juice until well coated. Add celery, raisins, and nuts; toss until mixed well. In a small bowl, stir enough milk into the mayonnaise to thin it; stir in the sugar until well blended. Toss the salad with the dressing until well coated. Chill.

Three-Bean Salad

1 can cut green beans

1 can wax (yellow) beans

1 can kidney beans

1 small green pepper, diced

1 small onion, diced

½ C. granulated sugar

⅓ C. vinegar

1 t. salt

¼ t. pepper

⅓ C. cooking oil

Combine all ingredients until well mixed. Chill for several hours before serving.

Best-Yet Macaroni Salad

¾ C. uncooked macaroni

1 C. ripe olives, sliced

2 eggs, hard-cooked and sliced

1 6½-oz. can tuna

2 C. finely shredded cabbage

½ C. mayonnaise

2 t. mustard

2 T. vinegar

1 t. salt

¼ t. pepper

Cook macaroni in boiling salted water until tender; drain, rinse with cold water, and chill until cold. Add olives, eggs, tuna, and cabbage; toss lightly until mixed. In a small bowl, combine mayonnaise, mustard, vinegar, salt, and pepper; beat well. Stir into salad until all is well coated. Chill.

Vienna Macaroni Delight

1 8-oz. pkg. elbow macaroni

1 C. chopped celery

3 T. onion, diced

1 can Vienna sausage, sliced thinly

1 C. mayonnaise

2 T. vinegar

1 t. salt

¼ t. pepper

2 eggs, hard-cooked and sliced

Cook macaroni in boiling salted water until tender; drain and rinse with cold water. Chill until cold. Add celery, onion, and Vienna sausage; toss lightly. In a small bowl, combine mayonnaise, vinegar, salt, and pepper; beat well. Stir into salad until all is well coated. Garnish with hard-cooked eggs. Chill several hours before serving.

Tangy Potato Salad

2 potatoes, cooked and cubed

1 T. chopped parsley

2 T. diced onion

½ t. salt

1 C. chopped celery

½ C. mayonnaise

3 radishes, sliced

Combine all ingredients; mix well. Chill for several hours. Serve on lettuce leaves and garnish with slices of radish and hard-cooked egg, if desired.

Picnic Salad

3 potatoes, cooked and cubed   ½ C. mayonnaise
1 C. celery, chopped   ¼ C. milk
1 C. cucumber, chopped   ½ t. salt
3 hot dogs, cooked and sliced dash pepper
2 T. chopped onion

Combine potatoes, celery, cucumber, and hot dogs in a salad bowl. In a small bowl, stir together onion, mayonnaise, milk, salt, and pepper; beat well. Stir into salad and toss lightly until well coated. Chill.

Nutty Chicken Salad

A great way to use leftover cooked chicken!

1 C. cooked, diced chicken
½ C. chopped celery
¼ C. chopped green pepper
¼ C. chopped nuts
½ C. mayonnaise
¼ t. salt
dash pepper
¼ t. curry powder, optional

Combine chicken, celery, green pepper, and nuts. In a small bowl, beat together mayonnaise, salt, pepper, and curry powder. Stir into salad; blend well. Chill.

Beefy Macaroni Salad

1 C. uncooked elbow macaroni   ½ t. salt
1 C. cucumber, diced   ¼ t. pepper
½ C. chopped celery   1 T. vinegar
2 T. grated onion   1 T. mustard
1 C. cooked cubed beef   2 eggs, hard-cooked and sliced
¾ C. mayonnaise

Cook macaroni in boiling salted water until tender; drain and rinse with cold water. Chill. Add cucumber, celery, onion, and beef. Mix together mayonnaise, salt, pepper, vinegar, and mustard; beat until smooth. Stir into salad until all is well coated. Garnish with eggs and chill before serving.

Tuna Mold

1 3-oz. pkg. lemon gelatin	3 T. chopped onion
½ C. boiling water	2 T. chopped celery
1 6½-oz. can tuna	½ C. mayonnaise
1 can chicken gumbo soup	¼ C. milk
3 T. chopped green pepper	

Dissolve gelatin in boiling water. Set aside. Rinse tuna well in a strainer to remove oil; stir into gelatin. Add remaining ingredients, stirring to mix well. Pour into greased bowl or pan. Chill until well set.

Spanish Chicken Salad

2 C. cooked chicken, cubed and chilled	½ C. green olives, sliced
1½ C. chopped celery	¾ C. mayonnaise
2 hard-cooked eggs, chopped	1 t. salt

Mix all ingredients well. Chill. Serve on lettuce leaves with a spoonful of mayonnaise and some chopped green pepper, if desired.

Mexican Salad

½ lb. ground beef	1 tomato, chopped
½ C. chopped onion	1 avocado, chopped (optional)
1 C. grated cheese	1 15-oz. can kidney beans
½ head lettuce, torn in large pieces	Thousand Island dressing

Brown ground beef and onions until beef is cooked and onions are transparent; drain. Rinse kidney beans well. Add all remaining ingredients. Serve over crushed corn chips and drizzle with dressing.

Tuna Cheese Salad

1 large potato, cooked
and sliced
2 T. Italian salad dressing
2 t. chopped parsley
½ C. cubed cheese
3 T. chopped onion

½ head lettuce, torn into pieces
2 hard-cooked eggs, sliced
¼ C. sliced ripe olives
¼ C. Italian dressing

In salad bowl, sprinkle potatoes with 2 T. salad dressing and parsley; chill thoroughly. Just before serving, toss with cheese, onion, lettuce, eggs, and olives; drizzle dressing over all. Serve immediately.

Salad on a Shoestring

4 carrots, shredded
½ C. chopped celery
¼ C. chopped onion
1 6½-oz. can tuna

¾ C. mayonnaise
2 T. French salad dressing
1 T. sugar
2 C. shoestring potatoes

In a salad bowl, combine carrots, celery, onion, and tuna. Stir until mixed. In a small bowl, beat mayonnaise, dressing, and sugar until smooth. Stir dressing into salad and chill. Just before serving, stir in shoestring potatoes.

Roast Beef Salad

Another super way to use leftover meat!

1 C. cooked beef, cubed
½ C. chopped celery
3 T. chopped onion
1 8-oz. can kidney beans,
drained
1 egg, hard-cooked and
chopped
2 T. pickle, chopped

½ C. mayonnaise
1 T. chili sauce
1 T. mustard
¼ t. salt
dash pepper

132

In a salad bowl, combine beef, celery, onion, beans, egg, and pickle; mix well. In a small bowl, beat mayonnaise, chili sauce, mustard, salt, and pepper until smooth; stir into salad and chill.

Turkey Salad

A delicious follow-up to Thanksgiving dinner.

2 C. cooked turkey, diced

½ C. chopped nuts

½ C. raisins

¼ C. shredded coconut

2 T. chopped onion

¼ C. chopped green pepper

½ C. mayonnaise

1 t. lemon juice

½ t. salt

dash pepper

½ head lettuce, separated into leaves

Combine turkey, nuts, raisins, coconut, onion, green pepper; in a small bowl, beat mayonnaise, lemon juice, salt, and pepper until smooth. Stir dressing into salad. Serve on lettuce leaves.

Favorite Ham Salad

A great way to use leftovers!

1 C. ham, cooked and diced

1 C. cooked peas

1 C. French dressing

1 egg, hard-cooked and sliced

Marinate ham and peas in French dressing overnight; drain. Serve on lettuce; garnish with egg.

Rice Salad

1 C. cooked rice

2 tomatoes, chopped

2 eggs, hard-cooked and chopped

1 6½-oz. can tuna, drained

2 t. cooking oil

½ t. vinegar

½ t. salt

dash pepper

Combine rice, tomatoes, eggs, and tuna. In a small bowl, combine oil, vinegar, salt, and pepper; pour over salad and stir until well mixed. Chill.

Salad Dressings

Cottage Cheese Dressing

1 C. low-fat plain yogurt
1 C. low-fat cottage cheese
½ C. chopped parsley
¼ C. vinegar

2 T. mustard
2 t. granulated sugar
1 T. salt
1 t. pepper

Combine all ingredients, stirring to mix well. Store, covered, in the refrigerator. Makes approximately 2 cups of dressing.

French Dressing

¾ C. salad oil
¼ C. lemon juice or vinegar
1 T. sugar
¾ t. salt

¼ t. paprika
¼ t. dry mustard
¼ t. pepper
¼ t. onion salt

Combine all ingredients in a jar with a tight-fitting lid. Shake until well mixed. Store, covered, in refrigerator. Makes about 1 cup of dressing.

Green Salad Dressing

1 C. mayonnaise or salad dressing
1 C. milk with 1 t. lemon juice added

Combine ingredients and gently add the following spices to desired taste: garlic powder, onion salt, celery salt, parsley (dried), salt and pepper.

Italian Dressing

1 C. cooking oil
½ C. vinegar
1 t. granulated sugar
½ t. salt

½ t. celery salt
¼ t. dry mustard
¼ t. red pepper
¼ t. garlic powder

Combine all ingredients in a jar with a tight-fitting lid. Shake until well mixed. Store, covered, in refrigerator. Makes about

1½ cups dressing.

Thousand Island Dressing

1 C. mayonnaise	1 T. finely chopped onion
2 T. catsup	1 egg, hard-cooked and
2 T. sweet pickle relish	finely chopped
1 T. finely chopped	½ t. salt
green pepper	dash pepper

Combine all ingredients in bowl and beat until smooth. Store, covered, in refrigerator. Makes about 1½ cups dressing.

Quick Thousand Island Dressing

1½ C. salad dressing	¼ C. pickle relish
⅓ C. chili sauce or catsup	1 T. grated or minced onion

Combine ingredients and mix well. Chill before serving. **Variations:** Add 2 t. chopped parsley and/or 1 finely chopped hard-boiled egg and/or 1 T. chopped green pepper.

Roquefort Dressing

2 oz. Roquefort cheese	1 t. salt
½ C. buttermilk	¼ t. pepper
½ C. mayonnaise	

Mash cheese with a fork; beat in buttermilk and mayonnaise until smooth. Add salt and pepper; beat well. Store, covered, in refrigerator. Makes about 2 cups of dressing.

Mayonnaise

You'll need a mixer or blender for this!

1 egg	½ t. salt
½ lemon	1 C. cooking oil
1 t. honey	

In a bowl or blender, combine egg, juice from lemon, honey, and salt. While beating or while blender is on, add oil, one drop at a time.

Store, covered, in refrigerator. Makes about 1 cup of mayonnaise.

Guacamole

1 ripe avocado, mashed	1 tomato, chopped
½ C. mayonnaise	1 t. salt
1 T. lemon juice	¼ t. chili powder
2 T. grated onion	dash pepper

Combine all ingredients. Store, covered, in refrigerator.

Diet Dressing

1 C. cold water	¼ C. catsup
1 T. cornstarch	½ t. paprika
½ t. dry mustard	½ t. Worcestershire sauce
¼ C. vinegar	½ t. salt

Stir cornstarch and dry mustard into cold water until dissolved. Cook over medium heat until thickened. Cool. Add remaining ingredients, beating until smooth. Cover and store in refrigerator.

Easy Dressing

1 C. mayonnaise
1 C. milk
1 t. lemon juice

Mix well and add the following to your taste:
seasoned salt
onion salt
garlic powder
celery salt
salt and pepper
parsley

Combine ingredients. Keeps well in refrigerator. For variation add ¼ cup crumbled bleu cheese.

MOM'S OLD Standbys

MAIN DISHES

Easy Chicken Bake

1 can cream of chicken soup	1 C. instant rice, uncooked
1 can cream of mushroom soup	1 pkg. dry onion soup mix
½ C. milk	1 fryer chicken, cut up

Combine soups and milk; stir until well blended. Sprinkle rice in a 9×13 greased baking pan. Arrange chicken pieces on top of rice. Pour soup mixture over chicken and rice, making sure all pieces of chicken are covered and that all rice is moistened. Sprinkle dry soup mix over chicken. Cover with foil and seal tightly. Bake at 325°F for 1½–2 hours, or until chicken is done and rice is tender.

Golden Chicken Bake

1 C. biscuit mix	dash pepper
1 t. salt	1 fryer chicken, cut up
1½ t. paprika	½ C. butter or margarine

Combine biscuit mix, salt, paprika, and pepper in a paper bag; one at a time, put chicken pieces in bag and shake to coat. Melt butter in baking dish; arrange chicken pieces in dish. Bake at 400°F for 1 hour, reducing heat to 375°F for the last 10 minutes.

Creamy Chicken Divan

2 pkgs. frozen chopped broccoli	½ t. curry powder
	½ C. bread crumbs
3 C. cooked diced chicken	2 T. butter or margarine, melted
3 cans cream of chicken soup	1 C. cheese, grated
1 C. mayonnaise	
2 T. lemon juice	

137

Cook broccoli according to package directions; drain well. Arrange in the bottom of a 9×13 pan. Arrange chicken pieces on top. Combine soup, mayonnaise, lemon juice, curry powder; stir well to blend. Pour over chicken. Combine bread crumbs and butter; sprinkle over top of casserole. Bake at 350°F for 30 minutes. Sprinkle with grated cheese and return to oven for 5 minutes or until cheese is melted.

Penny-Wise Salmon Bake

1 large potato, diced	½ t. salt
3 T. butter or margarine	⅛ t. pepper
3 T. flour	1½ C. milk
4 t. grated onion	1 can pink salmon, drained
1½ t. prepared mustard	

Cook potatoes in salted boiling water until tender, about 10 minutes. Drain well. Melt butter in saucepan; blend in flour, onion, mustard, salt, and pepper. Gradually add milk, stirring constantly, until thickened. Bring to a boil and cook 1 minute. Flake salmon, removing bones and skin. Stir salmon and potatoes into sauce. Spoon into greased baking dish and bake at 350°F for 15 minutes. Serve with peas.

Citrus Halibut Steaks

2 halibut steaks, about 1-inch thick

¼ C. butter or margarine

3 T. chopped onion

2 T. chopped parsley

1 6-oz. can frozen orange juice concentrate, thawed

1 lemon, sliced

¼ t. salt

dash pepper

Saute onion in butter until tender; stir in orange juice and salt and cook until heated through. Sprinkle halibut steaks with salt and pepper; brush with orange juice mixture. Broil approximately 5 minutes, or until fish flakes easily with a fork. Garnish with lemon slices and serve with remaining orange juice mixture.

Salmon Patties

½ C. flaked salmon

2 T. butter or margarine

1 T. flour

¼ C. milk

¼ C. bread crumbs

¼ t. lemon juice

⅛ t. salt

dash pepper

dash red pepper (optional)

Drain salmon well. In small saucepan, melt margarine; stir in flour. Beat in milk, a little at a time, stirring constantly and cooking until thickened. Add salmon, bread crumbs, lemon juice, salt, pepper, and red pepper. Form into patties. Saute in melted butter until heated through. Serve plain or on buns.

Scalloped Tuna and Potatoes

3 T. butter or margarine

3 T. minced onion

½ t. salt

dash pepper

3 T. flour

2 C. milk

1 6½-oz. can tuna,
    drained and flaked

3 large potatoes, thinly sliced

Saute onion in butter until tender. Stir in salt, pepper, and flour; whip in milk to make a sauce. Continue cooking, stirring constantly, until thickened. Add tuna and heat through. Layer potatoes in an 8×8 square pan; pour the tuna mixture over the potatoes. Bake, covered, at 350°F for 1 hour. Uncover and bake 30 additional minutes, or until potatoes are tender.

Crunchy Tuna Casserole

1 6½-oz. can tuna

1½ C. frozen peas, thawed

1 can cream of mushroom soup

1 C. cooked noodles

¼ C. bread crumbs

3 T. melted butter or margarine

1 small pkg. potato chips,
    crushed

Combine tuna, peas, soup, and noodles. Spoon into a greased baking dish. Moisten bread crumbs with melted butter; sprinkle over casserole. Top with crushed potato chips. Bake at 375°F for 35 minutes, or until bubbly hot.

Fried Fish the Easy Way

2 fish fillets	¼ t. onion salt
½ C. flour	¼ t. paprika
1 t. salt	2 T. butter or margarine
¼ t. pepper	2 T. cooking oil

Clean the fish carefully, removing all visible bones and skin; rinse thoroughly in cold running water. In a paper sack, combine flour, salt, pepper, onion salt, and paprika; shake to mix. One at a time, place fish in bag and shake to coat. Heat butter and oil in frying pan; cook fish, turning only once. Be careful not to overcook; fish should flake when gently probed with a fork, but should still look moist.

New England Cabbage Bake

3 small potatoes, sliced thinly	1 can corned beef
½ C. chopped onion	1 can cream of celery soup
½ t. salt	1 C. milk
¼ t. pepper	1½ t. prepared mustard
2 C. shredded cabbage	

Layer potato slices in a lightly greased baking dish. Sprinkle with onion, salt, and pepper. Arrange cabbage over potatoes. Crumble corned beef over cabbage. In a bowl, combine soup, milk, and mustard; spoon over casserole. Bake, covered, at 375°F for 1½ hours or until potatoes are tender.

Pepper Steak

1 lb. round steak, cut in strips
2 medium green peppers, cut in strips
2 medium tomatoes, chopped in large pieces
3 T. soy sauce
1½ T. sugar
3 C. cooked rice

Make a marinade by combining the soy sauce and sugar;

marinade beef strips several hours or overnight in refrigerator. When ready to eat, brown beef in small amount of cooking oil until browned. Remove from pan. Saute green peppers quickly, until bright but still crunchy, stirring constantly. Add tomatoes and return beef and marinade to pan. Heat through. Serve over hot cooked rice.

Beef Pot Roast

3 lb. beef pot roast

½ t. salt

¼ t. pepper

1 envelope dry onion soup mix

2 potatoes, quartered

1 onion, quartered

4 carrots, sliced lengthwise

2 stalks celery, sliced in quarters

½ C. hot water

3 T. flour

Wipe roast with a clean, damp cloth to remove juices. Place in a slow-cooking pot or heavy skillet with lid. Sprinkle with salt, pepper, and onion soup mix. Cover and cook on low to medium temperature for 2–2½ hours. About 1 hour before serving, add vegetables; keep covered. Immediately before serving, move meat and vegetables to a serving dish and keep warm in the oven. Combine hot water and flour in a small jar with a tight-fitting lid; shake to thoroughly mix. Stir into meat juices, stirring constantly during cooking, until slightly thickened to gravy consistency. Serve immediately.

Hamburger Pie

1 lb. ground beef

½ C. chopped onion

1 can cut green beans, drained

1 can condensed cream of tomato soup

4 servings mashed potatoes

1¼ C. grated cheese

Brown meat and onions until meat is cooked and onions are tender; drain fat. Stir in green beans and soup; heat through. Pour into lightly greased baking dish; top with mashed potatoes. Bake at 350°F for 25 minutes; sprinkle grated cheese over top, and bake 10 minutes longer or until cheese is melted and pie is bubbly.

Ham and Scalloped Potatoes

3 medium potatoes, sliced thin
2 medium onions, sliced and separated into rings
1 t. salt
½ t. pepper
½ C. milk
3 T. flour
1 can cheddar cheese soup
1½ C. grated cheese
3 C. cooked ham, cubed

Layer half the potatoes and half the onions in a baking dish. Sprinkle with half the salt and pepper. In a jar with a tight-fitting lid, combine milk and flour until completely blended. In a small saucepan, cook, stirring constantly, until thickened. Stir in soup and cheese until cheese is melted. Pour half of cheese mixture over potatoes and onions. Sprinkle with half the ham. Repeat layers. Bake at 300°F for 2–2½ hours, or until potatoes and onions are tender. Do not bake at too hot a temperature and do not undercook.

Easy Hamburger Stew

1 lb. ground beef
1 small onion, chopped
1 small green pepper, chopped
2 C. grated raw carrots
2 C. grated raw potatoes
1 can cream of mushroom soup
1 t. salt
½ t. pepper
½ C. water
¾ C. crushed potato chips

Brown ground beef, onion, and green pepper; add carrots and potatoes, stirring until well blended. Add salt and pepper and pour into baking dish. Combine water and soup; pour over meat and vegetables, stirring slightly to combine. Top with crushed chips. Bake at 350°F for 35–40 minutes or until bubbly.

Top-of-the-Stove Meatloaf

1 lb. ground beef
¼ C. cracker crumbs
½ can condensed tomato soup
4 T. minced onion
1 egg, slightly beaten
½ t. salt
⅛ t. pepper
2 t. cooking oil
⅛ C. water
2 t. mustard
2 t. catsup
4 slices cheese

Combine beef, crumbs, 3 T. soup, onion, egg, salt, and pepper; mix thoroughly. Mound in the middle of a frying pan and cut into four segments. Brown on both sides in cooking oil. Cover, reduce heat, and simmer for 20–25 minutes or until meat is done. Spoon off fat. Combine rest of soup with water; pour into skillet. Top each "loaf" with mustard, catsup, and a slice of cheese. Cook for 10 minutes or until cheese has melted.

Easy Beef Stew

1 lb. stewing beef	1½ C. water
½ C. flour	2 onions, sliced and separated
1 t. salt	3 potatoes, cubed
½ t. pepper	3 carrots, sliced
3 T. cooking oil	3 stalks celery, sliced

Cut meat into bite-sized pieces. In paper sack, combine flour, salt, and pepper; put pieces of meat in sack, a handful at a time, and shake to coat. Reserve flour. Brown meat in fat until browned on all sides. Add water, cover, and cook over low heat until tender, about 2½ hours. Add vegetables to pan and continue cooking until tender—about 30 minutes. If needed, thicken with reserved flour.

Ground Beef and Noodles

2 T. cooking oil	1 t. salt
1 lb. ground beef	4 C. hot water
¼ C. chopped parsley	1 C. uncooked noodles
1 C. chopped carrots	2 small tomatoes, seeded
½ C. chopped celery	and chopped
1 envelope dry onion soup mix	

Brown the ground beef in the oil, stirring frequently. Stir in parsley, carrots, celery, soup mix, salt, and water; bring to a boil, reduce heat, and simmer for 10–15 minutes, stirring occasionally, until vegetables are almost tender. Add noodles, cover, and cook until tender, about 10 minutes. Add tomatoes and heat through.

Corn and Franks

1 T. cooking oil
2 small potatoes, peeled
and diced
3 T. chopped onion
5 frankfurters, sliced

1 16-oz. can whole-kernel corn
½ t. salt
dash pepper
½ t. chili powder

Saute potatoes in oil until tender; add onion and frankfurters and cook over medium heat until frankfurters begin to brown. Stir in corn, salt, pepper, and chili powder; heat through.

Hamburger Stroganoff

1 lb. ground beef
1 small onion, chopped
1 can cream of mushroom soup
½ C. milk
2 C. cooked noodles

2 T. butter or margarine
1 t. salt
¼ t. pepper
½ C. sour cream

Brown ground beef; drain fat. Saute onions until tender. Stir in soup, milk, noodles, butter, salt, and pepper; simmer, covered, 10–15 minutes. Uncover and simmer 10 minutes. Remove from heat and stir in sour cream. Heat through but do *not* bring to a boil. Serve immediately.

Speedy Hamburger-Rice Casserole

½ C. chopped onions
1 T. butter or margarine
½ lb. ground beef
1 can condensed vegetable
soup
¾ C. water
1 T. catsup

1 T. mustard
¼ t. salt
dash pepper
1¼ C. water
1 C. instant rice

Saute onions in butter until tender; add meat and cook until browned. Stir in soup, ¾ C. water, catsup, mustard, salt, and pepper. Mix well. Bring to a boil, reduce heat, and simmer 15 minutes. While meat is simmering, bring 1¼ C. water to a boil in a

144

saucepan and cook rice according to package directions. Stir cooked rice into meat mixture; spoon into a baking dish and put under the broiler for 3–5 minutes, or until bubbly.

Pigs in Blankets

1 C. biscuit mix	2 T. pickle relish
¼ C. milk	4 skinless frankfurters
2 T. prepared mustard	

Combine biscuit mix and milk; turn onto slightly floured surface and knead until smooth. Roll into rectangle and cut into four pieces. Spread each piece with mustard and pickle relish, and wrap each piece around a frankfurter, pinching ends of dough to seal. Bake on greased cookie sheet at 400°F for 5–7 minutes, or until "blankets" turn a light golden color.

Quick Franks and Potatoes

6 frankfurters	4 servings mashed potatoes
6 T. tomato sauce	1½ C. grated cheese

Split each frankfurter lengthwise and arrange in baking dish; spoon 1 T. of tomato sauce into each pocket. Spoon mashed potatoes between frankfurters; top with grated cheese. Bake at 375°F for 25 minutes.

Savory Meatballs

½ lb. ground beef	½ t. garlic powder
1 envelope dry onion soup mix	2 small tomatoes, chopped
⅛ C. cracker crumbs	and seeded
1 egg, beaten	½ C. water
1 T. cooking oil	¼ C. sour cream
1 T. flour	

Thoroughly combine ground beef, half of onion soup mix, cracker crumbs, and egg; form into small meatballs. Brown in oil. Pour off fat. Add rest of soup mix, flour, garlic powder, tomatoes, water, and sour cream; cover and simmer for 10 minutes. Serve over cooked noodles or rice.

Meat Patties with Tomato Sauce

½ lb. ground beef

¼ C. quick-cooking oatmeal

½ t. salt

dash pepper

2 T. minced onion

1 egg, beaten

¼ C. milk

¼ C. catsup

1 T. brown sugar, firmly packed

2 t. prepared mustard

Combine beef, oatmeal, salt, pepper, onion, egg, and milk; mix thoroughly and form into patties. Brown patties on both sides. Combine catsup, brown sugar, and mustard; put a spoonful on each patty. Cover and simmer for 15–20 minutes or until meat is done.

Barbecued Beans and Franks

2 16-oz. cans pork and beans

¼ C. brown sugar, firmly packed

½ C. catsup

1 T. vinegar

1 T. Worcestershire sauce

¼ t. tabasco sauce

4 frankfurters

Combine beans, brown sugar, catsup, vinegar, Worcestershire sauce, and tabasco sauce; pour into a shallow baking dish. Arrange sliced frankfurters on top. Bake at 350°F for 30–35 minutes, or until bubbly hot.

Easy Swiss Steak

1 lb. steak

2 T. flour

1 t. salt

½ t. pepper

3 T. cooking oil

1 1-lb. can stewed tomatoes

1 carrot, diced

1 stalk celery, diced

¼ C. chopped onion

¼ C. chopped green pepper

1 C. grated cheese

Cut meat into serving pieces. In a paper sack, combine flour, salt, and pepper; shake to mix. Shake meat to coat. Arrange meat in skillet and cook in oil, browning both sides; arrange meat in bottom of baking dish. Add remaining flour mixture to oil; stir in stewed tomatoes, carrot, celery, onion, and green pepper. Bring rapidly to a boil and pour over meat. Bake, covered, at 375°F for 1½ hours or until vegetables and meat are tender. Uncover, top with grated cheese, and bake 10 minutes longer, or until cheese is melted.

Porcupine Meatballs

1 lb. ground beef

¼ C. uncooked rice

1 can cream of chicken soup

¼ C. minced onion

¼ C. minced green pepper

1 t. salt

¼ t. pepper

1 egg, beaten

1 C. water

Thoroughly combine ground beef, ¼ C. of the chicken soup, rice, onion, egg, salt, and pepper. Shape into meatballs and brown in large frying pan. Mix remaining soup with water; pour over meatballs, cover, and simmer for 30–40 minutes or until rice is tender.

Hawaiian Ham Delight

1 slice cooked ham,
  ½-inch thick

1 C. milk

2 T. mustard

1 can pineapple rings

1 apple, cored and sliced
  into rings

¼ C. granulated sugar

4 T. butter or margarine

1½ t. cinnamon

½ C. water

Spread ham with mustard and place in bottom of shallow baking dish. Pour ½ C. of the milk over the ham and bake at 350°F until milk has evaporated. While ham is cooking, heat pineapple rings, apple slices, sugar, butter, cinnamon, and water in small saucepan; simmer until apples are tender. Pour remaining milk on ham and cover with simmered fruit; cook an additional 10 minutes.

Oven Macaroni and Cheese

¾ C. canned milk

½ C. water

1 C. diced cheese

1½ T. butter or margarine

1 C. soft cubes of bread

2 T. diced onion

½ t. salt

dash pepper

2 eggs, beaten

2 C. cooked elbow macaroni

In a large saucepan, combine milk, water, cheese, and butter; heat to boiling, stirring constantly. When cheese melts, remove from heat. Stir in bread cubes, onion, salt and pepper. Fold in eggs and macaroni. Spoon into a greased baking dish and bake at 350°F for 30 minutes.

Corny Casserole

2 C. cooked noodles

1 7-oz. can corned beef, crumbled

¼ C. minced onion

¼ C. minced celery

1 can cream of mushroom soup

1 4-oz. can mushrooms, drained

½ C. canned milk

1 C. grated cheese

Combine all ingredients and pour into a greased baking dish. Top with bread crumbs or crushed potato chips if desired. Bake at 425°F for 10–15 minutes or until bubbly.

Beef Nachos

You can make a meal out of these!

½ lb. ground beef

½ C. minced onion

1 C. refried beans

1 t. salt

¼ t. pepper

1½ C. tomato sauce

4 T. chopped jalapeno peppers

1 large tomato, chopped and seeded

1 C. sliced ripe olives

1 pkg. nacho-flavored corn chips

1½ C. grated cheese

Brown ground beef and onion until meat is cooked and onion is tender; spoon off excess fat and stir in refried beans, salt, pepper, tomato sauce, and jalapeno peppers. Heat through. Arrange a generous serving of corn chips on each plate. Spoon beef/bean mixture on chips; sprinkle with tomato and olives; top with cheese. Place under the broiler until cheese melts, about 3 minutes. Serve immediately.

Easy Tamale Pie

½ lb. ground beef

½ C. minced onion

2 t. garlic powder

1 8-oz. can tomato sauce

½ C. milk

1 egg, slightly beaten

1 6-oz. can whole-kernel corn

¼ C. sliced olives

½ C. yellow cornmeal

1 t. chili powder

1 t. salt

Cook ground beef and onion with garlic powder until meat is brown and onion is tender. Stir in tomato sauce, milk, egg, corn, olives, cornmeal, chili powder, and salt. Spoon into an 8×8 square baking dish. Bake at 350°F for 40–45 minutes; knife inserted in the middle will come out clean. Cut in squares and serve immediately.

Speedy Spaghetti

1 small onion, chopped

1 t. garlic powder

1 T. cooking oil

½ lb. ground beef

½ t. salt

⅛ t. pepper

dash red pepper

¼ t. chili powder

¼ t. tabasco sauce

1 t. Worcestershire sauce

½ can cream of tomato soup

½ can cream of mushroom soup

1 4-oz. can mushrooms, drained

4 oz. dry spaghetti noodles

½ C. grated cheese

Brown the onion and garlic powder in the hot oil. Add the ground beef and cook until done. Spoon off excess fat. Add seasonings, soups, and mushrooms and simmer, covered, for 20–30 minutes. Cook spaghetti in boiling salted water; drain and rinse with hot water. Arrange on plates; spoon sauce over noodles and sprinkle with grated cheese. Serve immediately.

Crunchy Corn Dogs

½ C. flour

¾ t. baking powder

⅓ C. cornmeal

1 T. sugar

½ t. salt

½ C. milk

1 egg, beaten

1 t. cooking oil

4–6 frankfurters

Sift together flour, baking powder, cornmeal, and sugar. In a small bowl, stir together milk, egg, and oil; beat in dry ingredients. If desired, skewer each frankfurter on a wooden stick; dip in batter. Fry in hot oil and drain on paper towels. Serve hot.

Easy Barbecued Chicken

2 lbs. chicken pieces

2 T. Worcestershire sauce

1 T. vinegar

1 T. bottled meat sauce

1 T. granulated sugar

¼ C. catsup

Combine Worcestershire sauce, vinegar, meat sauce, sugar, and catsup until well mixed. Arrange chicken pieces, skin side up, in a greased baking dish. Brush liberally with sauce. Bake, uncovered, at 350°F for 1 hour.

To fry: As an alternative, fry chicken pieces for 35 minutes in small amount of cooking oil; turn frequently. Drain grease. Brush sauce on fried chicken, cover, and simmer for 10 minutes.

Meat Balls with Potatoes

½ lb. ground beef

¼ C. dry bread crumbs

¼ C. canned milk

1 egg, beaten

½ t. salt

¼ C. minced onion

2 T. flour

½ t. salt

¼ t. pepper

1 onion, sliced and
    separated into rings

2 large potatoes, sliced

½ t. salt

¼ t. pepper

½ C. boiling water

In a bowl, mix ground beef, bread crumbs, milk, egg, salt, and onion. Form into 6–8 large meatballs. In a paper sack, combine flour, ½ t. salt, and ¼ t. pepper; put meatballs in the sack, a few at a time, and shake to coat. Brown meatballs in 1–2 T. hot fat until done; push to side and brown onion rings. Layer sliced potatoes on top of meat and onion; sprinkle ½ t. salt and ¼ t. pepper on potatoes. Pour boiling water over potatoes. Cover and simmer for 15–20 minutes or until potatoes are done. Serve immediately.

Easiest-Ever Scalloped Potatoes

2 large potatoes	1 C. grated cheese
1 large onion	1 C. cooked ham, cubed
1 can cream of mushroom soup	

Scrub and cut potatoes in pieces; cut onions in pieces. Boil in salted water until tender; drain and set aside. Combine soup and cheese in saucepan; simmer until cheese melts. Add ham; heat through. Stir in potatoes and onions; heat through. Serve immediately.

Pork Chops and Rice

4 pork chops	2 T. chopped onion
½ C. flour	2 T. cooking oil
½ t. salt	2 T. chopped green pepper
¼ t. pepper	1 t. salt
½ C. uncooked rice	¼ t. pepper
2 C. stewed tomatoes	

Trim fat and bone from pork chops. Stir together flour, salt, and pepper; roll chops in flour mixture to coat, and brown in skillet in hot oil. Combine rice, tomatoes, onion, oil, green pepper, salt, and pepper; pour over chops in skillet. Cover and simmer for 45 minutes. Do *not* lift lid during cooking.

Stuffed Pork Chops

1½ C. soft bread crumbs	1 egg, beaten
½ t. salt	¾ C. yellow corn
2 T. minced green pepper	4 pork chops, 1-inch thick
2 T. minced onion	1 can cream of mushroom soup
2 T. melted butter	

In a small bowl, combine bread crumbs, salt, green pepper, onion, melted butter, egg, and corn into a stiff stuffing. Cut a slit in each chop and stuff with stuffing. Arrange chops in a greased baking dish; pour soup over chops. Cover and bake at 350°F for 1 hour.

Easy Meatloaf

1 lb. ground beef	¼ C. green pepper, diced
1 C. dry bread crumbs	1 t. salt
2 eggs, beaten	¼ t. pepper
½ C. onion, minced	2 C. tomato sauce

Combine ground beef, bread crumbs, eggs, onion, green pepper, salt, pepper, and 1 C. tomato sauce; use hands to knead the mixture until it is well combined. Shape into a loaf and bake at 350°F for 30 minutes. Pour remaining 1 C. tomato sauce over loaf and bake 30 minutes longer. Slice and serve immediately.

Tangy Chicken

1 lb. chicken pieces	1 C. water
½ C. flour	2 T. brown sugar, packed
1 t. salt	½ t. pepper
2 T. butter	½ C. chopped onion
½ C. chopped celery	1 C. catsup

Combine flour and salt; roll chicken pieces in flour mixture to coat. Fry in skillet in hot oil until browned on all sides. In a small bowl, combine melted butter, chopped celery, water, brown sugar, pepper, onion, and catsup; pour over chicken in skillet. Cover and simmer 30 minutes, or until thick and celery and onion are tender.

Beef Rolls

½ lb. ground beef	⅔ C. milk
½ C. chopped onion	2 T. flour
¼ C. catsup	2 C. hot water
1 T. Worcestershire sauce	2 beef bouillon cubes
¼ t. pepper	¼ t. salt
2 C. biscuit mix	dash pepper

Brown ground beef in large skillet; add onions and cook until tender. Stir in catsup, Worcestershire sauce, and pepper; set aside. In large bowl, combine biscuit mix and milk; knead until smooth. Roll out into a rectangle. Spread with meat mixture. Roll up and pinch seam shut. Slice, arrange on ungreased cookie sheet, and bake at 475°F for 10 minutes. In pan used to cook hamburger, stir in 1 T. flour. Dissolve bouillon cubes in hot water and pour into pan; cook, stirring constantly, until thickened. Season with salt and pepper. Pour gravy over beef rolls and serve immediately.

Tin Foil Roast

1 2½–3 lb. roast

1 envelope dry onion soup mix

1 can cream of mushroom soup

Place roast on a doubled sheet of heavy-duty tin foil. Stir together the soup and soup mix; pour on top of roast. Seal foil. Put roast in pot and cook in oven at 350°F for 1¼ hours. Use juice for gravy.

Easy Franks and Potatoes

4 small potatoes, cooked and cubed

2 small onions, chopped

3 T. butter or margarine, melted

4 frankfurters, cut up

Brown potatoes and onions in butter; add hot dogs and heat through. Serve immediately.

Hawaiian Chops

4 pork chops   ½ t. pepper
½ C. flour   4 slices of pineapple
1 t. salt

Trim excess fat from pork chops. In a bowl, combine flour, salt, and pepper; roll chops in flour mixture to coat. Arrange chops in a baking dish; bake at 375°F for 30 minutes. Lay a slice of pineapple on each chop; return to 350°F oven for 15 minutes.

Chops and Cheesy Potatoes

1 can potatoes, cut in pieces, or 2–3 cooked potatoes

1 T. onion, minced

1 can cream of mushroom soup

1 can cheddar cheese soup

4 pork chops

Combine potatoes, onion, mushroom soup, and cheese soup. Arrange pork chops in greased baking dish; top with potatoes. Bake at 350°F for 1 hour.

Upside-Down Meat Pie

½ lb. ground beef   ½ C. tomato sauce
¼ C. chopped celery   1 t. mustard
¼ C. chopped onion   1 C. biscuit mix
1 small carrot, grated   ¼ C. milk
¼ C. chopped green pepper   4 slices cheese

In small skillet, brown beef; add celery, onion, carrot, green pepper, and tomato sauce, cooking until vegetables are tender. Stir in mustard. In small bowl, combine biscuit mix and milk; knead and roll out into a circle. Spoon meat mixture into slightly greased pie plate; top with dough. Bake at 450°F for 10–15 minutes, or until dough is lightly browned. Turn upside down on serving plate and top with slices of cheese. Cut in wedges to serve.

Creamy Stuffed Potatoes

2 potatoes, baked in skins   ¼ C. flour

1 4-oz. pkg. dried beef   1½ C. milk

¼ C. butter or margarine

Split tops of potatoes. Snip beef into small pieces; brown very slightly in melted butter. Stir in flour; add milk, stirring constantly, until thickened. Pour beef "gravy" into potatoes. Serve immediately.

Tangy Spam Loaf

1 can Spam   1 egg, well beaten

1 C. onion, grated   4 T. catsup

1 large potato, grated   1 T. mustard

2 carrots, grated   1 C. milk

With a fork, mash Spam until it is broken up with a consistency similar to ground beef. Mix in onion, potato, carrot, egg, catsup, and mustard; knead with fingers to mix thoroughly. Mix in milk. Spread in a greased loaf pan. Bake at 350°F for 1 hour.

Hamburger Cheese Patties

Simple and delicious!

½ lb. ground beef   2 slices cheese

½ t. salt   1 small can tomato sauce

¼ t. pepper

dash red pepper or
  chili powder

Mix ground beef, salt, pepper, and red pepper until well blended. Form into four patties and press thin between two plates. Top two of the patties with first a slice of cheese and then another patty; pinch around the edges to seal. Brown on both sides; reduce heat, pour tomato sauce over patties, and simmer for 15–20 minutes. Serve immediately.

Easy Chicken Pie

A delicious use for leftover chicken!

4 T. butter or margarine	1 C. cooked carrots
4 T. flour	1 can green beans, drained
¼ t. salt	1 potato, cooked, peeled,
dash pepper	and cubed
1 C. hot water	1 can refrigerator biscuits
1 chicken bouillon cube	
1 C. milk	
2 C. cooked chicken, cut in cubes	

Melt butter; stir in flour, salt, and pepper. Dissolve bouillon cube in hot water; stir into flour mixture, add milk, and stir constantly over medium heat until thickened. Combine sauce with chicken and vegetables; pour into a lightly greased casserole dish. Arrange biscuits on top. Bake at 450°F for 10–15 minutes, or until bubbly and biscuits are lightly golden. Serve immediately.

Corn Dumpling Skillet Pie

½ lb. ground beef	¼ C. yellow cornmeal
1 T. flour	1 t. baking powder
¼ t. salt	½ t. salt
dash pepper	dash chili powder
1 C. cooked green beans	1 egg, beaten
1¼ C. tomato juice	½ C. milk
½ C. cooked whole-kernel corn	3 T. cooking oil
½ C. flour	

Brown ground beef; drain off excess fat. Stir in 1 T. flour, salt, and pepper. Stir in tomato juice gradually, stirring constantly, until thickened. Add beans and corn. In small bowl, sift together flour, cornmeal, baking powder, chili powder, and salt. In a separate bowl, beat together eggs, milk, and cooking oil. Pour liquid into flour mixture; stir with a fork, just until all ingredients are moistened. Bring hamburger mixture to a boil; drop cornmeal mixture onto meat mixture by spoonfuls. Cover; reduce heat and simmer for 15–20 minutes, or until dumplings are firm.

Enchiladas

½ lb. ground beef

¼ C. chopped onions

2 T. chopped green chilis (optional)

1 small can tomato sauce

¼ C. sliced ripe olives

8 corn tortillas

2 C. shredded cheese

1 can mild enchilada sauce

½ C. sour cream

½ head lettuce, shredded

In large skillet, brown hamburger, onions, and chilis until hamburger is cooked and onions are transparent. Stir in tomato sauce, olives, and 1 C. of the shredded cheese. Place a spoonful of the meat mixture in the center of each tortilla, roll tortilla up, and place in greased baking dish, seam side down. Pour enchilada sauce over tortillas; sprinkle with rest of cheese. Bake at 350°F for 20–25 minutes, or until bubbly and cheese is melted. Serve with a dollop of sour cream over a bed of shredded lettuce.

Ham and Cheese Pie

A delicious main-dish pie—and no bother with a crust!

4 T. butter or margarine

½ lb. mushrooms, sliced thinly

1 small onion, sliced and separated into rings

1 C. ham, cut in thin strips

1 C. Swiss cheese, grated

4 eggs, beaten well

1 C. canned milk

2 T. mustard

¾ t. salt

dash pepper

Melt butter or margarine in a large skillet. Saute mushrooms in butter until tender; remove from butter and layer on the bottom of a greased 9-inch pie plate. Saute onion rings in butter until limp and transparent; remove from butter and layer on top of mushrooms. Arrange strips of ham on top of onion rings. Sprinkle grated cheese over ham. Beat together melted butter, eggs, canned milk, mustard, salt, and pepper; pour gently over meat and vegetables in pie plate. Bake at 425°F for 15–20 minutes, or until knife inserted in center comes out clean.

Zucchini Casserole

A delicious main dish when you don't have meat.

¼ C. chopped onion
4 C. sliced, peeled zucchini
1 can cream of chicken soup
1 8-oz. pkg. herb-seasoned stuffing mix
½ C. butter or margarine, melted
1 C. sour cream
1½ C. shredded cheese

Cook onion and zucchini in boiling water for 5 minutes or until tender; drain. In a bowl, combine soup, sour cream, and shredded cheese. In a separate bowl, make stuffing according to package directions; stir in butter or margarine. Spread half the stuffing over the bottom of a baking dish; spoon on the zucchini and the soup mixture. Top with remaining stuffing. Bake at 350°F for 25–30 minutes, or until bubbling.

Hearty Hamburger Stew

¼ lb. ground beef
¼ C. onion, chopped
2 stalks, celery, sliced
1 16-oz. can tomatoes
2½ C. water
2 small carrots, diced

2 medium potatoes, cubed
¼ C. green pepper, chopped
¼ C. uncooked rice
1½ t. salt
½ t. pepper

Brown hamburger in a large skillet. Stir in onion, celery, tomatoes, water, carrots, potatoes, green pepper, rice, salt, and pepper; simmer, covered, for about 25 minutes, or until vegetables and rice are tender.

Easy Sloppy Joes

½ lb. ground beef
¼ C. catsup

2 T. minced onion
½ can chicken gumbo soup

Brown ground beef; stir in catsup, onion, and chicken gumbo soup. Cover and simmer 10–15 minutes, stirring occasionally. Serve on hamburger buns.

Chicken Divan

3 pkg. frozen broccoli, chopped
3 C. cooked chicken,
   cut in cubes
3 cans cream of chicken soup
1½ C. mayonnaise
1½ t. lemon juice
½ t. curry powder
1 C. bread crumbs
2 T. butter or margarine, melted
1 C. shredded cheese

Cook broccoli according to package directions; drain. Arrange in the bottom of a 9×13 baking dish. Arrange chicken on top of broccoli. In a large bowl, combine soup, mayonnaise, lemon juice, and curry powder; mix well. Pour over chicken. Combine bread crumbs and melted butter; sprinkle over casserole. Bake at 350°F for 25–30 minutes, or until bubbly hot. Remove from oven and sprinkle with cheese; return to oven for 5 minutes or until cheese is melted. Serve immediately.

Beef and Chili Beans

1 C. onions, chopped
½ green pepper, chopped
1 T. cooking oil
1 lb. ground beef
1 16-oz. can tomatoes
2 16-oz. cans chili beans,
   drained
1 t. salt
½ C. catsup
¼ t. chili powder
2 T. sugar
1 T. vinegar
dash red pepper
½ t. oregano

Cook onions and green pepper in cooking oil until tender. Add ground beef and brown thoroughly. Stir in tomatoes, beans, salt, catsup, chili powder, sugar, vinegar, red pepper, and oregano; bring to a boil, reduce to low, and simmer for 25–30 minutes, or until thick. Garnish with grated cheese or chopped onion, if desired.

Quick Taco Salad

¼ lb. ground beef
1 can kidney beans,
   rinsed and drained
¼ C. onions, chopped
½ head lettuce, shredded

1 green pepper, coarsely
   chopped
1 tomato, seeded and chopped
1 C. shredded cheese
2 C. corn chips

In a small skillet, brown the ground beef thoroughly; stir in the beans and heat through. In individual serving bowls, place 1 C. each of corn chips. Spoon half the ground beef-bean mixture in each bowl. Top each with half the onions, half the lettuce, half the green pepper, half the tomato, and half the cheese. Serve with catsup or taco sauce if desired.

Spaghetti and Meatballs

½ lb. ground beef
½ C. onion, finely chopped
½ t. salt
dash pepper
2 T. cooking oil

1 8-oz. can tomato sauce
¼ C. water
1 4-oz. can sliced
   mushrooms, drained
½ lb. spaghetti noodles
½ C. grated parmesan cheese

In a small bowl, combine ground beef, onion, salt, and pepper; shape into small meatballs. In large skillet, brown the meatballs in the cooking oil until browned evenly; drain off excess fat. Pour tomato sauce, water, and mushrooms over meatballs; stir to blend, and simmer, covered, over low heat about 10–15 minutes. In the meantime, heat 2 quarts of salted water to boiling; cook spaghetti noodles until tender, according to package directions. Rinse in hot water and drain well. Place half the spaghetti noodles on each plate; spoon over half the sauce, and sprinkle half the parmesan cheese over each. Serve immediately.

Polka-Dot Macaroni and Cheese

2 C. uncooked macaroni
1 can cheddar cheese soup
½ C. milk

1 t. Worcestershire sauce
2 frankfurters

Cook macaroni according to package directions; drain well. Pour into an 8-inch square baking dish; stir in cheddar cheese soup, milk, and Worcestershire sauce. Cut frankfurters into very thin slices and arrange on top of macaroni. Bake, uncovered, at 375°F for 25 minutes, or until bubbly.

Chili Mac

1 lb. ground beef

1 small onion, chopped

1 can tomatoes

½ C. macaroni

Brown ground beef and onions until meat is cooked and onions are tender. Stir in tomatoes and macaroni; cover and simmer until macaroni is tender, about 10 minutes. Salt and pepper to taste.

Vegetable Beef Casserole

1 lb. ground beef

1 10-oz. pkg. frozen peas

4 T. chopped onion

1 C. chopped celery

1 can cream of mushroom soup

½ t. salt

¼ t. pepper

3 T. canned milk

2 C. crushed potato chips

Brown ground beef until thoroughly cooked; spread in bottom of baking dish. In large bowl, combine peas, onions, celery, soup, salt, and pepper; pour over beef. Sprinkle with crushed potato chips. Bake at 350°F for 30 minutes.

Speedy Stroganoff

1 lb. ground beef

½ C. chopped onion

½ C. chopped celery

1 can cream of celery soup

1 C. sour cream

1 can sliced mushrooms, drained

2 T. tomato paste

buttered noodles, cooked

In large skillets, brown ground beef thoroughly; drain grease. Add onion, celery, soup, sour cream, mushrooms, and tomato paste; simmer over low heat for 5 minutes, or until heated through. Serve over buttered noodles.

Skillet Potpourri

6 slices bacon, cooked
and crumbled

1 12-oz. can corned beef, cubed

¼ C. chopped onion

1 can cream of chicken soup

¼ C. milk

1 T. mustard

1 16-oz. can whole potatoes,
drained and sliced, or
2–3 cooked potatoes

1 8-oz. can green beans,
drained

Cook corned beef and onion in 2 T. of the bacon drippings until onion is transparent. Combine soup, milk, and mustard; beat until well blended. Stir soup mixture, potato slices, and beans into corned beef; heat through, stirring frequently. Garnish with crumbled bacon.

Easiest-Ever Pizza

1 C. flour

1 t. salt

⅛ t. pepper

2 eggs, beaten

⅔ C. milk

1 lb. ground beef

1 4-oz. can mushroom pieces,
drained

1 8-oz. can tomato sauce

2 C. grated cheese

½ t. oregano

In large mixing bowl, combine flour, salt, pepper, eggs, and milk; beat until smooth and pour into a large pie plate or pizza pan. Make sure batter covers the bottom of the pan. Brown ground beef; drain well and sprinkle over crust batter. Sprinkle on mushrooms, pour on tomato sauce, and sprinkle cheese and oregano over the pizza. Bake at 425 °F for 20–25 minutes or until bubbling and cheese has melted.

Pizza Burger

1 lb. ground beef

1 t. salt

¼ t. pepper

1 large tomato, seeded
and chopped

1 C. grated cheese

½ t. oregano

1 T. chopped onion

Thoroughly mix the ground beef, salt, and pepper; pat in the bottom of a pie plate. Top with tomato, cheese, oregano, and onion. Bake at 350°F for 25–30 minutes. Cut into wedges to serve.

Cheesey Beef Casserole

This can be made ahead of time and refrigerated.

½ lb. ground beef

1 T. butter or margarine, melted

3 T. minced onion

1 8-oz. can tomato sauce

½ t. salt

dash pepper

½ C. sour cream

½ C cream-style cottage cheese

3 T. chopped parsley

½ C. cooked carrots, sliced

4 oz. noodles, cooked
    and drained

Brown ground beef in melted butter or margarine; add onions and saute. Stir in tomato sauce, salt, and pepper; simmer, uncovered, 5 minutes or until thickened. In a bowl, combine sour cream, cottage cheese, parsley, and carrots; gently stir in cooked noodles. In greased baking dish, layer half the meat mixture, half the cottage cheese mixture, half the meat mixture, and finish with half the cottage cheese mixture. Top with grated cheese and bake at 350°F for 25–30 minutes, or until bubbly.

Quickest-Ever Beef Stew

3 C. water

1 envelope dry onion soup mix

2 potatoes, peeled and cubed

1 10-oz. pkg. frozen mixed
    vegetables

2 T. flour

¼ C. water

2½ C. cooked beef, cubed

1 C. shredded cheese

Heat water to boiling; stir in soup mix, potatoes, and frozen vegetables. Cook for 10–12 minutes, or until vegetables are tender. Stir the flour into the ¼ C. water until well blended; stir into the vegetable mixture and heat, stirring constantly, until thickened. Stir in beef and heat through. Place in serving bowls; top with shredded cheese.

Barley Stew

3 T. cooking oil
½ C. shredded raw chicken
½ onion, minced
½ C. pearl barley
½ C. sliced mushrooms

2 C. hot water
2 chicken bouillon cubes
⅛ t. pepper
2 carrots, sliced thinly

Heat cooking oil; stir in chicken, onion, and barley, and saute until chicken is lightly browned. In a measuring cup, dissolve bouillon cubes in hot water; add to chicken/barley mixture. Stir in pepper and carrots. Bring to a boil, reduce heat, and simmer 25 minutes.

Chinese Casserole

1 lb. ground beef
1 small onion, chopped
2 C. cooked rice
1 can cream of chicken soup

1 can cream of mushroom soup
1 T. soy sauce
1 can Chinese noodles

Brown ground beef and onions until meat is well browned and onions are tender. In a large bowl, combine rice, cream of chicken soup, cream of mushroom soup, and soy sauce. In bottom of casserole dish, sprinkle half the Chinese noodles. Spread meat-onion mixture over noodles. Top with soup mixture, and sprinkle remaining noodles over the top. Bake at 350°F for 10–15 minutes, or until bubbly hot.

Chicken-Filled Dumplings

1 can cream of chicken soup
1 can golden mushroom soup
1 C. water
3 T. chopped onion
1½ C. cooked chicken, cubed

¼ C. celery, minced
2 T. onion, minced
¼ t. pepper
1 can refrigerated country-style biscuits

In large saucepan, combine cream of chicken soup, golden

mushroom soup, water, and 3 T. chopped onion; heat to boiling, reduce heat, and simmer. In small bowl, combine chicken, celery, onion, pepper; stir to blend. Separate biscuits and roll each out until thin. Spoon chicken mixture into the center of each; wrap dough around chicken mixture and pinch to seal. Place dumplings on top of simmering soup; spoon soup over dumplings. Simmer for 15–20 minutes, or until dough in dumplings is cooked. Serve immediately. Leftovers can be refrigerated and reheated by simmering for 15 minutes, or until heated through.

Mushroom Soup Casserole

1 lb. ground beef

1 can cream of mushroom soup

¼ C. milk

½ C. mushrooms

½ C. onion, chopped

1 C. sour cream

4 oz. cooked noodles

Brown ground beef until done; drain off grease. Stir in cream of mushroom soup, milk, mushrooms, onion, sour cream, and noodles; simmer, covered, for 5–8 minutes. Serve immediately.

New England Bake

2 medium potatoes, peeled and thinly sliced

2 C. shredded cabbage

2 T. butter or margarine, melted

1 T. flour

⅛ t. salt

¾ C. milk

1 T. prepared mustard

½ can corned beef, sliced

In large amount of boiling water, cook potatoes until tender, about 15 minutes; add cabbage and cook 5 minutes more. Drain. Meanwhile, in small saucepan stir melted butter and flour together into a paste; stir in salt and milk, gradually, stirring constantly until thickened. Stir in mustard and set aside. Stir mustard mixture into drained potatoes and cabbage. In casserole, spread half the potato/cabbage mixture; top with the corned beef slices. Top with remaining potato/cabbage mixture. Bake, covered, at 350°F for 20–25 minutes, or until heated through. Serve immediately.

It Doesn't End with Plucking: How to Bone a Chicken

Chances are, you'll never have to pluck a chicken—but if you want to savor one of nature's most economical and delicious meats, you should know how to cut and bone one! You can save a considerable amount of money if you buy stewing hens or whole fryers and cut them up yourself.

Boning a chicken is easy. You'll need a good pair of kitchen shears or scissors, a sharp paring knife, and an elementary knowledge of chicken anatomy. You can do it in less than a dozen steps:

1. Gather your equipment. Make sure the chicken is completely thawed before you attempt to cut it up. Choose an area where you'll be comfortable; you might want to sit at your kitchen table so that the chicken will be at a comfortable height.

2. Place the chicken breast side up. With your sharp knife, cut all the way through the skin and flesh in a lengthwise slit from the neck to the cavity. Turn the chicken over, and make another lengthwise slit through the skin and flesh on the underside.

3. Place the chicken breast side up. With the kitchen shears or scissors, cut through the ribs to one side of the breastbone.

4. Turn the chicken over; cut through the ribs to either side of the backbone, and remove the backbone.

5. Locate the natural division of the chicken that is just below the rib; using your shears, cut completely through the flesh so that the chicken is cut into four pieces.

6. If you are frying the chicken, you need to separate the drumstick from the thigh; to do it, bend the leg at the joint and cut through the joint with a sharp paring knife. If you are boiling the chicken, you can leave the leg attached to the thigh.

7. To separate the wings from the breast, bend the chicken at the joint as with the leg; again, use a sharp paring knife to cut completely through the joint.

8. To reduce calories in broiled chicken, remove the skin by slipping your fingers between the skin and the chicken's flesh. Pull the skin gently away; use a sharp paring knife to help cut the skin away where necessary. Trim off the excess fat that lies beneath the skin; it's yellow and usually lies in small pockets.

9. To remove the meat from the bones before cooking it, use a sharp paring knife; using short, quick strokes, coax the meat away from the bones.

10. Remember: don't throw out the bones! You can stew them and make your own chicken broth. Simply put them in a heavy saucepan, cover with hot water, put on a lid, and simmer. You can add salt, parsley, pepper, and other seasonings to taste. Simmer for at least an hour. When you've finished, put the broth in the refrigerator—the fat will rise to the top and congeal. Before warming the broth again, simply pick the hardened fat from the top.

MOM'S OLD Standbys

VEGETABLES AND RICE

Cheesy Broccoli Bake

1 pkg. frozen chopped broccoli	1 egg, beaten
½ C. mayonnaise	1½ C. grated cheese
½ C. cream of mushroom soup	1 C. crushed crackers

Cook broccoli according to package directions; drain well and cool. Combine mayonnaise, soup, egg, and grated cheese; stir in cooked broccoli. Pour into a buttered casserole dish, and sprinkle cracker crumbs on top. Bake at 325°F for 30 minutes.

Harvard Beets

¼ C. cider vinegar	2 t. flour
¼ C. granulated sugar	½ T. butter, melted
¼ t. salt	2 C. cubed cooked beets
½ t. prepared mustard	

Combine cider vinegar, sugar, salt, mustard, flour, and butter until well blended; cook over low heat, stirring constantly, until thick. Pour over cubed beets and stir to coat beets. Serve immediately.

Easy Pickled Beets

1 can small, whole beets

juice from 1 jar pickles

Drain the liquid from the canned beets; cover the beets with the pickle juice. Cover and chill for at least 4 hours. Can be served hot or cold.

Oriental Summer Vegetables

1 T. butter or margarine
1 T. cooking oil
1 chicken bouillon cube
2 medium-sized zucchini squash, sliced
¼ lb. fresh mushrooms, sliced

3 medium-sized carrots, sliced
1 small green pepper, cut in strips
½ C. sliced onion
1 T. lemon juice

Heat butter and oil over low heat until butter melts; add bouillon cube, stirring and mashing until dissolved. Add zucchini, mushrooms, and carrots and cook over medium heat, stirring constantly, about 3 minutes. Add green pepper and sliced onion and cook, stirring constantly, about 3 more minutes or until vegetables are crispy-tender. Add lemon juice and mix well. Can be served over cooked rice for a main dish.

Zucchini-Bacon Fry

3 slices bacon, cubed
2 C. peeled, cubed zucchini

dash salt
dash pepper

Fry cubed bacon until crisp; add zucchini, salt and pepper to taste, cover, and cook for 15–20 minutes, or until zucchini is tender.

Zucchini Bake

2 zucchini squash, peeled and cubed
2 eggs, beaten
¼ C. milk
1 t. baking powder
2 T. flour

½ lb. cheese, cubed
¼ C. onion, diced
¼ C. green pepper, diced

Cook zucchini in a small amount of boiling water until almost tender (about 5 minutes); drain and let cool. Combine eggs, milk, baking powder, cheese cubes, onion, and green pepper. Stir in zucchini. Bake in a greased casserole dish at 350°F for 35 minutes; let stand for 10 minutes before serving.

Scalloped Potatoes

4 or 5 potatoes   1 can cheddar cheese soup
1 onion sliced thin   1 can cream of mushroom soup

Peel and slice potatoes and onion. Layer in a greased casserole dish. Mix soups together and thin with 1 can of milk. Pour over potatoes. Cover and bake at 350°F for 1 hour or until done.

Cheesy Scalloped Potatoes

4 potatoes, cooked, peeled,   ¼ t. paprika
   and sliced   ¼ t. prepared mustard
3 T. salad oil   3 C. milk
3 T. cornstarch   2 C. cheese, grated
1 t. salt

Layer potatoes in a greased casserole dish. In a saucepan, combine salad oil, cornstarch, salt, paprika, mustard, and milk. Stirring constantly, bring to a boil. Remove from heat and add cheese; stir until cheese is melted. Pour sauce over potatoes. Bake at 350°F for 35 minutes.

Potato Onion Bake

2 potatoes, peeled and sliced   3 T. flour
1 large onion, sliced and   ½ C. milk
   separated into rings   1 C. cheese, grated
2 T. butter, melted   ¼ t. salt
1 can cheddar cheese soup   dash pepper

Layer a third of the potatoes and onions in a greased casserole dish. In a saucepan, combine the butter, cheese soup, flour, and milk; stirring constantly, cook until bubbly. Remove from heat and stir in grated cheese and salt. Pour a third of the sauce over the potatoes and onions in the casserole dish. Repeat these layers two more times. Cover with foil and cook at 300°F for 2½ hours, or until potatoes and onions are tender.

Baked Cheesed Potatoes

4 or 5 potatoes peeled

3 T. butter or margarine

1½ t. salt

dash pepper

¾ C. grated cheese

½ C. light cream

¼ C. milk

Cut potatoes in strips as for french fries. Place in center of strip of foil. Dot with butter or margarine, sprinkle with salt and pepper. Top with cheese. Fold up edges of foil to hold liquid and add milk and cream. Fold foil over and seal edges, allowing some space for steam. Bake 350°F for 50 minutes or until done.

Skillet Scalloped Potatoes

2 potatoes, peeled and
thinly sliced

2 T. cooking oil

¼ t. salt

dash pepper

1 C. canned milk

Brown potatoes in heavy skillet in cooking oil. When tender, sprinkle with salt and add canned milk. Simmer, covered, over low heat for 10 minutes, or until milk has formed a sauce. Serve immediately.

Creamed New Potatoes and Peas

8 small (new) potatoes,
cooked but not peeled

¼ C. butter or margarine

3 T. flour

1½ t. salt

¼ t. pepper

1½ C. milk

1 C. canned milk

1 10-oz. pkg. frozen peas

½ C. finely diced onion

4 slices bacon, cubed and
cooked crisp

Cut potatoes in half and place them in a greased casserole dish. Cook peas according to package directions and sprinkle over potatoes. In a saucepan, melt butter or margarine over medium heat; stir in flour, salt, and pepper. Add milk and canned milk and cook, stirring constantly, until thickened. Pour sauce over vegetables and stir gently to combine. Top with crisp bacon. Heat for 20 minutes in a 325°F oven.

170

Ranchero Potatoes

4 sliced, cooked potatoes

¼ C. margarine

2 T. flour

1 C. milk

½ t. salt

¼ t. pepper

½ C. finely diced onions

¼ C. barbecue sauce

1 C. cheese, grated

Layer half the potatoes in an 8×8 casserole dish. In a saucepan, melt the butter over medium heat; stir in the flour, and add the milk gradually, stirring constantly, until thickened. Remove from heat and stir in salt, pepper, onions, and barbecue sauce; stir in cheese until melted. Pour half the sauce over the potatoes; repeat the layers. Bake at 350°F for 25 minutes.

Seasoned Sliced Potatoes

Slice a potato (with the peeling left on) into thin slices. Spread a little oil on both sides of the slices and sprinkle with garlic and onion powder. Brown on both sides under the broiler of the oven. If you want crispier potatoes, cook longer. Good nutritional quick snack.

Onion Rings

2 sweet Spanish onions, sliced and separated into rings

½ C. flour

½ t. baking powder

¼ t. salt

1 egg, well beaten

½ C. milk

1 T. cooking oil

Blend flour, baking powder, and salt; set aside. Beat together egg, milk, and oil, and stir into flour/salt mixture. Heat frying oil in a deep pan to about 375°F (watch to make sure it's not too hot—it should not start smoking). Dip onion rings, a few at a time, into the batter; drop into hot fat, and turn over as they brown. When rings are a light golden brown in color, lift out and drain on paper towels. Salt the rings and serve hot.

Speedy Baked Beans

1 28-oz. can pork and beans
6 strips bacon, cooked and
  crumbled
½ C. chopped onions
¼ C. catsup

1 t. mustard
1 t. salt
½ C. brown sugar,
  firmly packed

Cook bacon until crisp; saute onions in bacon drippings and drain. Stir in all remaining ingredients; cook for 10 minutes over medium heat. Serve hot or cold.

Chinese Fried Rice with Vegetables

1 T. cooking oil
½ C. onions, chopped
1 C. *cold* cooked rice
1 egg, beaten

1 T. soy sauce
¼ t. salt
1 C. chopped vegetables
  (carrots, celery,
  green pepper, etc.)

In a hot skillet, heat oil; stirring constantly, cook onions until lightly browned. Add rice and saute (rice *must* be cold before you begin—chill it in the fridge). Beat together eggs, soy sauce, and salt; add to rice mixture. Stirring constantly, add vegetables until done. This is a perfect use for leftover rice!

Spanish Rice

3 slices bacon, cubed
1 C. chopped onion
½ C. chopped green pepper
2 cans condensed tomato soup

½ C. uncooked rice
½ C. water
3 whole cloves
1 bay leaf

Cook bacon in skillet until crisp; remove. Saute onion and green pepper in bacon drippings until tender. Add soup, rice, water, cloves, and bay leaf; cook, uncovered, until rice is tender, about 40 minutes. Remove cloves and bay leaf. Top with bacon and serve.

Perfect Rice

To cook perfect rice, pour the desired amount of rice into a saucepan. Fill the saucepan slowly with hot water until it is one knuckle deep above the rice. Cook over medium high heat, uncovered, until "pocks" form in the rice. Remove from heat, cover, and let stand 10–15 minutes. Rice will be tender and perfectly steamed.

German-Style Red Cabbage

1 small head red cabbage, shredded

1 small onion, diced

4 strips bacon, cubed

2 T. flour

½ C. brown sugar

½ C. vinegar

½ C. water

Cook cabbage in boiling water until tender; drain. Fry bacon until crisp; saute onion in bacon drippings. In a saucepan, combine flour, brown sugar, vinegar, and water; cook, stirring constantly, until thick. Stir sauce into cabbage, onion, and bacon; serve immediately.

Easy Bean Casserole

2 cans French-style green beans, drained

1 can cream of mushroom soup

1 can French fried onion rings

Stir beans and soup together and spoon into a greased pie plate or casserole dish. Top with onion rings. Bake at 325°F for 20 minutes, or until bubbly hot. Serve immediately.

Quick Sweet and Sour Beans

1 can pork and beans

1 can (8 oz.) pineapple chunks, drained

1 small green pepper, cut in strips

¼ C. onion, diced

¼ C. brown sugar, firmly packed

2 T. vinegar

3 T. soy sauce

Combine all ingredients in a greased casserole dish. Bake at 350°F for 35 minutes, stirring once or twice during baking time. Serve piping hot.

Chinese Vegetables

3 slices bacon
1 C. celery (sliced diagonally)
½ green pepper, sliced
½ onion, chopped
salt to taste

2 C. cabbage, shredded
1 large carrot (sliced diagonally)
1 t. sugar

Brown bacon, add vegetables and stir fry for 5 minutes. The last minute of cooking time sprinkle with 1 t. sugar and continue cooking.

Basic Gravy

4 T. boiled meat drippings
4 T. flour
2 C. hot water
salt and pepper to taste

Pour off excess fat drippings from skillet or roasting pan. Add one half to one cup hot water, boil to loosen browned bits. Combine four tablespoons boiled drippings and four tablespoons flour. Stir over heat until smooth. While stirring add two cups hot water, and salt and pepper to taste. Makes 2 cups.

Variations: You can add onion salt, celery salt, garlic salt or seasoning salt. Next time you have fried meat, cook in hot skillet and fix gravy this way.

Easy Instant Gravies

1 C. condensed soup
boiled meat drippings
water or milk

Drain off surplus fat. Add choice of soup and stir over low heat. If need be, add water or milk for correct consistency.
Variations:
LAMB OR CHICKEN: 1 C. Condensed Cream of Chicken Soup
PORK: 1 C. Condensed Cream of Celery Soup
HAM: 1 C. Condensed Cream of Mushroom Soup

_____

_____

_____

_____

_____

_____

_____

_____

_____

_____

_____

_____

_____

_____

_____

_____

_____

_____

_____

_____

_____

_____

_____

_____

_____

CAKES AND DESSERTS

Applesauce Cake

This moist cake is mixed in the same pan you bake it in!

2 C. flour	1 C. granulated sugar
1 t. cinnamon	1 T. cocoa
1 t. baking powder	1 C. sweetened applesauce
½ t. nutmeg	½ C. cooking oil
½ t. cloves	

Mix flour, sugar, and spices in a greased 9-inch frying pan until well blended. Stir in applesauce and cooking oil. Bake at 350°F for 35 minutes.

Crunchy Applesauce Bars

1 C. granulated sugar	1 t. nutmeg
1 C. sweetened applesauce	¼ t. cloves
½ C. shortening	¼ t. salt
2 C. flour	1 C. raisins
1 t. baking soda	¼ C. chopped nuts
1½ t. cinnamon	1 t. vanilla

Combine sugar and applesauce; blend in melted shortening. Sift together flour, baking soda, cinnamon, nutmeg, cloves, and salt; add to applesauce mixture. Stir in raisins, nuts, and vanilla. Spread in a greased 9×13 pan. Sprinkle on the following topping:

⅔ C. crushed corn flake cereal	¼ C. chopped nuts
¼ C. granulated sugar	2 T. butter or margarine

Combine crushed corn flakes, sugar, and nuts; cut in butter until the mixture is crumbly. Press into batter. Bake at 350°F for 30 minutes. Cool and cut into bars.

Spicy Apple Gingerbread

⅔ C. butter or margarine

1 C. granulated sugar

2 eggs

1⅓ C. molasses

4 C. sifted flour

4 t. baking powder

½ t. baking soda

4 t. ground ginger

2 t. cinnamon

1 t. salt

1½ C. buttermilk

3 C. chopped peeled apples

Cream butter and sugar until fluffy; beat in eggs. Add molasses, and beat until well blended. Sift together flour, baking powder, baking soda, ginger, cinnamon, and salt. Add half of the flour mixture to the molasses mixture, stirring well. Add half the buttermilk, stirring until well blended. Add the rest of the flour mixture, stirring well, and the rest of the buttermilk, beating the mixture until well blended. Stir in the apples. Spread batter in a greased and floured 9×13 pan. Bake at 350°F for 50 minutes, or until a toothpick inserted in the center comes out clean.

Variations: For a different but delicious gingerbread, try one of the following: Add 1 C. raisins and 1 C. chopped nuts; increase baking time to 55 minutes. Omit ½ C. flour, and add ½ C. cocoa for a chocolate gingerbread. Pour ½ C. melted butter in the bottom of the pan; sprinkle 2 C. firmly packed brown sugar over the butter, and arrange 6 sliced and peeled apples over the mixture. Spread the batter over the apple slices and bake as usual.

Picnic Cake

1½ C. boiling water

1 heaping C. pitted, chopped dates

1 t. baking soda

1 C. granulated sugar

¾ C. shortening

2 eggs

1½ C. + 2 T. flour

½ t. salt

1 t. cinnamon

1 t. vanilla

½ C. brown sugar, firmly packed

½ C. chopped nuts

½ C. chocolate chips

Pour boiling water over dates; let stand until cool. Stir in baking soda. Mix granulated sugar, shortening, and eggs until fluffy; add to date mixture. Stir together flour, salt, cinnamon, and vanilla; add to the date mixture. Pour into a greased 9×13 pan. Combine brown sugar, nuts, and chocolate chips; sprinkle over the top of the cake batter. Bake at 350°F for 40 minutes.

Carrot Cake

1 C. cooking oil	1 t. cinnamon
2 C. granulated sugar	1 t. baking soda
3 eggs, well beaten	1½ C. chopped nuts
2 C. grated carrots	1½ C. raisins
1 flat can crushed pineapple	1 t. vanilla
3 C. flour	

Combine oil and sugar until well mixed. Add eggs, carrots, and pineapple. Sift together flour, cinnamon, soda *twice*; stir into batter and blend well. Stir in vanilla, nuts, and raisins until all ingredients are moistened and blended. Spread batter in a well-greased 9×13 pan. Bake at 350°F for 45–50 minutes, or until center springs back when lightly touched. Cool on rack before frosting with a mixture of cream cheese and milk.

Disco Crazy Cake

3 C. flour	2 t. vinegar
2 C. granulated sugar	2 t. vanilla
1 t. salt	2 t. baking soda
²/₃ C. cocoa	2 C. cold water
¾ C. cooking oil	

Sift the flour, sugar, salt, and cocoa into a 9×13 ungreased pan. Spread the mixture evenly in the pan, and create three small "wells" in the mixture. Into the first, pour the oil; into the second, pour the vinegar; and into the third, pour the vanilla. Pour the cold water over the entire cake and mix well with a fork. Bake at 350°F for 40 minutes. Cool on rack and frost.

Three-Minute Cobbler

It only takes three minutes to mix up!

½ C. butter or margarine
1 C. flour
1 C. granulated sugar
2 t. baking powder

¾ C. milk
¼ t. salt
1 16-oz. can fruit pie filling or fruit

Melt butter in a casserole dish. Stir in flour, sugar, baking powder, milk, and salt until all lumps are gone. Dump the fruit on top, but don't stir it in. Bake for 1 hour at 350°F.

Apple Squares

1 pkg. yellow cake mix, reserving 1 C.
½ C. melted butter or margarine
1 egg
2 cans apple/cherry pie filling

¼ C. melted butter or margarine
¼ C. granulated sugar
1 t. cinnamon

Grease the bottom only of a 9×13 pan. Stir together in the pan the cake mix, melted butter, and egg. Spread the pie filling on top of the batter. Combine the 1 C. reserved cake mix, ¼ C. melted margarine, sugar, and cinnamon, and sprinkle over the pie filling. Bake at 350°F for 45 minutes.

Pudding Cake

1 C. flour
¾ C. granulated sugar
2 T. cocoa
2 t. baking powder
¼ t. salt
½ C. milk

2 T. cooking oil
1 C. finely chopped nuts
1 C. brown sugar, firmly packed
¼ C. cocoa
1¾ C. hot water

Combine in a large bowl flour, sugar, 2 T. cocoa, baking powder, salt, milk, oil, and nuts; beat vigorously until well blended. Pour into a greased 8-inch square pan. In same bowl, mix brown sugar, ¼ C.

cocoa, and hot water; pour slowly over the batter in the pan. Bake at 350°F for 45 minutes: the "pudding" becomes thick and rich and sinks to the bottom of the pan.

Dump-It Cake

Grease a 9×13 pan well. Dump 1 can of sweetened applesauce into it. Dump 1 can of crushed pineapple on top of that. Spread 1 pkg. of dry yellow cake mix over the pineapple. Melt 1 C. (2 cubes) of butter or margarine and pour it on top of the cake mix. Sprinkle 1½ C. chopped nuts over the melted butter. *Do not stir.* Bake at 350°F for 1 hour. Top with whipped cream if desired.

Easy Lemon Cake

1 pkg. white cake mix	3 eggs
1 3-oz. pkg. lemon gelatin	½ C. cold water + ½ C.
½ C. cooking oil	cold water

Stir cake mix and gelatin until well mixed. Beat in oil, eggs, and ½ C. water until smooth. Add another ½ C. water, and beat 1 minute (about 300 strokes by hand). Pour into a greased and floured 9×13 pan. Bake at 375°F for 30–35 minutes.

Chocolate Mayonnaise Surprise Cake

The surprise is the mayonnaise: it makes a delicious, moist cake!

2 C. flour	1 C. granulated sugar
2 t. baking soda	1 C. mayonnaise
4 T. cocoa	(*not* salad dressing)
1 C. water	2 t. vanilla

Sift flour, baking soda, and cocoa. Set aside. In a large bowl, beat together the sugar, mayonnaise, water, and vanilla. Stir in the flour mixture until well blended and all ingredients are moistened. Pour batter into two greased and floured layer pans or a greased and floured 9×13 pan. Bake at 350°F, 30–35 minutes for layer pans or 30 minutes for an oblong pan. Cool and frost.

Spicy Breakfast Cake

½ C. brown sugar,
firmly packed

⅓ C. chopped nuts

1½ t. cinnamon

¾ C. butter or margarine

1½ C. granulated sugar

3 eggs

1½ t. vanilla

3 C. flour

1½ t. baking powder

1½ t. baking soda

¼ t. salt

1½ C. sour cream

In a small bowl, combine the brown sugar, chopped nuts, and cinnamon until the mixture is crumbly. Set aside. In a large bowl, cream the butter and sugar until fluffy. Stir in eggs and vanilla until well blended. Sift together the flour, baking powder, baking soda, and salt; stir it into the batter alternately with the sour cream. Pour a third of the batter into a 9-inch square pan that has been greased and floured. Sprinkle half of the cinnamon mixture over the batter. Put another third of the batter in the pan, and sprinkle with the rest of the cinnamon mixture. Top with the rest of the batter. Bake at 350°F for 50–60 minutes. Cool on a wire rack until warm; cut and serve warm with cold milk.

Peach Shortcake

1 pkg. yellow cake mix

3½ C. sliced peaches

½ C. cold water

½ C. granulated sugar

2 T. cornstarch

2 T. butter or margarine

⅛ t. nutmeg

½ C. whipping cream, whipped

Prepare and bake cake mix according to package directions in a 9×13 pan; cool completely and remove cake from pan. Set aside. In a large saucepan, combine peaches, water, sugar, and cornstarch. Cook over medium heat until thickened, stirring constantly. Remove from heat; stir in nutmeg and butter. Spoon whipped cream over cooled cake, and pour peach mixture over the whipped cream. Serve immediately.

Triple Fudge Cake

1 pkg. devil's food cake mix

2 C. prepared chocolate
pudding

1 egg

½ C. semisweet chocolate chips

1 C. coarsely chopped nuts

In a large bowl, combine dry cake mix, pudding, and egg; beat well for 2 minutes (about 600 strokes by hand). Pour batter into a 9×13 greased pan. Sprinkle batter with the chocolate chips and nuts. Bake at 350°F for 30 minutes. Cool and top with whipped cream.

Lazy Oatmeal Cake

1¼ C. boiling water

1 C. quick-cooking oatmeal

½ C. softened butter or
margarine

1 C. granulated sugar

1 C. brown sugar,
firmly packed

1 t. vanilla

2 eggs

1½ C. flour

1 t. baking soda

½ t. salt

¾ t. cinnamon

¼ t. nutmeg

¼ C. melted butter or
margarine

⅔ C. brown sugar
(firmly packed)

½ C. shredded coconut

½ C. chopped nuts

½ C. raisins

3 T. milk

Pour boiling water over oatmeal; let stand for 20 minutes. Beat butter until it is creamy, and gradually beat in granulated and brown sugars. Blend in vanilla and eggs until mixture is well blended. Stir in flour, baking soda, salt, cinnamon, and nutmeg until all ingredients are blended and moistened. Pour into a greased and floured 9-inch square pan. Bake at 350°F for 50 minutes. Cool. Combine melted butter, ⅔ C. brown sugar, coconut, nuts, raisins, and milk, and beat until well blended. Spread over cooled cake.

One-Bowl Cake

2¼ C. flour, sifted

1½ C. granulated sugar

3 t. baking powder

1 t. salt

½ C. shortening

1 t. vanilla

⅔ C. milk

⅓ C. milk

2 eggs

Sift together flour, granulated sugar, baking powder, salt; stir in vanilla and ⅔ C. of milk. Beat in shortening until all ingredients are smooth and well blended. Beat in ⅓ C. milk and eggs. Pour into two greased and floured layer pans. Bake at 350°F for 30–35 minutes. Cool and frost with chocolate, caramel, or butter icing.

Easy Chocolate Icing

1 4-oz. pkg. chocolate pudding mix (not instant)

1¼ C. cold milk

½ C. butter or margarine

½ C. shortening

1 C. powdered sugar, sifted

1 t. vanilla

¼ t. salt

Cook pudding according to package directions. Set aside. Cream butter, shortening, and sugar until light and fluffy; stir in vanilla and salt. Gradually add pudding, beating well. Makes enough frosting to frost 2 layers or one oblong cake.

Fudge Icing

1½ oz. baking chocolate

1½ C. granulated sugar

7 T. milk

2 T. cooking oil

2 T. butter

1 T. light corn syrup

1 t. vanilla

¼ t. salt

Grate the baking chocolate until it is in fine pieces. In a large saucepan, combine it with the sugar, milk, oil, butter, corn syrup, and salt. Bring to a full rolling boil, stirring constantly; boil for 1 minute. (If in a humid climate, boil 1½ minutes.) Cool slightly, and add vanilla; beat vigorously until of a spreading consistency. Add a few drops of milk if the frosting is too thick.

Easy Chocolate Fudge Frosting

3 C. sifted powdered sugar   1 t. vanilla

2 T. melted butter   2 T. cocoa

Beat all ingredients until well blended; add milk, a few drops at a time, until frosting is of spreading consistency.

Nutty Coconut Icing

1½ C. granulated sugar   1 C. shredded coconut

½ can sweetened condensed   ½ to 1 C. chopped nuts
    milk

½ C. butter or margarine

Combine sugar, milk, and butter in a saucepan; bring to a boil, and boil for 3 minutes, stirring constantly. Remove from heat; stir in coconut and nuts.

Creamy Caramel Frosting

½ C. butter or margarine   2 C. powdered sugar, sifted

¼ C. milk   1½ t. vanilla

1 C. brown sugar,
    firmly packed

In a saucepan, combine butter, milk, and brown sugar. Heat to boiling, and cook for 2 minutes, stirring frequently to prevent scorching. Cool. Stir in powdered sugar, and beat until smooth. Add vanilla, and beat until well blended.

Easy Penoche Icing

½ C. butter or margarine   ¼ C. milk

1 C. brown sugar,   1¾ C. sifted powdered sugar
    firmly packed

Melt butter in a saucepan. Stir in brown sugar; bring to a boil, and boil for 2 minutes, stirring constantly. Stir in milk, and bring to a boil again, stiring constantly. Remove from heat as soon as the mixture starts to boil. Cool to lukewarm. Gradually add powdered sugar, beating well. If frosting is too stiff, add a few drops of hot water.

Creamy Butter Frosting

½ C. butter or margarine
3½ C. powdered sugar, sifted
few grains salt

2 egg whites or 1 egg
1½ t. vanilla

Cream butter and eggs until light and fluffy. Add sugar gradually, beating well. Add salt and vanilla; beat until fluffy. Add a few drops of milk if frosting is too thick. Makes enough to frost two layers or an oblong cake.

Basic Glaze

½ C. boiling water
1 C. sifted powdered sugar

Combine well and pour over cake.

Lemon Glaze

½ C. boiling water
1 C. sifted powdered sugar
1 T. evaporated milk

1 t. lemon juice
½ t. grated lemon peel

Combine boiling water and sugar until smooth; stir in milk, lemon juice, and lemon peel. Pour immediately over cake or doughnuts.

Fresh Peach Pie

1 C. fresh mashed peaches
¾ C. water
1 C. granulated sugar
3 T. cornstarch

1 t. cinnamon
1 baked pie shell, cooled
3 C. fresh sliced peaches

In a saucepan, combine the mashed peaches with the water, sugar, and cornstarch. Bring to a boil, reduce heat, and simmer for 5 minutes, stirring constantly until thickened. Stir in cinnamon. Arrange the sliced peaches in the pie shell; pour the hot peach mixture over the sliced peaches. Chill in the refrigerator until set. Top with whipped cream if desired.

Chocolate Banana Pie

1 pkg. instant chocolate
pudding
1¼ C. cold milk
1 8-oz. pkg. cream cheese,
softened

2 or 3 bananas, sliced
1 baked 9-inch pie shell

Beat milk into softened cream cheese; add pudding mix, and beat according to package directions, until thick. Arrange sliced bananas in bottom of pie shell; pour prepared pie mixture over the bananas. Chill until set. To serve, whip cream with 1 sliced banana; top with sliced banana.

Easy Strawberry Pie

1 C. granulated sugar
½ C. mashed strawberries
3 T. cornstarch
2 drops red food coloring

1 T. lemon juice
1 baked 8-inch pie shell
2 C. sliced strawberries
2 sliced bananas

Add enough water to the mashed berries to make 1 cup. Set aside. In saucepan, combine sugar, berries, water, cornstarch, and food coloring; cook over medium heat until thick. Fill the pie shell with sliced strawberries and sliced bananas; pour glaze over the top. Chill. Top with whipped cream, and garnish with whole strawberries.

Strawberry Pie

3 T. strawberry gelatin
1 C. sugar
3 T. cornstarch
pinch salt

1 C. water
3 drops red food coloring
3 C. sliced strawberries
1 baked 9-inch pie shell

Combine gelatin, sugar, cornstarch, and salt to make a paste with ⅛ C. of the water. Set aside. Boil ⅞ C. of the water and gradually add the paste, stirring constantly to prevent lumping. Cook until thickened. Cool for 2 hours. Arrange sliced strawberries in pie shell. Stir food coloring into cooled glaze and pour over strawberries. Cool completely; chill. Top with whipped cream.

Easy Apple Pie

1 quart sliced, peeled apples	1 t. cinammon
¾ C. granulated sugar	¼ t. nutmeg
¾ T. flour	Pie crust

Combine sugar, flour, cinnamon, and nutmeg until well blended; stir in apples. Pour the mixture into a pie crust; dot with 1 T. butter or margarine. Bake for 350°F for 30 minutes.

Chocolate Macaroon Pie

3 squares unsweetened chocolate	½ C. flour
	1 t. vanilla
½ C. butter or margarine	⅔ C. sweetened condensed milk
3 eggs, slightly beaten	
¾ C. granulated sugar	2⅔ C. shredded coconut

In a saucepan, melt the chocolate and butter over low heat, being careful not to scorch; stir in eggs, sugar, flour, and vanilla. Pour into a greased 9-inch pie plate. Combine milk and coconut; batter will be stiff. Spoon over chocolate mixture, leaving a 1-inch border around the outside. Bake at 350°F for 30 minutes. Store in refrigerator.

Fresh Fruit Pie

There's no sugar in this delicious pie!

¾ C. unsweetened apple juice concentrate

¾ C. water

1 T. lemon juice

3 T. cornstarch

4 C. diced fruit (apples, bananas, strawberries, etc.)

1½ C. Grape Nuts cereal

¾ C. unsweetened apple juice concentrate

In a saucepan, mix apple juice concentrate and water; cook over medium low heat until thickened. Remove from heat; stir in lemon juice and set aside to cool. Mix ¾ C. apple juice concentrate with

Grape Nuts, and let soak for 10 minutes. Press into a 9-inch pie plate. Bake at 350°F for 12 minutes. Let cool. Gently fold cooled apple mixture over diced fruit until well blended. Pour into cooled shell and chill.

Favorite Apple Pie

3 C. sliced, peeled apples	2 T. butter or margarine
1 C. water	2 T. cornstarch
1 C. sugar	1 t. cinnamon

Combine all ingredients in a large saucepan; bring to a boil, boil for 3 minutes. Remove from heat and cool to lukewarm. Pour in a pie crust. Bake at 350°F for 50 minutes.

Creamy Pumpkin Pie

1 pkg. instant vanilla pudding	1 C. cooked pumpkin
½ C. milk	¾ t. pumpkin pie spice

Combine all ingredients in a large bowl; beat slowly until well blended. Pour into a cooked pie shell. Chill for about 2 hours. Top with whipped cream.

Cherry Cheese Cake

1 graham cracker crumb crust

1 can sweetened condensed milk

1 8-oz. pkg. cream cheese, softened

1 t. vanilla

¼ C. lemon juice

1 can cherry pie filling

In a large bowl, beat the cream cheese until it's fluffy. Slowly add the milk, continuing to beat the mixture, until well blended. Add vanilla and lemon juice. Blend well. Pour into the pie crust. Chill for 3–4 hours or until firm. Top with cherry pie filling and serve. Store in refrigerator.

Lemon Cream Pie

1 can frozen lemonade concentrate

1 9-oz. container Cool Whip

1 can sweetened condensed milk

1 graham cracker crust

Combine lemonade, Cool Whip, and milk; beat until creamy. Pour into crust. Chill.

Incredible Coconut Pie

½ C. flour

1 C. granulated sugar

¼ C. melted butter or margarine

4 eggs, well beaten

2 C. milk

1 t. vanilla

1 7-oz. pkg. shredded coconut

In mixing bowl, combine flour and sugar. Add butter, eggs, milk, and vanilla, mixing well. Stir in coconut. Pour into a buttered 10-inch pie plate. Put in a cold oven; turn oven on to 350°F, and bake 45 minutes. Cool.

Graham Cracker Crust

1½ C. graham cracker crumbs

2 T. brown sugar, firmly packed

¼ t. cinnamon

⅛ t. nutmeg

¼ C. butter or margarine, melted

Combine all ingredients until well blended. Press into a 9-inch or 10-inch pie plate. Bake at 350°F for 8 minutes.

Never-Fail Pie Crust

1½ C. flour

¼ t. salt

¾ C. shortening

2½ T. cold water

1½ t. vinegar

1 egg, slightly beaten

In a mixing bowl, blend flour, salt, and shortening; use a pastry blender or two knives to cut shortening into the flour and salt. Combine water, vinegar, and the egg; blend it well into the flour mixture. Shape the dough into two balls. The ball of dough can either be used immediately, or wrapped and frozen for later use. To use, flatten the ball and use a flour-dusted rolling pin to roll the dough into a circle about 2 inches larger than the rim of the pie plate. Put the dough in the plate, prick the bottom with a fork, and moisten the rim slightly. Bake at 475°F for 8 minutes or until lightly browned. Let cool.

Easiest-Ever Pie Crust

1½ C. flour (white or
   whole wheat)
½ C. cooking oil
¾ t. salt

2 T. granulated sugar
2 T. cold water or milk

Dump flour in an ungreased pie plate. Add the oil, salt, sugar, and stir well. Pour in the water or milk, and mix with a fork into a stiff dough. Press into shape in the pie plate. Bake at 350°F for 10–12 minutes, or until lightly browned.

Bread Custard

4 slices bread
butter or margarine
brown sugar
cinnamon
⅓ C. raisins

3 eggs
⅓ C. granulated sugar
1 t. vanilla
dash salt
2½ C. scalded milk

Toast the four slices of bread. Butter each one, and sprinkle each with brown sugar and cinnamon. Put two slices together as for sandwiches; repeat with the other two slices. Cut each "sandwich" into quarters. Arrange in the bottom of a buttered casserole dish. Sprinkle with raisins. Combine the eggs, granulated sugar, vanilla, salt, and milk; stir until well blended. Pour over the bread. Put the casserole dish in a pan of 1-inch-deep water. Bake at 350°F for 75–80 minutes.

Apple-Banana Delight

Here's a pudding without sugar!

2½ C. unsweetened apple juice

2 bananas

5 T. cornstarch

Blend the bananas and apple juice in a blender; add cornstarch and mix until well blended. Cook over medium heat until thickened, stirring constantly. Arrange sliced bananas in the bottom of a serving dish; pour hot mixture over the bananas. Chill until set.

One-Pan Rice Pudding

½ C. regular rice (long grain)	½ C. sugar
1 C. water, slightly salted	1 C. raisins (optional)
1 quart milk	½ t. vanilla
¼ C. butter	3 T. sugar
3 eggs	1 T. cinnamon

Pour rice slowly into boiling water. Cover and cook seven minutes. Add the milk and butter. Stir a little, bring to a boil, cover, and turn to low and cook for 1 hour. Meanwhile, beat eggs, add sugar, raisins and vanilla. Pour mixture into rice, stirring slowly until rice starts to thicken and bubbles. Serve hot or cold with a mixture of cinnamon and sugar sprinkled on top.

MOM'S OLD Standbys

COOKIES AND BARS

Chocolate Chip Bars

2¾ C. flour

2½ t. baking powder

½ t. salt

⅔ C. shortening

1 1-lb. pkg. brown sugar

3 eggs

1 12-oz. pkg. chocolate chips

1 C. chopped nuts

Sift together the flour, baking powder, and salt; set aside. Cream the shortening and brown sugar, and add the slightly beaten eggs until well blended. Add the flour mixture, and stir until moistened. Stir in the chocolate chips and the nuts. Spread the batter in a greased 9×13 pan. Bake at 350°F for 25 minutes. Cool and cut into squares.

Crunchy Caramel Layers

1 C. flour

¼ t. salt

¼ t. baking soda

½ C. brown sugar, packed

¾ C. quick-cooking oatmeal

½ C. butter or margarine

24 caramels

2 T. cream

2 T. flour

½ C. semi-sweet chocolate chips

Combine flour, salt, baking soda, brown sugar, and oatmeal; cut the butter in until the mixture is crumbly. Press all but 1 cup of the mixture into the bottom of an 8-inch square pan. Bake at 350°F for 10 minutes. Combine the caramels and the cream in the top of a double boiler, cooking and stirring frequently until the caramels are melted. Blend in 2 T. flour. Spread the caramel mixture carefully over the baked mixture; sprinkle the chocolate chips over the caramel mixture, and sprinkle the 1 cup of mixture over the top. Bake at 350°F for 12–15 minutes, or until lightly browned.

Lemon Drifts

1 C. butter or margarine, softened
½ C. powdered sugar
2 C. flour
4 eggs, beaten

2 C. granulated sugar
½ C. lemon juice
5 T. flour
1 t. baking powder

Beat butter, powdered sugar, and 2 C. flour together until smooth. Spread into a greased 9×13 pan; bake at 350°F for 20 minutes. Beat together the eggs, granulated sugar, lemon juice, 5 T. flour, and baking powder until well blended; the mixture will be thin. Pour over the top of the baked crust, and continue baking at 350°F for 25 minutes. Sprinkle with powdered sugar, cool, and cut into bars.

Nutty Raisin Bars

1 C. brown sugar
⅓ C. shortening
2 C. raisins
2 C. sifted flour
1 t. baking powder
¼ t. cloves

1¼ C. water
1 t. salt
2 t. cinnamon
½ t. nutmeg
1 C. chopped nuts

Combine water, brown sugar, shortening, and raisins in a large saucepan; bring to a boil, boil for three minutes, and cool. Sift together flour, baking powder, cloves, salt, cinnamon, and nutmeg into the cooled raisin mixture. Stir until well blended. Add chopped nuts, stirring until the nuts are evenly distributed. Grease and flour a 9-inch square pan; spread the mixture evenly in the pan. Bake at 325°F for 50 minutes; cool and cut into bars. Store in a tightly covered container. These bars can be frosted if desired.

Marshmallow Dreams

½ C. butter or margarine
¼ C. cocoa
1 C. granulated sugar
2 eggs

¾ C. flour
1 C. chopped nuts
1 t. vanilla
½ lb. miniature marshmallows

Cream the butter, sugar, and cocoa together until well blended. Add the eggs, one at a time, beating well after each one. Stir in the flour, nuts, and vanilla until well blended. Spread the batter evenly in an 8-inch square greased pan. Bake at 350°F for 20 minutes. Remove from the oven, and cover the top with a single layer of miniature marshmallows. Return the bars to the oven for about 3 minutes, or until the marshmallows are a light golden color. Remove from the oven and cool completely. Frost the bars with this icing:

¼ C. butter or margarine   ¼ C. cocoa

¼ C. evaporated milk   1 C. powdered sugar

Beat until smooth, and spread over Marshmallow Dreams.

Chewy Cookie Bars

1½ C. crushed corn flake cereal   1½ C. chocolate chips

3 T. granulated sugar   1½ C. sweetened coconut

½ C. butter or margarine   1 can sweetened condensed

1½ C. chopped nuts   milk

Melt butter or margarine in a 9×13 pan; stir in granulated sugar and crushed corn flake cereal until well mixed, and press with the back of a spoon until the mixture forms a crust in the bottom of the pan. Sprinkle the nuts evenly over the crust; sprinkle the chocolate chips evenly over the nuts; sprinkle the coconut evenly over the chocolate chips; pour the can of sweetened condensed milk evenly over the mixture. Bake at 350°F for 20–25 minutes, or until the mixture is lightly browned around the edges. Cool and cut into bars.

Orange Cookies

1 pkg. chocolate cake mix   2 C. quick-cooking oatmeal

1 orange peel, grated   2 eggs

1 C. chopped nuts   ¾ C. cooking oil

Stir together cake mix, orange peel, chopped nuts, and oatmeal; set aside. In small bowl, beat together eggs and cooking oil; add to flour mixture until well blended. Drop by spoonfuls onto greased cookie sheet; bake at 375°F for 12 minutes. Cool on wire rack.

English Toffee Bars

¼ C. granulated sugar   ½ C. butter

¼ C. brown sugar   1 egg yolk

1 C. sifted flour   ½ t. vanilla

¼ C. finely chopped nuts   1 6-oz. pkg. chocolate chips

Cream granulated sugar, brown sugar, and butter together until well blended; add the egg yolk and the vanilla, stirring until well blended. Mix in sifted flour, and spread evenly in a greased 8-inch square pan. Bake at 250°F for 15 minutes. Remove from oven; immediately sprinkle chocolate chips over the surface. When chips have melted completely, spread them evenly over the surface and sprinkle with nuts. Cool and cut into small squares.

Pumpkin Cookies

1¼ C. flour   ½ C. pumpkin, cooked

2 t. baking powder   ½ t. vanilla

¼ C. shortening   ½ C. chopped nuts

½ C. granulated sugar   ½ t. lemon extract

1 egg, beaten   ½ C. raisins

Sift flour and baking powder together; set aside. Cream shortening and sugar until well blended; stir in flour mixture until moistened. Stir in egg, pumpkin, vanilla, nuts, lemon extract, and raisins; drop by spoonfuls onto cookie sheet covered with aluminum foil. Bake at 350°F for 15 minutes.

Carrot Cookies

¼ C. butter or margarine   1 C. sifted flour

½ C. granulated sugar   1 t. baking powder

1 egg, beaten   pinch salt

½ t. vanilla   ½ C. grated carrots

½ t. lemon extract

194

Cream butter and sugar until well blended; stir in egg, and add vanilla and lemon extract. Sift together flour, baking powder, and salt; stir into creamed mixture until moistened. Beat in grated carrots until well blended. Drop by spoonfuls on greased cookie sheet; bake at 375°F for 10–13 minutes.

Banana Raisin Delights

1 pkg. yellow cake mix	2 medium-ripe bananas
2 C. quick-cooking oatmeal	1 C. sweetened flaked coconut
2 eggs	1 C. raisins
¾ C. cooking oil	½ C. chopped nuts

Beat eggs well, and add cooking oil; beat until well blended. Mash bananas with a fork; stir into egg/oil mixture. Set aside. In a large mixing bowl, stir together the cake mix, coconut, and oatmeal; blend in the banana mixture until moistened. Stir in the raisins and nuts. Drop by spoonfuls on greased cookie sheet. Bake at 375°F for 10–15 minutes. Cool on a rack.

Crunchy Applesauce Oatmeal Cookies

1 C. granulated sugar	½ t. salt
½ C. shortening	1 t. nutmeg
1 egg	1 t. cinnamon
1 C. applesauce	1 C. quick-cooking oatmeal
1 t. baking soda	1 C. raisins
1¾ C. flour	1 C. chopped nuts

Cream sugar and shortening until well blended. Stir in egg, and beat until smooth. Combine applesauce and baking soda, and add to mixture. Set aside. In large mixing bowl, sift together flour, salt, nutmeg, and cinnamon; stir in egg mixture, and blend well. Add oatmeal, raisins, and nuts; stir until mixture is well moistened. Drop by spoonfuls onto greased cookie sheet. Bake at 425°F for 10 minutes. Cool on wire rack.

Apple Raisin Cookies

2 eggs
¾ C. cooking oil
1 C. diced peeled apple
1 pkg. white cake mix
2 C. quick-cooking oatmeal

1 t. cinnamon
1 t. nutmeg
1 C. raisins
1 C. chopped nuts

Beat together eggs and cooking oil; stir in diced apple. Stir in cake mix and oatmeal until well moistened; add cinnamon and nutmeg, stirring until well blended. Stir in raisins and nuts. Drop by spoonfuls onto greased cookie sheets; bake at 375°F for 12 minutes. Cool on wire rack.

Peanut Butter Cookies

1¼ C. flour
¼ t. salt
¼ t. baking soda
½ C. butter or margarine

½ C. peanut butter
½ C. granulated sugar
½ C. brown sugar
1 egg

Combine flour, salt, and baking soda, and set aside. In large mixing bowl, mix butter and peanut butter until well blended; add granulated and brown sugar, mixing well, and beat in egg. Stir flour mixture into peanut butter mixture until well blended. Drop by spoonfuls onto lightly greased cookie sheet; flatten with a fork, and sprinkle lightly with granulated sugar. Bake at 375°F for 10–15 minutes, or until lightly browned. Cool on wire rack.

Giant Chocolate Chippers

⅓ C. butter or margarine
¼ C. firmly packed brown sugar
¼ C. granulated sugar
1 egg
½ C. sifted flour
⅛ t. baking powder

⅛ t. salt
¼ t. baking soda
½ C. crushed wheat flake cereal
½ C. quick-cooking oatmeal
¼ C. sweetened flaked coconut
1 6-oz. pkg. chocolate chips

Cream together butter, brown sugar, granulated sugars, and egg until the mixture is fluffy. Sift together flour, baking powder, salt, soda, and add to creamed mixture until well blended. Stir in remaining ingredients. Drop by large chunks onto greased cookie sheet; bake at 375°F for 12 minutes or until lightly browned. Do not overbake; cookies should be moist when removed from oven.

Spicy Nut Bars

½ pkg. spice cake mix   ½ C. raisins

1 egg   ½ C. chopped nuts

½ C. cooking oil   ½ C. plain yogurt

1 C. quick-cooking oatmeal

Blend all ingredients until well blended and completely moistened. Spread mixture in a greased 8-inch square pan. Bake at 375°F for 15 minutes; cool pan on wire rack, and cut into bars.

Chocolate Chippies

1 pkg. chocolate cake mix   1 egg

¼ C. butter or margarine   1 6-oz. pkg. chocolate chips

⅓ C. milk   1 C. chopped nuts

Beat together cake mix, butter, milk, and egg until well blended; stir in chocolate chips and nuts. Drop by spoonfuls on a greased cookie sheet; bake at 375°F for 12 minutes. Cool on wire rack.

Chocolate Drops

½ C. shortening   ¾ C. flour

1 C. granulated sugar   ½ t. baking soda

1 egg, beaten   ½ t. salt

¾ C. buttermilk   ½ C. cocoa

1 t. vanilla   ½ C. chopped nuts

Cream shortening and sugar until fluffy; stir in egg and vanilla. Blend in buttermilk. Sift together flour, baking soda, salt, and cocoa; stir into buttermilk mixture until well moistened. Stir in chopped nuts. Drop by spoonfuls onto greased cookie sheets. Bake at 350°F for 9 minutes. Frost with chocolate icing if desired.

197

Classic Chocolate Chip Cookies

1 C. shortening

1 C. granulated sugar

½ C. brown sugar,
firmly packed

2 eggs, beaten

1 t. vanilla

1 t. baking soda

2 T. warm water

½ t. salt

3 C. flour

1 C. chopped nuts

1 12-oz. pkg. chocolate chips

Cream together shortening, granulated sugar, brown sugar, eggs, and vanilla until fluffy. Add water, flour, salt, and baking soda; stir until well moistened. Add chocolate chips and nuts. Bake at 375°F for 8–10 minutes; do not overbake. Cool on wire rack.

Brownie Nuggets

½ C. shortening

2 C. granulated sugar

2 eggs

1 t. vanilla

1 C. milk

3½ C. flour

4 t. baking powder

1 t. salt

1 C. cocoa

1 C. chopped nuts

1 C. raisins

Cream shortening and sugar until fluffy; add eggs and vanilla. Sift together flour, baking powder, salt, and cocoa. Stir in half of the flour mixture with the creamed mixture; stir in half the milk; stir in the rest of the flour mixture, and then the rest of the milk. Stir in nuts and raisins. Drop by spoonfuls onto greased cookie sheets. Bake at 350°F for 12 minutes; do not overbake. Great for a crowd: makes about 5 dozen cookies!

Cherry-Chocolate Chiparoons

4 eggs

½ t. salt

1½ C. sugar

1 C. flour

2 T. cooking oil

2 t. almond extract or vanilla

4½ C. shredded coconut

1 12-oz. pkg. chocolate chips

½ C. chopped maraschino
cherries

Beat eggs and salt until frothy; gradually add sugar, beating well until thick and lemon-colored (about 5 minutes). Stir in flour, oil, and almond extract or vanilla; blend well. Fold in coconut, chocolate chips, and cherries. Drop by spoonfuls onto greased cookie sheets. Bake at 325°F for 12–15 minutes. Cool on wire racks. Makes about 7 dozen cookies—a real crowd-pleaser!

Peanut Butter Cups

4 large graham crackers

1 C. peanut butter

½ lb. powdered sugar

½ C. butter or margarine

1 large chocolate bar

Put graham crackers in a plastic bag or between sheets of waxed paper; crush with a rolling pin or hammer. (Graham crackers can also be crushed in a blender.) Set aside. In a large saucepan, slowly melt butter over low heat. Remove from heat. Blend in crushed graham crackers, peanut butter, and powdered sugar until completely mixed. Press into an 8-inch square pan. In the top of a double boiler, melt a large chocolate bar; spread on peanut butter mixture. Let cool, and cut into bars.

Soft Zucchini Cookies

A great way to use up that squash!

½ C. shortening

½ C. granulated sugar

1 C. brown sugar

2 eggs, beaten

3 C. peeled, coarsely grated zucchini

2½ C. flour

2 C. quick-cooking oatmeal

1 t. baking powder

½ t. baking soda

1 t. cinnamon

½ t. salt

1 C. chopped nuts

1 C. raisins

Cream shortening, granulated sugar, brown sugar, and eggs until fluffy; stir in zucchini. Sift together flour, baking powder, baking soda, cinnamon, and salt; add to zucchini mixture. Stir in oatmeal until well blended. Add nuts and raisins. Drop by spoonfuls onto greased cookie sheets. Bake at 375°F for 12–15 minutes.

Peanut Crispies

1 C. raw peanuts
¾ C. shortening
½ C. granulated sugar
1 C. brown sugar,
    firmly packed
2 eggs

1 t. vanilla
1½ C. flour
½ t. baking soda
½ t. salt
2 C. quick-cooking oatmeal

    Chop the peanuts and spread them on a cookie sheet; bake at 325°F for 15 minutes, or until golden and crispy. Set aside. Cream shortening, granulated sugar, brown sugar, eggs, and vanilla until fluffy. Blend in flour, baking soda, and salt until well moistened. Stir in oatmeal and peanuts until well blended. Drop by spoonfuls onto greased cookie sheet; bake at 375°F for 12 minutes or until lightly browned. Cool on wire rack.

Moist Sugar Cookies

½ C. butter or margarine
½ C. granulated sugar
1 egg
½ C. cooking oil

½ C. powdered sugar
½ t. cream of tartar
½ t. baking soda
2 C. flour

    Cream butter and sugar until fluffy; add the rest of the ingredients in the order listed. Stir until well blended. Keeping the drops small, drop by spoonfuls onto ungreased cookie sheets. Dip the bottom of a glass in granulated sugar, and press cookies slightly. Bake at 350°F for 7 minutes. Do not overbake. Cool on wire rack.

Chocolate Drop Cookies

½ C. butter or margarine
¾ C. granulated sugar
1¾ C. sifted flour
1 egg, beaten
½ t. baking soda

½ t. salt
3 T. cocoa
1 t. vanilla
½ C. milk
1 C. chopped nuts

Cream butter, sugar, and egg until fluffy. Set aside. Sift together flour, baking soda, salt, and cocoa. Stir into creamed mixture. Blend in vanilla, milk, and nuts. Drop by spoonfuls onto greased cookie sheets. Bake at 350°F for 8 minutes. Cool on wire rack.

No-Bake Orange Coconut Balls

2 C. finely crushed graham crackers

1 C. sweetened flaked coconut

1 C. powdered sugar

¾ C. frozen orange juice, thawed and undiluted

Mix graham cracker crumbs, powdered sugar, and coconut until well blended. Add orange juice concentrate and stir until dough is stiff. Form into small balls and roll balls in powdered sugar. Store in a covered container for 8 hours or overnight.

Boiled Cookies

1½ C. granulated sugar	1½ C. quick-cooking oatmeal
¼ C. butter or margarine	½ C. coconut
⅛ t. salt	½ t. vanilla
1½ T. cocoa	1 C. chopped nuts
¼ C. milk	

Mix sugar, butter, salt, cocoa, and milk in a saucepan; bring to a boil, and boil for 1 minute. Remove from heat and stir in oatmeal, coconut, vanilla, and nuts. Drop by spoonfuls onto waxed paper and let cool until firm.

Peanut Butter Drops

¼ C. butter or margarine	¼ C. peanut butter
¼ C. milk	½ t. vanilla
1 C. granulated sugar	1½ C. quick-cooking oatmeal

Mix butter, sugar, and milk in a saucepan; bring to a boil, and boil for 1 minute. Remove from heat. Stir in peanut butter, vanilla, and oatmeal. Drop by spoonfuls onto waxed paper and chill in the refrigerator until firm.

Moist Oatmeal Cookies

¾ C. shortening

1 C. brown sugar

½ C. granulated sugar

¼ C. water

1 egg

1 t. vanilla

1 C. flour

½ t. baking soda

1 t. salt

3 C. quick-cooking oatmeal

1 C. chopped nuts

1 C. raisins

Cream together shortening, brown sugar, granulated sugar, water, egg, and vanilla until fluffy. Sift together flour, baking soda, salt, and add to creamed mixture. Stir in oatmeal until well blended. Fold in nuts and raisins. Drop by spoonfuls onto greased cookie sheets. Bake at 350°F for 12–15 minutes, or until slightly golden. Cool on wire rack.

Oatmeal Spice Cookies

1 C. quick-cooking oatmeal

¾ C. flour

¼ C. buttermilk

2 eggs

½ C. shortening

1 C. raisins

¼ t. cinnamon

½ C. granulated sugar

½ t. baking soda

1 C. chopped nuts

Mix all ingredients until well blended. Drop by spoonfuls onto greased cookie sheets. Bake at 375°F for 8–10 minutes.

Classic Chocolate Chip Cookies

½ C. butter or margarine

6 T. granulated sugar

6 T. brown sugar

1 egg

1½ C. flour

½ t. baking soda

½ t. salt

1 t. hot water

1 C. chopped nuts

1 6-oz. package chocolate chips

½ t. vanilla

Cream together butter, granulated sugar, and brown sugar; add egg and beat well. Sift together flour, baking soda, and salt, and add to creamed mixture. Stir until well moistened. Stir in nuts, chocolate chips, and vanilla. Drop by spoonfuls onto greased cookie sheets. Bake at 375°F for 8–10 minutes.

Butterscotch Angel Cookies

¾ C. butterscotch chips

2 T. butter or margarine

2 eggs, well beaten

1 t. vanilla

⅛ t. salt

2 C. sifted powdered sugar

4 C. miniature marshmallows

1 pkg. flaked coconut

1 C. chopped nuts

Melt butterscotch chips and butter in the top of a double boiler. Remove from heat, and stir in eggs, vanilla, salt, powdered sugar, marshmallows, and nuts. Form into small balls and roll in coconut. Store in the refrigerator.

No-Bake Caramel Drops

1 T. butter

6 T. evaporated milk

24 caramel candies

3 C. crisped rice cereal

2 C. corn flake cereal

1 C. chopped nuts

Melt butter and caramels in a heavy saucepan over low heat, stirring frequently to prevent scorching. Stir in milk. Stir together rice cereal, corn flake cereal, and nuts in a large bowl; pour caramel mixture over the cereals. Lightly butter hands; mix and form into small balls.

No-Bake Peanut Butter Cookies

½ C. dark corn syrup

½ C. granulated sugar

½ C. peanut butter

½ t. vanilla

2 C. corn flakes or Special K cereal

Mix corn syrup and sugar in a saucepan; bring to a boil, stirring frequently, and boil 1 minute. Remove from heat and add peanut butter, vanilla, and cereal. Blend well. Drop by spoonfuls onto waxed paper and let cool until firm.

Applesauce Brownies

1 C. shortening

3 1-oz. squares baking chocolate

2 C. granulated sugar

4 eggs, well beaten

1 C. sweetened applesauce

2 t. vanilla

2 C. flour

1 t. baking powder

½ t. baking soda

½ t. salt

1 C. chopped nuts

Melt shortening and chocolate together in the top of a double boiler. Blend in sugar, eggs, applesauce, and vanilla. Sift together flour, baking powder, baking soda, and salt; add to chocolate mixture. Stir in nuts. Spread in a greased and floured 9×13 pan. Bake at 350°F for 30 minutes. Cool in pan. Cut into squares and roll in sifted powdered sugar. Great for parties!

Peanut Butter Brownies

2 eggs

¾ C. granulated sugar

⅓ C. brown sugar, firmly packed

¼ C. peanut butter

⅛ C. shortening

1½ t. vanilla

1 C. unsifted flour

1½ t. baking powder

1½ t. salt

½ C. chopped peanuts

Cream eggs, granulated sugar, brown sugar, peanut butter, shortening, and vanilla until fluffy. Add flour, baking powder, and salt, stirring only until moistened. Stir in chopped peanuts. Spread into a lightly greased 9×13 pan. Bake at 325°F for 25 minutes. Cool and cut into squares.

Chewy Chocolate Brownies

1 large package regular chocolate pudding mix
   (do not use instant pudding)

1 C. flour

½ t. baking powder

⅔ C. butter or margarine

1⅓ C. granulated sugar

4 eggs

2 t. vanilla

1 C. chopped nuts

Stir together pudding mix, flour, and baking powder until well blended. Set aside. Melt butter in saucepan over low heat; remove from heat. Stir in sugar until well blended; beat in eggs one at a time. Blend in vanilla and pudding mixture. Stir in nuts. Spread in a greased 9×13 pan. Bake at 350°F for 20–25 minutes; do not overbake. Cool and cut into bars.

Easy Brownies

½ C. butter or margarine   ¼ C. cocoa
1 C. granulated sugar   ¾ C. flour
1 t. vanilla   ½ C. chopped nuts
2 eggs

Melt butter and let cool. Stir in granulated sugar and vanilla. Beat in eggs, beating well between each one. Stir cocoa and flour together, and blend into creamed mixture. Blend in nuts. Press into greased and floured 8-inch square pan. Bake at 350°F for 25–30 minutes. Do not overbake! Cool pan on wire rack before cutting into squares.

Butterscotch Brownies

1 6-oz. pkg. butterscotch chips   ½ t. vanilla
¼ C. butter or margarine   1 egg
¾ C. flour   1 6-oz. pkg. chocolate chips
⅓ C. brown sugar   1 C. miniature marshmallows
1 t. baking powder   ½ C. chopped nuts
¼ t. salt

In a large saucepan, melt butter and butterscotch chips over low heat; stir constantly to prevent scorching. Remove from heat and cool to lukewarm. Stir in flour, brown sugar, baking powder, salt, vanilla, and egg, blending well. Fold in chocolate chips, marshmallows, and nuts. Spread into a greased 8-inch square pan. Bake at 350°F for 20–25 minutes; do not overbake. The center will still be soft when the brownies are removed from the oven.

Frying Pan Cookies

¾ C. sugar

1 C. chopped dates

2 eggs

1 t. vanilla

1 C. chopped nuts

1 C. cornflakes

1 C. rice krispies

coconut

In a heavy frying pan, mix sugar, dates and well-beaten eggs. Cook over medium heat, stirring constantly until mixture pulls away from sides of pan (about 5 minutes). Cook 3 minutes longer, then add vanilla and nuts. Carefully add cornflakes and rice krispies. Wet hands in cold water and form into balls about the size of walnuts. Roll in coconut. Cool.

Wafer No Bake Cookies

1 pkg. chocolate chips (6 oz.)

½ C. sugar

3 T. light corn syrup

1/3 C. orange juice

1 pkg. vanilla wafers (7¼ oz.), finely crushed

1 C. nuts, chopped

Melt chocolate in top of double-boiler over hot water, remove from heat and stir in sugar, syrup and juice. In mixing bowl, combine wafer crumbs and nuts. Stir into chocolate mixture, blend well. Immediately shape into 1-inch balls. Store for several days in airtight container.

MOM'S OLD Standbys

CANDIES

Raspberry Popcorn Balls

1 C. light corn syrup

1 3-oz. pkg. raspberry gelatin

1 C. granulated sugar

6 quarts popped popcorn

Stir together corn syrup and gelatin; stir in sugar. Cook over low heat until sugar is completely dissolved. Pour over popcorn, and form into balls. Store in covered container, or wrap individual balls in plastic wrap or foil.

Caramel Corn

1 can sweetened condensed milk

2 C. brown sugar, firmly packed

½ C. butter or margarine

1 C. light corn syrup

pinch salt

Cook all ingredients in a heavy saucepan to soft ball stage (a little of the mixture dropped in cold water forms a soft ball). Pour over popcorn until all popcorn is evenly coated. Form into balls, and store in covered container.

Easy Caramel Corn

1 C. brown sugar, firmly packed

½ C. butter or margarine

30 large marshmallows

Melt ingredients in a heavy saucepan over medium heat, stirring frequently to prevent scorching. Pour over popcorn until all popcorn is evenly coated. Form into balls. Wrap each ball in plastic wrap.

Candied Popcorn

¾ C. light corn syrup

4 T. butter or margarine

2 T. water

1 C. miniature marshmallows

1 lb. powdered sugar, sifted

¼ t. red food coloring

Blend corn syrup, butter, and water in a large saucepan over low heat; add marshmallows and stir constantly until completely melted. Add powdered sugar and food coloring, stirring until completely dissolved and bubbly, about 2 minutes. Pour slowly over popped popcorn and stir until all popcorn is coated. Cool.

Baked Caramel Corn

1 C. brown sugar,
  firmly packed

½ C. butter or margarine

¼ C. light corn syrup

½ t. salt

½ t. baking soda

½ C. chopped nuts

3 quarts popped popcorn

Stir together brown sugar, butter, corn syrup, and salt in a saucepan; bring to a boil, and boil for 5 minutes. Remove from heat; stir in baking soda. Combine nuts and popcorn in a large bowl; pour boiled mixture over popcorn/nut mixture and stir until all nuts and popcorn are coated. Spread on a cookie sheet. Bake in a 200°F oven for 1 hour, stirring every 15 minutes. Let cool, and store in a covered container.

Mixed Up Candy

2 C. corn flake cereal

2 C. crisped rice cereal

½ C. salted peanuts

½ C. shredded coconut

½ C. dark corn syrup

½ C. granulated sugar

¼ C. milk

¼ t. vanilla

Mix corn flake cereal, crisped rice cereal, and peanuts in a bowl, and stir to blend. Cook corn syrup, sugar, and milk in a kettle, stirring constantly, to 236°F. Remove from heat, add vanilla, and pour over cereal and nut mixture. Mix thoroughly, stirring in coconut. Spread on buttered cookie sheets.

208

Rice Balls

½ C. peanut butter   ¼ C. granulated sugar

½ C. honey   puffed rice cereal

Simmer peanut butter, honey, and sugar until smooth. Pour over puffed rice cereal, and form into balls. Store in a covered container.

Marshmallow Squares

¼ C. butter or margarine

4 C. miniature marshmallows

¼ C. peanut butter

5 C. Kix, Cheerios, or Rice Krispies

Melt butter in a heavy saucepan over low heat; add marshmallows, and cook for 2 minutes or until marshmallows are melted. Remove from heat and stir in cereal until well coated. Press into a buttered 9×13 pan. Cool and cut into squares.

Chocolate Crunch Candies

1 large chocolate candy bar

Corn flakes

Melt chocolate bar over low heat, stirring constantly to prevent scorching. Slowly add corn flakes until mixture is stiff. Drop by spoonfuls onto waxed paper. Let cool.

Chewy Corn Flake Clusters

¾ C. granulated sugar   ⅜ C. water

dash salt   1 t. vanilla

½ C. light corn syrup   ¼ C. chunk-style peanut butter

⅛ C. butter or margarine   4½ C. corn flakes

Combine sugar, salt, corn syrup, butter, and water in a saucepan; bring to a boil, reduce to medium heat, and cook to 236°F. Remove from heat; stir in vanilla and peanut butter. Put corn flakes in a large buttered bowl; pour cooked mixture over corn flakes until all are well coated. Drop by spoonfuls onto waxed paper. Cool.

Fudgesicles

1 pkg. chocolate pudding mix (not instant)

2 C. milk

1 C. evaporated milk

¼ C. granulated sugar

In a saucepan, combine pudding mix, sugar, and milk; cook according to pudding package directions, until thick, stirring constantly. Pour into a pan and put in freezer until partially frozen. Stir and spoon into paper cups; insert wooden sticks or toothpicks for handles. If desired, freeze in pan and cut into squares; roll in chopped nuts.

Butterscotch Freeze

1 pkg. instant butterscotch pudding mix

1 C. cold root beer

1½ C. cold water

Combine and beat according to pudding mix package directions. Pour into a pan and freeze. Cut into squares and roll in chopped nuts or flaked coconut.

Frozen Bananas

4 bananas

2 small chocolate candy bars

1 C. chopped nuts

Melt chocolate bars over low heat, stirring constantly. Peel bananas, and roll in melted chocolate. Roll in chopped nuts. Wrap in plastic wrap and put in freezer until frozen.

Eggnogsicles

2 C. vanilla ice cream

1 6-oz. can frozen orange juice concentrate, thawed and undiluted

1 egg

1½ C. cold milk

Combine ice cream, orange juice concentrate, and egg in a large bowl; beat until smooth. Gradually add milk, beating constantly. Pour into pan and freeze. Cut into squares and roll in shredded coconut.

Popsicles

1 3-oz. pkg. gelatin (any flavor)   2 C. hot water
1 C. sugar   2 C. cold water
1 envelope powdered punch
    mix (any flavor)

Combine gelatin, sugar, and punch mix; stir in hot water until completely dissolved. Blend in cold water. Pour into paper cups and freeze.

Fantastic Fudge

1 can sweetened condensed   ½ t. salt
    milk   1 t. vanilla
3½ C. milk chocolate chips

Bring milk and chocolate chips to a boil, but don't cook. Remove from heat and add salt and vanilla; stir until well blended. Pour into a buttered dish and cool. Cut into squares.

Peanut Butter Fudge

4 C. granulated sugar   1 12-oz. pkg. semisweet
1⅓ C. cold milk   chocolate chips
1 pint marshmallow creme   2 t. vanilla
2 C. chunk-style peanut butter

Butter sides of a heavy saucepan. Combine sugar and milk in saucepan; heat and cook over medium heat to boiling. Cook to soft ball stage. Remove from heat, add remaining ingredients, and stir until mixture is well blended. Pour into buttered 9×13 pan. Cool and cut into squares.

Rocky Road

1 12-oz. pkg. butterscotch chips   2 C. chopped nuts
2 T. shortening   1 12-oz. pkg. chocolate chips
1 pkg. miniature marshmallows   2 T. shortening

Melt butterscotch chips and 2 T. shortening in top of double boiler; pour into greased 9×13 pan. Combine marshmallows and nuts; spread over the top and press in slightly. Melt chocolate chips and 2 T. shortening over double boiler; pour over top, and smooth with a spatula. Refrigerate until firm. Cut into squares.

Creamy Fudge

¾ C. butter or margarine   1 lb. powdered sugar
1 lb. brown sugar   1 t. vanilla
⅔ C. evaporated milk   1 C. chopped nuts

Melt butter in a heavy saucepan. Add brown sugar and milk; stir to blend well. Bring to a boil and cook for exactly 3 minutes, stirring down sides of pan frequently. Remove from heat and cool for 2 minutes. Beat powdered sugar into the candy until well blended; stir in vanilla and nuts. Pour into a buttered 9×13 pan; refrigerate. Cut into squares when cool.

Five-Minute Fudge

⅔ C. evaporated milk   2 C. miniature marshmallows
2 T. butter or margarine   1½ C. semisweet chocolate
1⅔ C. granulated sugar   chips
½ t. salt   1 C. chopped nuts
                            1 t. vanilla

In a saucepan over medium heat, combine milk, butter, sugar, and salt; bring to a boil, and cook for 5 minutes (begin timing when bubbles form around the edge of the mixture). Stir constantly during cooking. Remove from heat. Stir in marshmallows, chocolate chips, nuts, and vanilla; stir vigorously until marshmallows and chocolate chips are completely melted. Pour into buttered 8-inch square pan. Cool and cut into squares.

212

Virginia Fudge

A delicious variation on an old favorite!

¼ C. butter or margarine
¼ C. evaporated milk
1 C. brown sugar,
  firmly packed

¼ C. chopped nuts
1 t. vanilla
1¼ C. sifted powered sugar

Melt butter in a saucepan over low heat. Add milk and brown sugar, stirring constantly until sugar dissolves. Bring to a boil and cook for 3 minutes. Remove from heat and add powdered sugar; beat until creamy and smooth. Add vanilla and nuts. Pour into a buttered pan. Cool and cut into squares.

Holiday Candy Logs

Make these and give as Christmas gifts.

1 pkg. graham crackers
1 egg
1 C. sifted powdered sugar

2 T. butter or margarine
1 6-oz. pkg. chocolate chips
1 pkg. miniature marshmallows

Crush graham crackers; set aside. Mix egg and powdered sugar, and beat until well blended. Melt butter and chocolate chips over low heat; stir into powdered sugar mixture. Stir in marshmallows until well blended. Form into 8 logs; roll in graham cracker crumbs, wrap in foil, and freeze. To serve, slice.

Candied Walnuts

½ C. brown sugar,
  firmly packed
¼ C. granulated sugar
¼ C. sour cream

½ t. vanilla
1½ C. whole walnut halves

Combine brown sugar, granulated sugar, and sour cream in a saucepan; cook to soft ball. Cool to lukewarm. Stir in vanilla. Stir in nuts until all are well coated; dump out onto aluminum foil, breaking nuts apart. Cool.

Peanut Brittle

2 C. granulated sugar
½ C. light corn syrup
1 C. water

2¼ C. salted peanuts
1 t. butter or margarine
¼ t. baking soda

Spread peanuts evenly over a well-buttered cookie sheet. Set aside. Combine sugar, corn syrup, and water in a saucepan; cook until the color of a brown paper bag, stirring frequently (takes 25 to 30 minutes). Remove from heat. Stir in butter and baking soda. Pour immediately over peanuts. Cool. Break into pieces with a wooden spoon.

Gumdrops

4 T. flavored gelatin
1 C. cold water

4 C. granulated sugar
1½ C. boiling water

Soften gelatin in cold water; set aside. Combine sugar and boiling water; boil for five minutes. Add gelatin, and stir until completely dissolved. Reduce heat, and boil gently for 15 minutes. Tint with food coloring if desired, and add flavoring if desired. Dip a pan in cold water, and pour mixture into pan. Let stand overnight. Cut into squares, and roll in granulated sugar. Let stand until firm.

Hopscotch Candy

1 6-oz. pkg. butterscotch chips
½ C. peanut butter
1 3-oz. can chow mein noodles
2 C. miniature marshmallows

Melt butterscotch chips in double boiler over boiling water. Stir in peanut butter until mixture is smooth and creamy. In a large bowl, mix marshmallows and chow mein noodles. Pour butterscotch mixture over the marshmallow/noodle mixture. Stir until well coated. Drop by spoonfuls onto waxed paper and chill until set, or pour mixture into buttered 9-inch square pan and chill until set; cut into squares.

MOM'S OLD Standbys

Y ou overslept, and you're in a big hurry to get dressed. The race is on: you paw frantically through your drawers, shove your clothes to one end of the closet. You're out of luck—it seems that everything you own is either dirty, wrinkled, or hopelessly in need of repair. The clock ticks on, and you stand by helplessly.

You wend your way out of the theatre, crowded behind the family with all the children—you know, the ones who started throwing popcorn halfway through. Just as you get into the glare of the lobby lights, you see it: a huge blob of mustard, sitting on the front of your new plaid shirt, absent without leave from the foot-long hotdog you eagerly ate in the first minutes of the movie. Ruined. And it was your favorite shirt.

Disaster? No—not if you act quickly, that is!

What you wear is important: it forms a statement about you and what you represent. We're all judged on the basis of first impressions, and our clothing is a big part of that.

Keeping your clothes in good condition can be easy, once you learn the basics of doing laundry and the secrets behind stain removal.

SORTING

Want to keep whites white and colors bright? Take the time to sort your laundry before you dump it in the washing machine!

Sorting is really quite simple:

Wash whites *only* with other whites. To qualify for the "white" load, there can be *no* color on the article of clothing—not even a small red stripe around the top of your athletic socks.

Wash colored clothing with other colored clothing of the same intensity: in other words, wash light-colored clothing with other pieces of light-colored, and wash darks together.

Pay attention to how dirty your clothes are, too: if you have a few items that are extremely dirty, wash them together in their own load.

215

When you put heavily soiled clothes with clothes that are only lightly soiled, some of the soil may get distributed to the cleaner clothes, and may not be completely removed during washing. If clothes are extremely soiled, they should be soaked in soapy water and rinsed before laundering.

An important part of sorting is checking clothing condition.

Summertime . . . And the Mildew is Blooming

If you're in a humid area, watch out when it gets warm: molds that are always present in the air thrive in warm, moist surroundings, and the result is mildew—on your towels, your sheets, your white shirts, even your books!

If you've never seen mildew, you might not recognize it. It's a dark, furry growth that smells dank and musty; it leaves behind a stain—and, when it's left too long, it can actually rot leather, paper, and all kinds of fabrics.

To get rid of mildew on clothing, check the information on page 224. Check to make sure there isn't any mildew in your drawers or on the walls or shelves in your closet; if you do find mildew, wipe down the closet and inside of your drawers with vinegar. Leave your closet door open for a few days, and, if you can, take your empty drawers outside and leave them in the sun for a day or two.

To get rid of mildew between bathroom tiles, mix a cup of liquid laundry bleach with a cup of water; apply the solution generously to the tiles. Rinse the solution off with clear water after half an hour. (Make sure you don't breathe the fumes directly, and don't get the solution on the shower curtain or your clothing.)

To help prevent mildew, try the following:

- Hang up your wet towels when you're finished showering
- Leave the shower curtain pulled closed so it can dry out
- Never put damp clothing in a hamper or laundry basket; hang it out to dry first
- Never leave damp or wet clothes or towels on the floor
- Don't use starch in your laundry— mildew feeds on it
- Keep your laundry up—don't leave soiled clothing in hampers or laundry baskets longer than a week
- If the air outside is cooler and drier than the air inside, open your windows for ventilation while you're home

216

Look for loose buttons or torn seams, and repair them before washing the clothes. If you have pockets, check to make sure they're empty: there's nothing more frustrating than an important phone number or address, shredded into tiny pieces of lint in the bottom of the washer—or a ballpoint pen that leaks all over your white shirts. And make sure you remove pins or name badges.

As you toss each item of clothing into the washer, brush off any loose dirt, lint, or debris first.

REMOVING STAINS

It's essential that you treat stains *before* you do the laundry: stains are set by heat, and once you've washed them in warm water and dried them in the heat of a dryer, most are difficult—if not impossible—to remove.

For best results in removing any stain, treat it as soon as possible: freshest stains are easier to completely remove. The longer the stain is on the fabric, the more difficult it will be to get out. Even though you might not be doing your laundry until Saturday, take the time after dinner on Wednesday night to treat the stain from the beef gravy you spilled. Once the stain has been treated, you can swish the shirt in the sink, hang it up to dry out, and then wash it as usual on Saturday.

Before you toss your clothes into the washer, check each one carefully for stains. You can expect extra soil on cuffs and necklines; check the seats and knees of washable slacks or Levis and the fronts of everything—that's where spills are most likely to occur.

If you don't have *any* stain remover at all, you can still help remove stains with your regular detergent. If you're using a powdered detergent, mix a little with water to make a paste, and rub the paste into the stained area; if you're using a liquid or concentrate,

It's Not Spaghetti in that Pot!

Do your white socks look like you walked a thousand miles in them? Then try this simple trick:

Bring half a gallon of water to a boil in a large saucepan or kettle; throw in a few slices of lemon, and toss in your dingy—but freshly laundered—socks. Boil for half an hour, drain, and launder again as usual. You'll be amazed at the difference!

217

rub a little into the stain. Use a fingernail brush to lightly scrub the stain, and then launder as usual.

For most effective stain removal, you can use either a commercial product—many come in spray or squirt bottles—or you can use products from your kitchen to get rid of stains. Consult the following for specific stain removal:

TYPE OF STAIN	HOW TO REMOVE IT
Blood	Try one of the following methods: 1. Make a paste of meat tenderizer and water; rub it in the stain, and let it set for 30 minutes; rinse the clothing in a mixture of 2 quarts cool water and 1 tablespoon ammonia; rinse in cool water; let dry in the sun. 2. Flush the stain with cool water before it dries; soak in cold water for 30 minutes; rinse; work detergent into stain; wash, using bleach safe for fabric. 3. Sponge the stain with cool water; work a spoonful of 3% hydrogen peroxide into the stain; when foaming stops, rinse in cool water; if stain is gone, launder as usual. 4. Make a paste of powdered starch and water; rub it into the stain; let it dry; peel the dried paste away; rinse in cool water, and launder as usual.
Butter or Margarine	Try one of the following methods: 1. For whites, scour stain with kitchen cleanser; let stand for 15 to 30 minutes; rinse with cool water; if stain is gone, launder as usual. 2. Combine borax, cleanser, and water into a paste; test it on a small, concealed area of fabric; if fabric does not discolor, work the paste into the stain; launder as usual, without first rinsing the paste out of the fabric.
Candle Wax	Scrape as much of the wax off as you can with a dull knife; place the stained area between two

paper towels or two pieces of brown paper sack; press with a warm iron until wax has melted and been absorbed into towel or sack; launder in hottest water safe for fabric.

Carbon Paper   Make a paste of detergent and water, or use liquid detergent; work into stain; rinse with cool water; if stain is gone, launder as usual. If stain remains, before laundering work a little household ammonia into stain and launder as usual.

Catsup   Scrape off excess; sponge with cool water; soak the stained area in cool water overnight; work either powdered or liquid detergent into stain; rinse with cool water; launder as usual.

Chewing Gum   Try one of the following methods:
1. Put the article of clothing in a plastic bag in the freezer for several hours; scrape the frozen gum off the clothing with a dull knife.

Getting a Fresh Blast of Steam

To prevent hardwater and mineral deposits from building up in your steam iron, you should use only distilled water in it. But if you don't have access to distilled water—and your iron is hopelessly clogged up—here's how to blast it free:
1. Dump out any water that is still in your iron.
2. Fill the iron with white vinegar, set the control on "steam," and let the iron heat for five minutes.
3. Unplug the iron and let it cool completely; empty the vinegar out of the iron, and refill it with clean water.
4. Plug the iron back in, set the control on "steam," and iron a rag or scrap of fabric you can throw away; loosened residue will escape with the steam. Keep ironing until no more residue escapes.
5. Empty the water out of the iron, refill the iron with clean water, and resume ironing.
Or, use the frost from your refrigerator/freezer compartment. Melt desired amount and use in place of distilled water.

2. Sponge the gum with turpentine or kerosene before washing as usual.

3. Rub the chewing gum with beaten egg white until the gum dissolves and comes off; launder as usual.

4. Rub the gum with an ice cube; when cold and hard, scrape off with a dull knife; launder in hottest water safe for fabric.

5. Soak the stained area in white vinegar until gum dissolves or can be pulled off; launder as usual.

Chocolate
Make a paste of borax and cold water; rub into stain, and let stand for 15 minutes; rinse in cool water; launder in hottest water safe for fabric.

Cosmetics
To remove mascara, eyeshadow, rouge, pancake powder, or liquid foundation from clothing, rub a paste of powdered detergent and water into the stain (or use a small amount of liquid detergent); rinse with cool water; launder as usual. (See page 224 for procedure on removing lipstick.)

Crayon
Loosen the crayon with shortening; scrape off with a dull knife; rub detergent into stain; wash in hottest water safe for fabric with detergent and 2 cups of baking soda; repeat if necessary before putting clothing in dryer.

The Worst Ring of All

Oh, no . . . you've got ring around the collar!

"Those dirty rings," the woman on the ad moans at us, her face writhing with pain. "I've tried soaking . . . I've tried scrubbing . . . but still I get ring around the collar!"

If your white shirt collars have rings, try one of these easy methods:

1. Add enough vinegar to baking soda to make a thick paste; rub it in with an old toothbrush or small nail brush, and launder as usual.

2. With an old toothbrush or small nail brush, rub shampoo into the collar and cuffs; shampoo is specially designed to dissolve hair oils.

3. Mix a solution of ¼ cup liquid dish soap, ¼ cup household ammonia, and ¼ cup water; pour a little on collar and cuffs, rubbing well until the fabric is saturated. Launder as usual.

Deodorant	Try one of the following methods: 1. Sponge the stain with ammonia, and launder as usual. If the fabric is silk or wool, dilute the ammonia with one part water. 2. Sponge the stain with white vinegar; if stain remains, soak in rubbing alcohol for 30 minutes; rinse thoroughly with cool water; wash in hottest water safe for fabric. (**Note:** These methods work only for actual deodorant stains; if the stain is from perspiration, see page 225–226.)
Dye	If one article of clothing "bleeds" during washing and discolors other clothing, wash the discolored clothing immediately in a color-safe bleach.
Egg	Scrape the dried egg off the fabric with a dull knife; soak in cold water for 30 minutes; work detergent into the stain; launder in hottest water safe for fabric.
Fruit, Fruit Juice	Try one of the following methods: 1. Stretch the stained area over a large bowl; pour boiling water through the stain from a height of several feet; repeat until stain is gone; launder as usual. 2. Rub 3% hydrogen peroxide into the stain; when peroxide stops foaming, rinse thoroughly with cool water; repeat until stain is gone; launder as usual. 3. Rub lemon juice into the stain; let stand for 15 minutes; rinse thoroughly with cold water; repeat until stain is gone; launder as usual. 4. If the stain is fresh, sponge the stained area with cold water; soak in cold water for 30 minutes; launder as usual with bleach safe for fabric added to wash water.
Grass	Try one of the following methods: 1. Soak in cold water for 30 minutes; rinse thoroughly; rub detergent into the stained area; wash in hottest water safe for fabric with

Pressing Like a Pro

Want the crispest shirt ever? It's not really that difficult —by following a few simple steps, you, too, can master the fine art of ironing.

To get started, you'll need two basic tools: an iron and an ironing board. Your ironing board should have a snug-fitting cover to make the job easier and to prevent bunching and wrinkling while you iron. Your iron can be either a dry or a steam iron; if you don't have a steam iron, you'll need to dampen your clothes before you iron them. (Never dampen or steam silks —they get water spots!)

Regardless of what you're ironing, follow these guidelines:

- If you'll be ironing right after you do laundry, take your clothes out of the dryer while they're still damp—it will save time. If you have to iron later, dampen clothes about an hour before you start to iron: sprinkle your clothes generously with warm water and roll them up to distribute the moisture evenly.

- Start out cool: begin with a low temperature, and iron those things that need a lower temperature. Iron those things that need a hot temperature last—you'll prevent accidental scorching.

- Use a light hand. You don't need to exert a lot of pressure when you iron; keep a basic back-and-forth motion, and never stretch or pull the fabric while you iron it (you'll stretch it out of shape).

- In places where the fabric is double thick—such as cuffs, collars, hems, pocket flaps, and some yokes—iron on the inside first, then the outside.

- To get crisp seams, spritz them with a mixture of one part water to one part white vinegar, then press open from the inside before pressing on the outside.

- Never iron directly over buttons, snaps, zippers, or hooks and eyes.

- Start with the smallest parts of the piece of clothing, and progress to the largest; on a shirt, start with cuffs and collars, then do sleeves, and then do the front and back.

- To keep them from getting shiny, iron wools, silks, rayons, and dark-colored fabrics on the wrong side. If you have to do a minor touch-up on the right side of the fabric, put a lightweight clean cloth between the iron and the fabric.

- To get a sharp crease, dampen the crease a little more than usual, then press. If you need to, redampen and press again.

- To iron lace, put it on a clean bath towel, and use a lightweight clean cloth between the iron and the lace.

222

bleach added to wash water.

2. For silk, wool, or colored fabrics, soak stained area in 2 cups of water mixed with 1 cup of rubbing alcohol; rinse thoroughly, and launder as usual.

3. Dip a strip of white fabric in kerosene; rub the grass stain with the strip of fabric until the stain is completely saturated; wash in small amount of sudsy water; rinse thoroughly; launder as usual.

Grease	Try one of the following methods:

1. Rub detergent into the stain; wash in small amount of warm sudsy water; rinse thoroughly; launder as usual.

2. Sprinkle talcum powder, cornstarch, or cornmeal onto the stain; let stand for 15 minutes; brush off; work small amount of liquid shampoo into the stain; wash in hottest water safe for fabric.

3. For knits, rub stain with club soda; launder as usual.

4. For suede, sponge with vinegar; brush with a suede brush to restore nap.

Indelible Pencil	Rub stain with alcohol until stain disappears; launder as usual.

Ink (Ballpoint Pen)	Try one of the following methods:

1. Saturate stain with hairspray; immediately rub with a soft, clean cloth; rinse thoroughly; launder as usual.

2. Combine ½ cup rubbing alcohol with 1 cup water; rub into stain until stain disappears; rinse thoroughly; launder as usual.

Ink (Fountain Pen)	As soon as possible, pour cold water through the stain until it is gone or until no more color comes out; rub stain with a paste of detergent and lemon juice; let stand for 5 to 10 minutes; launder as usual.

Iodine	Try one of the following methods:

1. Moisten a cotton ball with rubbing alcohol; rub the stain until it is gone; rinse thoroughly; launder as usual. (Dilute the alcohol with two parts water for silk or wool fabrics.)

2. Soak the stained area in cool water; rub detergent into the stain; rinse in warm sudsy water; rinse thoroughly; launder as usual.

Lipstick   Rub stained area with petroleum jelly; wash in warm sudsy water; rinse thoroughly; launder as usual.

Mildew   Try one of the following methods:

1. Mix 1 tablespoon of chlorine bleach in 2 cups of warm water; test on a small concealed area of fabric; if fabric doesn't discolor, soak stained area for 15 minutes; rinse and launder as usual. Do *not* use this method on wool or silk.

2. Add ½ cup Lysol to wash water.

3. Make a paste of 1 teaspoon salt and the juice of 1 lemon; rub into fabric; without rinsing, let the stained area dry in the sun; launder, using hottest water safe for fabric.

4. Brush mildew off fabric; rub detergent into stained area; wash; if any stain remains, sponge with hydrogen peroxide and let dry in sun. Launder again, using bleach safe for fabric and hottest water safe for fabric.

Milk,   Immediately flush with cold water; soak
Milk Products   stained area in cold water for 30 minutes; rub detergent into stained area; wash. If stain hasn't disappeared, work a few drops of 3% hydrogen peroxide into stain and wash again.

Mucus   Scrape away excess; sponge with ¼ cup salt dissolved in 1 quart warm water; launder as usual.

Mud   Let mud dry completely; rub off with a stiff-bristle brush; sponge stained area with cool water; if stain remains, sponge with rubbing alcohol until gone; launder as usual.

Mustard	Moisten stain with cool water; rub detergent into stained area; rinse with cool water; soak overnight in sudsy water; wash in hottest water safe for fabric with bleach safe for fabric.
Pencil (Lead)	Try to "erase" the stain with a pencil eraser; rub detergent into stain; rinse thoroughly; if stain remains, rub ammonia into stain; rinse thoroughly; launder as usual.
Perspiration	Try one of the following methods:

1. If stain is fresh, sponge immediately with warm water and detergent or ammonia; soak for 30 minutes in warm water; launder in hottest water safe for fabric.

2. If stain has dried, sponge with vinegar;

Banishing Spots Forever: Rely on Your Kitchen Cupboard

Want to keep your clothes looking their best—but don't have a fancy spot remover?

Don't worry—many of the basics in your kitchen cupboards (and a few from your bathroom, too) can get out even the most stubborn stain.

Many commercial spot removers are really quite simple: they're not much more than a basic base of two parts water to one part rubbing alcohol. And scan through your cooking and first aid supplies to get some of the following:

Cornmeal. Sprinkled over a greasy stain, it helps absorb the grease: you can combine it with water to make a paste, or shake it right out of the box.

Cornstarch. If you use it while the stain is still fresh, cornstarch, too, absorbs grease—either as a powder or a paste.

Petroleum jelly. Good for getting off the crusty part of many stains—such as tar or dried-on food. Use it to loosen and soften the residue, then just scrape or lift it off.

Salt. Great for absorbing grease—shake it on right out of the shaker, right at the dinner table for best results! The sooner you get the salt on the stain, the more likely the stain will come right out.

Talcum powder. Another great grease absorber: shake it on and rub it in!

Vinegar. White vinegar works well to remove acidic stains, like those from fruits and fruit drinks.

225

	soak in warm water for 30 minutes; launder in hottest water safe for fabric.
	3. Rub stain with a paste of warm water and meat tenderizer; let stand for 1 hour; rinse thoroughly with cool water; launder as usual.
Rust	Try one of the following methods:
	1. Spread the stained area over a bowl or pan of boiling water; pour lemon juice through stain; rinse thoroughly; launder as usual.
	2. Make a paste out of lemon juice and salt; rub into stain; let dry in sun; rinse dried paste out of fabric with warm water; launder as usual.
Scorch	Put stained area on ironing board. Cover the stained area with a cloth that has been soaked in 3% hydrogen peroxide; cover the first cloth

---

A Bottle of Bleach on Your Shelf and a Song in Your Heart

You've got catsup on your white shirt, grass stains on your Levi's, and . . . well, socks that could curl your hair. Seems like a big order, but you can confront almost any laundry problem with a few washday basics.

Obtain the following, and keep them together in one spot between laundry days; if you stain an article of clothing, take care of it right away for best results.

A laundry basket. An inexpensive plastic one will work fine; just make sure it's large enough to hold your week's worth of laundry. If you have to travel to a laundromat, you can use the basket to tote your laundry supplies, too.

Detergent. The brand is really up to you; whatever you decide on, follow label directions carefully for best results. Make sure you consider how dirty your clothes are and whether you're washing in hard water—both conditions require slightly more detergent, as does a large-capacity load.

Bleach. Choose a good liquid chlorine bleach for whites and, if you want one, a powdered bleach that's safe for colored clothing. You won't need to use bleach in every load, but you'll find that bleach is also invaluable as a general cleaning product and disinfectant.

Fabric softener. Fabric softeners eliminate static cling from clothing; you can buy either the liquid kind that you add to rinse water in the washing machine, or sheets that you toss in the dryer with your clothes.

Spot remover (optional). You'll need to treat stains before you wash, so you'll need to use either a commercial spot remover (many are available in squirt or spray bottles) or a spot remover that you mix from household products.

	with a clean, dry cloth; press with iron set at hottest temperature safe for fabric; rinse thoroughly; launder as usual.
Shoe Polish	Rub stained area with rubbing alcohol; use alcohol straight on white fabrics, diluted with two parts of water on colored fabrics; rinse thoroughly; launder as usual.
Soft Drinks	Sponge immediately with rubbing alcohol diluted with one part water; rinse thoroughly; launder as usual.

Note: At first, it may not look like a soft drink has left a stain, but soft drinks leave a yellow stain when they dry; you must remove the stain before laundering, since washing and drying will set the stain.

LOADING THE WASHER

One of the main causes of dingy wash is improper loading: stuffing too many clothes in the washer. Most washing machines have a line that indicates maximum load capacity; keep your load a little smaller than that. If the washing machine allows you to select water level, make sure you fill the washer with enough water to allow free agitation of the clothes. When the washer has filled and the cycle has started, lift the lid and check to make sure that the clothes are agitating freely.

If you're washing knits, keep the load small to avoid excess wrinkling.

CHOOSING THE WATER TEMPERATURE

The wrong temperature can wreak considerable havoc: your clothes can shrink, colors can bleed, and whites can turn gray.

As a rule, use the following water temperatures for fabric types:

White shirts. Hot water wash, cold rinse.

White underwear. Warm water wash, cold rinse.

Wash-and-wear colored fabrics. Warm water wash, cold rinse.

Elastic fabrics. Warm water wash, cold rinse.

Synthetic fabrics. Warm water wash, cold rinse.
Colored fabrics that bleed. Cool water wash, cold rinse.
Woolens. Cool water wash, cold rinse.

CHOOSING DETERGENT

There are hundreds of brands of detergents on the market, and you can choose one in powdered, liquid, solid, or concentrated form. The detergent you choose is largely a matter of personal choice, but read the label—make sure you're getting a detergent that works in hard water if you have hard water (it's more difficult to get clothes clean in hard water).

Button, Button . . . Who's Got the Button?

There's nothing worse than losing a button . . . unless it's tearing the inseam out of your pants, that is!

Be prepared for any eventuality by assembling a small clothing repair kit. It's easy and inexpensive. You'll need the following:

Something to keep it in. This doesn't have to be fancy—even an empty bandage tin will do! Whatever you decide on, keep it small, and make sure it closes tightly.

Thread. Visit a fabric store, and ask for the smallest spools available. You'll only need a few: white, black, and gray are usually enough. Use the white thread for whites and light-colored clothing, and the black for navy and dark brown.

Needles. Needles are available in a small pack of assorted sizes from any fabric or variety store.

Straight pins. You'll only need a few. Try sticking them in a chunk of Styrofoam or keeping them together on a strip of masking tape.

Safety pins. Again, you'll only need a few—and remember: they're only for emergencies! Resist the urge to permanently hold yourself together with a maze of skillfully placed safety pins.

Buttons. You should make every effort to salvage the button you lose. But just in case you can't, keep a few buttons on hand as replacements; visit a fabric or variety store, and choose buttons that will closely match your suits and shirts.

Something to cut the thread with. A small pair of scissors is ideal. If you can't find any, try a razor blade—but keep the sharp edge covered to avoid cutting yourself.

228

Regardless of the detergent you choose, follow label directions for amount; you'll need to consider size of load, type of fabric, and amount of soil. The label will tell you how. Remember—some detergents are low-sudsing, designed to work without foamy suds; don't make the mistake of pouring more detergent in the washing machine just because you don't see suds.

SOAKING

To get better results, let the washer fill with water; pour in the designated amount of detergent, and swish it around with your hand until it dissolves; then add clothes. With the washer shut off, let the clothes soak in the soapy water for fifteen minutes, then reactivate the washing cycle. Soaking will help loosen stubborn dirt and will give the detergent time to start working on the clothing.

BLEACHING

In most cases, you won't need to use bleach in your laundry. Occasionally, though, bleach can be used to remove excessive soil, to help remove stains, and to help brighten white fabrics.

Liquid bleach can be used safely on white cottons; for other fabrics, you should choose a powder bleach with a label that specifies its safety for colored fabrics. Because the powder dissolves slowly in the wash water, the concentration of bleach remains low, and the clothing is not damaged.

Check all clothing labels before using any bleach—some will warn you against using any kind of bleach at all.

If you do use liquid bleach, use extreme care—make sure none of it splashes on dry clothing, and make sure the clothes are in the washer no longer than ten minutes after you add bleach to the wash water.

USING FABRIC SOFTENER

Fabric softener helps eliminate static cling from fabrics and results in softer, fresher laundry. There are two basic kinds of fabric softener: a liquid that you add to rinse water, and a small sheet that you toss in the dryer. The kind you choose depends on personal preference. Both kinds have advantages: liquid fabric softener dissolves in the rinse water, allowing for even distribution among clothing; fabric softener sheets are more convenient, since they don't require measuring and don't require monitoring of the wash cycle.

Whichever type you choose, follow label directions carefully.

RINSING

Rinsing is critical to a clean batch of laundry: it's essential that you remove all the soapy residue from the clothing if you want clothes to look clean and bright. Cold water rinses are best—besides saving energy, they tend to cut and remove soapy residue better than warm or hot water.

If you added extra detergent to a load of heavily soiled clothing, run the clothes through an extra rinse cycle to remove all traces of soap.

DRYING

If you're using a clothes dryer, check the lint filter before you start the dryer—clean all lint and dust from the filter, which usually looks like a screen. Select the right temperature if the dryer has a temperature control; you can dry most clothing on a medium heat, but use high heat for heavy fabrics, such as denims.

It's best to slightly under-dry: check the load periodically to make sure the clothes don't get too dry. Many articles of clothing won't need to be ironed if you remove them from the dryer when they are slightly under-dry and hang them on a hanger immediately. If you'll be ironing your clothes immediately, remove them from the dryer while they're still quite damp, roll them up, and put them in your laundry basket.

Let Your Seat So Shine . . .

We have all experienced having a shine on the seat of our pants, skirts, etc., after repeated wearing of a particular article of clothing. This shine is the result of the fibers in the clothing being repeatedly pressed and packed; therefore, to rid this shine, those fibers need to be released. To do this, dip a clean soft cloth in white vinegar, slightly wring it out, then vigorously rub the shiny area. Do not press the fabric afterwards unless it is absolutely necessary, but if you do be sure to use a press cloth between the iron and fabric. If there still seems to be too much shine, try rubbing a very fine grade of sandpaper gently over the shiny area. Before using the sandpaper, test a hidden area to see if the sandpaper might do too much damage.

230

If you're hanging clothing on a clothesline, shake the article of clothing so some of the wrinkles fall out before you hang it up. Hang it as straight as you can, and take it off the line while it's still slightly damp so you can iron it.

KEEPING CLOTHES IN GOOD REPAIR

Periodically check your clothing to see whether it needs repair; common problem areas are hems, buttons, armhole seams, and crotch seams. The old adage, "A stitch in time saves nine," is certainly true: take the time to repair a problem area as soon as you discover it, or you might have a much bigger problem on your hands.

For any hand repair, double the thread: put one end of the thread through the needle, pull it even with the other end of the thread, and tie a firm knot, holding both ends of the thread together.

To make your repair job easier, keep the length of thread relatively short—long thread gets tangled and knotted easily. Check to make sure you're using a sharp needle; blunt needles are hard to work with, and can snag and run fabrics.

Never pull a thread that's hanging from a hem or seam: cut it off, and make necessary repairs.

Sewing on Buttons

Check your buttons regularly—it's best to repair a button while it's loose than to try and find a button that matches after you've lost the original. It's also easier to sew the button in the right place, aligned with the buttonhole, before it has fallen off completely.

To sew on a button, begin with the needle on the underside of the fabric; push the needle up through the fabric and through one of the holes in the button, holding the button down firmly with the edge of your thumb. Pull the thread all the way through until the knotted end is taut against the underside of the fabric. Push the needle down through the other hole, pulling the thread all the way through again. Repeat until finished.

While buttons should be sewn firmly to the fabric, they should not be so tight that they can't be buttoned and unbuttoned easily; check periodically as you sew to make sure that you aren't pulling the thread too tight. A helpful hint to allow for this spacing is to slip a straight pin between the fabric and the button, and proceed to sew the button on, then slip the pin out when through.

To finish, make sure you knot the thread well on the underside of the fabric.

If you have a button on a coat or suit jacket that is constantly coming loose, try sewing it with fine fishing line.

Repairing Seams

To repair a seam that has ripped, follow these guidelines:

1. To make the repair durable, use doubled thread.

2. Turn the garment inside out; match the thread that was used to sew the garment originally as closely as you can. Never use anything but white thread on an article of white clothing; use black or navy on dark clothing, gray on gray clothing, and white on light-colored clothing.

3. With the clothing turned inside out, locate the tear. Matching the edges of the seam together, use a series of straight pins to hold the seam securely closed, as you want it to be when you finish.

4. Using a running stitch to repair the seam, keep your stitches small, and overlap them slightly. If you're working on knitted fabric, sew your running stitch in a slightly zig-zag pattern to allow for stretch.

5. If the seam is one that is constantly stressed, such as an armhole or crotch seam, sew a double line of stitching for reinforcement.

6. Knot the thread securely. Press the seam flat open on the inside, spritzing it with a little vinegar to set the seam. Turn the garment right side out, and press the seam on the outside for a finished look.

Repairing a Hem

Check hems periodically to make sure the threads are holding securely; if you can see that a hem is coming unraveled, repair it immediately. If you have a hem that does come out, follow these guidelines:

1. Using the old crease as a guideline, use straight pins to pin the hem back up.

2. With your thread doubled, take small stitches around the hem; as you complete each stitch, take up only a few threads of the fabric

on the right side of the garment, and finish the stitch by making a small knot in the thread.

3. Knot the thread securely when you have finished.

4. Press the hem on the inside, dampening it or using the steam setting on your iron; turn the garment right side out and press the hem on the outside, again dampening or using steam.

A Thick Wool Blanket Takes a Bath

Wool blankets *can* be successfully washed in a normal washing machine—but if you don't follow the proper procedure, your blanket may end up the size of a small bath towel! To avoid shrinkage and distortion, follow this simple procedure:

1. Check the blanket before you wash it to see if there are any spots of heavy soil. Use a nail brush or a vegetable brush and warm soapy water to remove any obvious spots.

2. Fill the washing machine with warm water—it should feel comfortably warm, but not hot, to your hand. Add the amount of detergent recommended for a full load, and agitate the machine until the detergent has completely dissolved.

3. Stop the washer's agitation. Submerge the blanket in the water, and let it soak for 20 minutes; during soaking time, swish the blanket two or three times by hand.

4. Turn the dial to the "spin" setting, and let the washer spin until the water has spun out of the blanket.

5. Allow the washer to fill with rinse water, and then stop the washer; the rinse water should be the same temperature as the wash water. Let the blanket soak, submerged in water, for five minutes; turn the dial to "spin" so the water will drain out of the washer, but don't let the washer spin yet. Repeat the rinsing process, letting the blanket soak in clear water another five minutes. Swish the blanket by hand a few times during the soaking period.

6. Turn the dial to "spin," let the washer drain, and let the blanket spin to get rid of excess water.

7. Put five or six large bath towels in the dryer, and run it on high heat for five minutes; remove the towels, wrap the blanket gently around them, and return the towels and blanket to the dryer.

8. Dry on high heat for approximately fifteen minutes; check frequently, and remove the blanket from the dryer while it is still damp (drying it completely will cause shrinkage).

9. With your companion on the other end of the blanket, pull it and stretch it vigorously to reshape it; brush it with a nylon- or metal-bristle brush to raise the nap and make the blanket look like new.

10. Drape the blanket over a rack or rod to let it completely dry.

I t's happened: you've burned yourself on the stove. Gotten a nosebleed. Scalded yourself in the shower. Fallen off your bike. Been blistered with a sunburn.

Minor accidents *can* be easily handled with a few simple first aid procedures; usually, that's all the help you'll need. But learn to use your common sense. Remember: first aid is only a temporary measure in terms of a more serious injury, such as fracture or a serious burn. Do what you can to help yourself, and then seek medical attention.

Use the following first aid practices to soothe your minor hurts. You should always seek medical help if you have a burn that has blistered, if you suspect you have broken a bone, or if you detect signs of infection—redness, pain, swelling, and fever.

BLEEDING

1. Grab the cleanest material you can find—a handkerchief works well, as does a clean washcloth or a strip of sterile gauze.

2. Cover the wound with the cloth, and apply firm pressure to the wound with your hand, holding the edges of the wound together.

3. Maintain firm pressure on the wound until the bleeding has stopped.

4. When bleeding has stopped completely, sponge the wound gently with an antiseptic, such as rubbing alcohol or hydrogen peroxide; gently spread a thin layer of antiseptic or antibiotic ointment over the wound.

5. Cover the wound with a bandage.

Note: If you can't control bleeding within a few minutes, you should seek medical help—stitches may be needed.

BLISTERS

1. Sterilize a needle by holding it for ten seconds in the flame of a sulphur match.

2. Carefully puncture the *edge* of the blister next to the skin.

3. Apply gentle pressure, squeezing the accumulated fluid out of the blister; make sure not to peel back or brush off the skin that formed over the blister—it helps guard against bacterial infection.

4. Treat the blister with either antibiotic ointment or rubbing alcohol.

5. Cover the blister with several layers of sterile gauze.

Note: You can prevent some blisters from forming by covering the area with several layers of sterile gauze at the first sign of discomfort.

BOILS

1. Soak the boil for 30 minutes at a time in the hottest water you can stand. If the boil is on your hand or foot, immerse it in hot water; if the boil is on an area of your body that cannot be easily immersed, soak it with a washcloth dipped in hot water; renew the cloth often to keep up the temperature.

2. Do *not* puncture the boil.

3. When the boil comes to a head, it will eventually burst open on its own. When that happens, apply *gentle* pressure and keep bathing the boil with hot water to help drain all infected matter.

4. Treat the boil with antibiotic ointment or rubbing alcohol and cover it with a sterile bandage.

BREATHING DIFFICULTIES

To help a person who has stopped breathing, follow these steps:

1. Position the victim on his back; take necessary precautions if you suspect that the person may have sustained a back or neck injury.

2. Tilt the victim's head so that his chin is pointing up by placing one of your hands under his neck; lift up gently while you press down gently on the victim's forehead. Check to make sure that the victim's tongue is not blocking his throat.

3. Using the hand that is on the victim's forehead, pinch his nostrils shut to prevent leakage of air. Open your mouth wide, take a deep breath, and seal your mouth over the victim's mouth. Blow four quick breaths into the victim as quickly as you can; pause

between each breath only long enough to lift your head and inhale.

4. If the victim does not begin to breathe on his own after the four quick breaths, continue to breathe into his mouth at the rate of one breath every five seconds, or 12 times per minute. Continue mouth-to-mouth resuscitation until help arrives.

If the victim is an infant, you should breathe gentle puffs of air at the rate of one every three seconds, or 20 times per minute.

If the victim has also obviously lost his heartbeat, you should institute cardiopulmonary resuscitation (CPR). Since this technique is somewhat complicated and can result in life-threatening injury if done improperly, you should receive training in the CPR procedure from a licensed practitioner. Most communities offer free training through the Red Cross or some other service group.

BRUISES

1. Apply a cold compress to the bruised area immediately after the injury, if possible—a washcloth or face towel soaked in cold water will work well.

2. To alleviate subsequent pain and swelling, apply cold compresses or an ice bag to the bruised area for 15 minutes at a time several times a day.

BURNS

Note: You should attempt first aid treatment only for first-degree burns—those in which the skin is reddened, slightly swollen, and sometimes covered with welts. If you receive a second- or a third-degree burn—one in which the skin is blistered or charred—or if the burn covers a large area of skin, you should seek medical treatment immediately. For first-degree burns, follow these guidelines:

1. Immediately immerse the burn in cold water, and keep it immersed until you no longer feel pain; if necessary, periodically add ice cubes to the water to keep it cold. Do *not* put butter or any other greasy product on the burn.

2. Apply one of the following to the burn: (a) a commercial burn ointment, (b) a thick layer of honey, (c) petroleum jelly, or (d) a thin paste of baking soda and water.

3. Cover the burn with a loose protective bandage that allows some exposure to air.

CHEMICAL BURNS

1. Irrigate the burned area with plenty of running cold water to completely flush away any traces of the chemical.
2. Apply one of the agents listed under Item 2 of "Burns."
3. Cover the area with a loose protective bandage.

Note: If the chemical burn involves the eye, immediately flush the eye with plenty of running water, cover the eye with a sterile pad to keep the lid still, and obtain immediate medical help.

CHOKING

Choking—getting a piece of food trapped in the throat, which subsequently cuts off breathing—is a life-threatening emergency. The *worst* thing to do is slap the victim on the back; forceful blows to the back can act to push the food further into the windpipe, lodging it more tightly. Likewise, you shouldn't attempt to reach the chunk of food with your fingers—you're likely to push it further into the windpipe.

The Heimlich Maneuver, designed to rescue choking victims, can be performed on victims who are either conscious or unconscious and can be performed on victims who are standing, sitting, or lying down. You can even perform the maneuver on yourself if you are alone or there is no one present who can help you.

For a victim who is standing:

1. Stand behind the victim and wrap your arms around the victim's waist.
2. Grasp your hands in front of the victim; the hand that is resting against the victim's abdomen should be in a fist. Make sure that the fist is positioned between the tip of the breastbone and the navel.
3. With your hands tightly grasped, press your fist into the victim's abdomen, using a quick, upward thrust. The piece of food should come flying out of the victim's mouth with force. If it doesn't, repeat the thrusting motion several more times until the food is dislodged.

For a victim who is sitting:

Repeat the procedure as with a victim who is standing; stand behind the chair, and grasp the victim around the waist.

For a victim who is lying down:

1. Roll the victim onto his or her back. Kneel at the victim's side, straddle his hips, or straddle one of his thighs. Your position isn't that important: choose the one that is most comfortable and that will allow you the greatest strength as you thrust.

2. Place one of your hands on top of the other; the heel of your bottom hand should be positioned between the tip of the breastbone and the navel. Move forward so that your shoulders are directly above the victim's abdomen.

3. Press your hands forcefully into the victim's abdomen with a rapid, upward thrust. Repeat the thrusting until you can see the piece of food; you may have to fish it out of the victim's mouth. Act quickly so that the victim doesn't breathe it in again.

For a victim who is a child:

1. Place the child on its back across your thigh.

2. Using two or three fingers of one hand, position your fingers between the tip of the breastbone and the navel.

3. With a quick, upward thrust, push your fingers into the child's abdomen. Don't use as much force as you would use with an adult.

To perform the maneuver on yourself:

1. Quickly locate a firm, rigid, preferably nonmovable object that is about the height of your abdomen; rest your abdomen across it so that it is positioned between the tip of your breastbone and your navel. You can use the edge of a counter, the edge of a table, or the back of a chair.

2. Quickly and forcefully press your weight downward so that the object works to thrust upward into your abdomen.

3. Repeat this thrusting motion until the food is dislodged.

CUTS

1. Wash the affected area with warm water and soap.

2. If bleeding is severe, apply pressure as described in "Bleeding." If bleeding is minor, apply moderate pressure until it stops.

3. Apply an antibiotic ointment or rubbing alcohol, thoroughly

cleansing the wound and removing any debris, such as gravel.

4. Cover the cut with an adhesive strip; if the cut is large, use sterile gauze and adhesive tape.

5. To relieve initial pain or throbbing, hold an ice bag over the bandaged cut for 15 to 20 minutes.

6. Change the bandage daily and monitor the cut for signs of infection; reapply antibiotic ointment or rubbing alcohol each time you change the bandage.

EAR, FOREIGN OBJECT IN

1. Lay on your side with the affected ear up.

2. Put several drops of warm mineral oil or warm olive oil into your ear until you feel a sensation of fullness; wait five minutes.

3. Sit up and tilt your head to the side, with the affected ear pointed downward. If the object was small or was an insect, it should float out in the oil.

Note: Do *not* put oil in your ear if the object is one that would swell—a bean, wood, or any other absorbent object. If a large object is lodged in your ear, or if your first aid treatment is unsuccessful, seek medical help.

Basic First Aid Supplies

You've probably seen plenty of first aid kits—from fancy ones in hinged boxes, complete with twenty graduated sizes of bandages, to the not-so-fancy: a shoe box stuffed with everything from tincture of iodine to syrup of ipecac.

You need something in between: the sheer basics, so you're equipped to handle most minor emergencies, and a spot to keep them in. The spot is up to you—a shelf or two in your bathroom cabinet works fine, as does a shoe box tucked in the corner of your closet shelf. As for the basics, use the following checklist:

1 box bandaids in assorted sizes
1 roll guaze bandage
1 roll adhesive tape

1 pint rubbing alcohol (70%)
1 tube antibiotic ointment
1 bottle aspirin or nonaspirin pain reliever
1 bottle petroleum jelly
Cotton balls and cotton swabs
1 bottle hydrogen peroxide (optional)
1 tube burn ointment (optional)
1 bottle Calamine lotion (optional)

240

EYE, FOREIGN OBJECT IN

1. If you can see the object, lift it gently away from your eye with the corner of a clean handkerchief or a clean cotton swab.

2. If you can't see the object, gently pull your upper eyelid out and down over your lower lid; the tears should wash the particle from your eye.

3. If you still aren't successful, gently pull your upper lid upward, inverting it; if you see the object, remove it with a cotton swab or the corner of your handkerchief.

4. If you still haven't found the source of irritation, gently pull your lower lid outward and remove the object.

5. Irrigate your eye gently with clear, cool water.

Note: If you are unable to remove a large object or if you have particles of metal in your eye, seek medical help immediately. You should also seek medical help if your eye burns for a prolonged period after removing the foreign object or if the surface of your eye is cut.

FAINTING

1. If you feel faint, immediately lie down; if you can't lie down, sit down and put your head between your knees. If you can, lie or sit in fresh, cool air. Stay in a head-down position for at least ten minutes.

2. If someone does faint, help him or her to lie down in a comfortable position, preferably with his/her head lower than the rest of the body.

3. After regaining consciousness, rest in a lying-down position for at least ten minutes before resuming activity.

FRACTURES

Note: Fractures *must* receive medical attention. To avoid further injury, don't try to move the fractured area; if you suspect injury to the neck or spine, don't move the person at all—send for medical help. If the fracture is compound—the bone is sticking out of the skin—take measures to stop bleeding while medical help arrives.

FROSTBITE

Note: Frostbite initially looks like a reddened first-degree burn;

a tingling sensation follows, ice crystals may form in the skin, and the skin will become a yellowish–gray color and feel numb.

1. Rewarm the frozen skin by submerging it in warm, *not hot,* water. *Do not* rub the frozen skin to warm it with friction!

2. When a reddish color returns to the frostbitten skin, take it out of the warm water and gently pat it dry; take care not to break any blisters that may have formed, and do not rub the skin.

3. Cover the skin with a loose bandage and seek medical help immediately. If the feet or legs are frostbitten, don't try to walk.

NOSEBLEED

Note: If you suspect that your nose is broken, do not try to treat it yourself; seek medical help immediately.

For minor nosebleeds that result from minor injury, allergy, or change in altitude, follow these guidelines:

1. Sit down and tilt your head back.

2. Apply pressure to your nose by firmly grasping the area just below the bridge of your nose between your thumb and forefinger; apply pressure for five to ten minutes.

3. If bleeding does not stop within ten minutes, pack the bleeding nostril with sterile gauze and apply firm pressure at the tip of the nose.

4. Apply a cold compress or ice bag to your face and to the base of your skull at the neck.

5. Once the bleeding has stopped, remain quiet and avoid laughing or blowing your nose.

Note: If you cannot control bleeding within 15 to 20 minutes, seek medical help—the nosebleed may be due to high blood pressure or to a fracture of the nose.

PUNCTURE WOUNDS

1. Wash the wound well with soap and hot water.

2. If bleeding is present, control it by applying direct pressure.

3. When bleeding has stopped, cover the wound with sterile gauze.

4. Seek medical help in all cases of deep puncture wounds; a tetanus shot may be needed if you have not been immunized against tetanus within the previous one to five years.

242

SHOCK

Note: Shock, which generally occurs to some degree after any injury, can, when severe, cause death. A person who is in shock may look dazed and confused; he may either be pale or flushed, depending on the type of injury; he will probably be breathing irregularly, and his breathing may be weak. He may vomit; in severe cases, he will lose consciousness. *Immediate* medical attention is needed. Until medical help arrives, follow these guidelines:

1. Have the person lie down on his/her back; keep the head level with the body or slightly elevated. Do *not* tilt the person so that the head is lower than the body.

2. Loosen tight clothing at the chest and neck.

3. If the skin is pale and cool, cover the person with one or more blankets to provide warmth, but be careful not to overheat the person; if the skin is hot and red, apply bath towels soaked in cool water until the skin returns to normal temperature, and then cover the person with a blanket to keep him/her warm.

4. *Never* give a person in severe shock anything to eat or drink.

SPLINTERS

1. Thoroughly wash the area around the splinter with soap and warm water; rinse well. Swab the area gently with rubbing alcohol.

2. Hold the end of a needle in the flame of a match for ten seconds.

3. If the end of the splinter is sticking out of the skin, grasp it with a pair of tweezers and gently pull it out of your skin at the same angle it entered. Go slowly and gently to avoid breaking the splinter off beneath the surface of your skin.

4. If the end of the splinter is visible but is beneath the surface of the skin, use the needle to gently loosen the skin around the splinter and expose its end; then grasp the end with the tweezers and remove it gently.

5. Gently squeeze the wound to encourage slight bleeding, which will wash out some bacteria.

6. Apply antibiotic ointment or swab the wound with rubbing alcohol.

7. Cover the wound with a bandage.

Note: You should seek medical help if the splinter is buried too deep to be removed, if infection develops (signalled by redness, pain, tenderness, pus, or fever), or if the splinter was deep and you have not been immunized against tetanus within the last five years. Seek medical help if the splinter breaks during removal and you are unable to completely remove the remainder of the splinter.

SPRAINS

1. Immediately immerse the sprained area in ice water for 20 minutes to control swelling. Repeat, using ice water or cold compresses, every four hours until the swelling has stopped.

2. Elevate the sprained limb to at least waist level until swelling has stopped.

3. Once the swelling has stopped, soak the sprained area in contrasting baths three times a day: first in very warm water for 20 minutes, then in icy water for 20 minutes.

4. Once the swelling has stopped, begin gently exercising the sprained area by moving it slightly from side to side—an important step in maintaining flexibility. Don't move it so rapidly or so far that you cause much pain; continue these flexibility exercises several times daily until pain begins to diminish.

5. Limit use of the sprained area; if it is an ankle, you need to use crutches until the motion of walking slowly heel-to-toe no longer hurts. If it is a wrist, avoid using your hand to eat, write, or do other things until a waving motion no longer causes pain.

SUNBURN

1. Apply cool compresses to the burned area to reduce pain and swelling, or take a cool shower. If the sunburn involves your back or an area you can't reach, soak in a tub of cool water.

2. Take aspirin or another nonaspirin pain reliever to reduce pain.

3. Apply a thin paste of baking soda and water to alleviate pain; calamine lotion can also relieve pain and reduce swelling.

4. If blisters form, *never* break them intentionally. If blisters do break, apply an antibiotic ointment and cover the blisters with a sterile dressing.

Note: Most sunburn is minor, but you should seek medical help if the sunburn is severe, covers more than one-fourth of your body, or involves extensive blistering.

Y
ou've felt it before: the scratchy throat. The throbbing head. The burning brow. The queasy stomach.

It's natural to worry a little when you don't feel good—but how can you tell when your worry is unfounded and when you should indeed seek medical help?

If you're suffering from a stabbing ear, an itching eye, or a spotty rash, find your symptom—or any of dozens others—on the chart below to determine whether you need medical help.

How to Determine When You Need Help

Regardless of the symptom or symptoms that you have, you should seek medical help in two general situations: first, if your symptoms continue to worsen despite your attempts to treat them and the passage of time; and, second, when you feel intuitively that you are very ill. It's always better to make an unnecessary call to a doctor than to risk a serious illness going undetected.

Canker Sores

Canker sores, reddish punched-out sores that occur inside the mouth, can follow illness or irritation to the mouth; some people get canker sores from eating too many nuts, heavily spiced foods, salty foods, or foods that are high in acid (such as tomatoes, oranges, grapefruit, or lemons).

Treatment
1. Rinse your mouth with warm water several times a day.
2. Use aspirin or a nonaspirin pain reliever on a limited basis.

Seek Medical Help When:
1. Your gums begin to bleed.
2. The canker sores themselves begin to bleed.
3. There are more than three canker sores at the same time.
4. You have a fever higher than 101° F.

Cold Sores

Cold sores, usually occurring outside the mouth near the lips, look like blisters; beginning with an uncomfortable tingling feeling, they erupt into large red lesions and eventually begin to ooze. Cold sores are highly contagious and are easily spread from one person to another. As cold sores heal, they begin to crust over and eventually dry up; *never* pick at the sores or remove the scabs.

Treatment

1. Dab alcohol or witch hazel on the sores to help dry them.
2. Apply a local anesthetic to relieve pain.
3. Apply a local antibiotic cream if sores appear to be infected.

Seek Medical Help When:

1. The cold sore gets larger.
2. The cold sores appear to be spreading.
3. Additional sores start forming near the original sore.
4. The sore lasts longer than a week without definite signs of healing.

Common Cold

The common cold is caused by a virus—and, as a result, there is no known cure. You may feel as though you will die, but you simply have to "ride it out." Certain treatment techniques, while they won't *cure* the cold, will help provide relief from symptoms while the cold runs its course.

Treatment

1. Use a vaporizer or humidifier to keep your respiratory tract moist, easing sore throat and making it easier to breathe.
2. Gargle with hot salt water to ease sore throat.
3. Take aspirin or a nonaspirin substitute to reduce fever and relieve aches and pains.
4. Use a cough syrup or cough drops at night if coughing keeps you awake.

Seek Medical Help When:

1. You run a fever of 101° F or higher for a continuous twenty-four-hour period.
2. You have a cough that lasts longer than twenty-four hours.

3. Your nasal discharge is greenish, thick, pus-like, or has a foul odor.

4. You have a sore throat that lasts longer than two days.

5. You have severe pain in your ears.

6. Your cold lasts longer than ten days without definite signs of improvement.

Constipation

Occasional constipation is normal and can result from many things—such as stress, not drinking enough liquids, eating too fast, not eating enough fiber, or ignoring the urge to use the bathroom. Occasional constipation usually responds well to treatment.

Treatment

1. Drink at least eight large glasses of water per day.

2. Drink fruit juices or eat fresh fruits.

3. Improve the diet to add plenty of bulk and fiber; try eating bran, vegetables and fruits that have skins and seeds, and whole wheat products.

4. Use a mild laxative product if the constipation becomes uncomfortable and does not respond to other treatment.

Seek Medical Help When:

1. You experience severe abdominal pain.

2. You have an unexplained weight loss.

3. You notice blood in your stool (either bright red streaks of blood or areas of dark blood).

4. You experience repeated dizziness.

5. The constipation becomes chronic—that is, you suffer repeatedly or are unable to gain relief from the constipation.

Cough

Cough can accompany a number of conditions—most commonly, it is a symptom of upper respiratory tract infection. Many coughs result from irritation to the bronchial tubes or to the throat from the mucous that accompanies a cold; you can obtain some relief from taking a decongestant that helps to dry up the mucous.

Treatment

1. Use a vaporizer or humidifier at night.

2. Take a mild cough suppressant before going to bed.

3. Prop your shoulders and head up with several pillows to reduce irritation from mucous drainage.

Seek Medical Help When:

1. You run a fever higher than 101° F for twenty-four continuous hours.

2. You cough persistently during the day.

3. The cough persists for longer than a week or accompanies a cold that lasts longer than ten days.

4. You begin wheezing.

5. You experience difficulty in breathing that lasts longer than fifteen or twenty minutes.

6. You begin to cough up material that is pus-like in appearance, thick and foamy, or has a foul odor.

7. Your cough is accompanied by severe chest pain.

Diarrhea

Diarrhea, like constipation, can be a symptom of many different illnesses and can result from many different factors. There are many different definitions of diarrhea, too: generally, the diarrhea you should be concerned about is signalled by loose, watery stools that are passed more often than six times a day. Diarrhea is often caused by a virus, making it resistant to treatment; the major danger from diarrhea is dehydration.

Treatment

1. Use a mild over-the-counter diarrhea medication to help control the diarrhea.

2. Drink plenty of water and other clear liquids.

3. Avoid drinking milk and eating milk products.

4. Eat a diet of bland foods until the stools become firm again.

Seek Medical Help When:

1. The diarrhea persists longer than three days.

2. You notice blood or mucous in the stool.

3. You are also vomiting.

4. You have a fever higher than 100° F that lasts longer than twenty-four hours.

5. You do not pass any urine for eight hours.

6. The diarrhea stubbornly resists treatment.

248

Earache

There are two general kinds of earache, and both of them require a doctor's attention. The first kind, sometimes called "swimmer's ear," is an infection of the ear canal; swimmer's ear, or external otitis, results in pain when you pull on the ear or when you press on the cartilage area just in front of the ear. External otitis must be treated with ear drops, usually containing antibiotics.

The second kind of ear infection, otitis media, affects the middle ear and is more common than swimmer's ear. You may suddenly wake up with a painfully stabbing earache, and it may be preceded for several days by a mild cold. In some cases, the pain may subside after a few hours, but the infection continues—so it is important to get antibiotic treatment. Since the infection is on the other side of the eardrum, ear drops are not effective in treatment of otitis media.

Treatment

In addition to the ear drops or antibiotics prescribed by a physician, you can do the following things to reduce the pain of an earache:

1. Take aspirin or a nonaspirin pain reliever as directed on the product label.

2. Apply gentle heat to the ear with a heating pad, hot water bottle, or warm washcloth.

3. With your doctor's approval, take a decongestant to reduce inflammation.

4. In cases of swimmer's ear, avoid getting water in your ears for at least two weeks. Use ear plugs or cotton plugs coated with petroleum jelly during swimming, showering, and while you wash your hair.

5. In cases of otitis media, avoid changes in pressure and altitude; if possible, avoid flying.

Seek Medical Help When:

1. A severe pain persists longer than an hour.

2. You have a less severe nagging pain that persists longer than two hours, even if it disappears on its own.

3. You run a fever of 101°F for longer than one hour.

4. There is any kind of discharge from the ear.

Fever

Most often, fever is the body's response to infection, but there can be other causes of an elevated temperature, too: certain medications (including antibiotics) can cause fever, as can chronic disease (such as cancer), vigorous exercise, or heatstroke. The main danger from fever is dehydration—the body literally dries out as it perspires in an attempt to lower the temperature. When high fevers occur—such as those above 105° F—convulsions may result. You *cannot* correctly diagnose a fever by feeling your forehead: the only accurate diagnosis occurs when you use a fever thermometer.

To take your temperature, grasp the thermometer firmly at the non-bulb end and shake it sharply until the mercury falls below 94° F. Tuck the mercury bulb under your tongue and leave it in place for five minutes. Do not breathe through your mouth while you are taking your temperature, and don't attempt to get a reading within half an hour after you have consumed hot or cold foods or liquids.

Treatment

1. Take aspirin or a nonaspirin medication designed to reduce fever; take the medication every three to four hours until the fever has been gone for twenty-four hours.

2. Bathe in a tub full of lukewarm—*not* cold—water.

3. Get plenty of rest.

4. Eat nutritious, light foods to keep up your strength.

Many doctors recommend letting a fever run its course unless it is extremely high or unless it carries with it extreme discomfort; you should generally let a fever run its course for twenty-four hours before beginning treatment.

Seek Medical Help When:

1. The fever reaches 105° F.

2. The fever persists for twenty-four hours after you begin treatment.

3. The fever is accompanied by other troublesome symptoms.

4. Your condition worsens instead of improving after you have been treating it for twenty-four hours.

5. You feel extremely ill, cannot stay awake, or feel confused and disoriented.

Headache

While it is the most feared, brain tumor is the *least common* cause of headache. Your headache is much more likely to fall into one of the following categories:

Tension headaches are a result of stress, which causes the muscles in the neck and shoulders to tighten up. Pain is most severe in the back of the head and in the neck, sometimes radiating into the shoulders. The neck and shoulders feel tight and are often tender to the touch.

Migraine headaches are caused by too much blood circulating to the brain—pain results from the increased pressure. Migraines often run in families, and can be triggered by stress, chemicals in foods (especially cheese, chocolate, and sausage), or illness. A migraine headache usually involves only one side of the head and may affect vision; migraines are often accompanied by nausea and/or vomiting. Prescription drugs are usually recommended to ease the pain of migraine headaches.

Allergy or *infection* can lead to headache. Hay fever is a common culprit; the headache will be accompanied by classic hay fever symptoms, such as itchy or runny nose, itchy eyes, and sneezing. Sinus infections lead to severe headaches; they are accompanied by tenderness in the face and around the eyes, toothache, and nasal discharge that is foul-smelling or contains pus.

Eyestrain does not actually cause headache, but causes the eyes to ache—a symptom that is often misinterpreted as headache.

Treatment

1. Take aspirin or a nonaspirin pain reliever once every three to four hours; if the headache accompanies a cold or hay fever, take the decongestant recommended by your doctor.

2. Get some sleep if possible.

3. If the headache appears to be tension-related, try to remove the source of tension; lie down with a heating pad on your shoulders and neck, or have someone gently massage your neck and shoulder muscles.

4. Get outside for some fresh air.

5. Get some mild exercise.

6. Take care of any other problems, such as constipation.

Seek Medical Help When:

1. A headache follows a blow to the head.

2. The headache persists for longer than twenty-four hours and does not respond to treatment.

3. The headache is particularly severe, so much that it interferes with your ability to carry on your work.

4. The headache is accompanied by other symptoms of illness.

5. The headache is accompanied by clumsiness, dizziness, or problems with vision.

6. You suffer from chronic headache, frequent headache, or a disturbing pattern of headaches.

Take Two Aspirin and Call Me in the Morning

It's a familiar refrain . . . but too many of us have relied too heavily on the good old aspirin tablet! Aspirin *does* have a number of benefits: it relieves pain and reduces fever, to name a few. But, as with all other medication, moderation is the key. To wisely use aspirin for all its good effects, and to escape some of its possible bad effects, follow these guidelines:

• Follow directions on the label closely. The label will not only specify dosage amount and timing, but will indicate under what conditions you should *not* take aspirin.

• Unless your doctor tells you to, don't take more than three aspirin tablets at a time, don't take aspirin more often than once every four hours, and don't take more than ten aspirin tablets in a twenty-four–hour period.

• Don't take aspirin for longer than two weeks unless your doctor has told you to; you should never take regular doses of aspirin over a prolonged period unless you are under your doctor's supervision.

• Always drink a full eight ounces of liquid with your aspirin—it helps the aspirin tablet dissolve and lessens the likelihood of upset stomach.

• Since aspirin reduces your blood's ability to clot, you should not take aspirin within a week of undergoing elective surgery, within a week of your estimated due date if you are pregnant, or while you are taking anticoagulant drugs.

• If you notice that you have adverse effects when you take aspirin—if you suffer from extreme indigestion, for example, or if you break out in hives—consider acetaminophen. It has many of aspirin's good qualities, but does not contain aspirin.

Influenza

Caused by virus, influenza *cannot* be treated with antibiotics—unfortunately, you just have to let the influenza (or "flu," as it is more commonly called) ride its course. If you are young and normally healthy, flu probably won't be a serious threat; those with diabetes, respiratory disease, heart disease, or chronic kidney diseases, as well as the elderly, can be adversely affected and should consider with their physicians getting flu shots. Classic influenza is signalled by fever (sometimes high), fatigue, achiness, nausea, sore throat, and a bad cough.

Treatment

1. Get plenty of rest—at least four days, recommend most doctors—and get it as soon as symptoms appear. The sooner you get to bed, the less likely you will have an extended bout with the illness.

2. Drink plenty of fluids to replace lost fluid and to help keep the lungs clear.

3. Take aspirin or nonaspirin pain reliever to relieve aches and pains.

4. Treat isolated symptoms with appropriate medication—throat lozenges for a sore throat, for example. Most doctors recommend against cough suppressants except at night if the cough interferes with sleep.

Seek Medical Help When:

1. You have a fever over 104° F that lasts longer than one day.

2. Your flu symptoms last longer than one week.

3. The symptoms worsen instead of improve as time goes on.

4. You are troubled by insomnia and are unable to sleep.

5. You have a low fever (100–101° F) that lingers for longer than four days, despite efforts to treat it.

Pink Eye

Highly contagious, pink eye (conjunctivitis) is an infection of the membranes of the eyelids that causes severe irritation to the eye. The white part of the eye often turns dark pink or red, the inside of the eyelids is red, and there is usually a creamy or pus-like discharge from the eye. While it is most often caused by bacteria, pink eye can follow a cold and be caused by virus. To avoid spreading pink eye, use your own washcloth and towel; launder your bedding frequently. Wash your hands thoroughly after touching your eyes, and avoid contact with others.

Treatment

1. Wipe away any discharge with a moist cotton ball; dispose of the cotton ball carefully to avoid contamination.

2. Lie down with a cool cloth over your eyes to relieve discomfort.

Seek Medical Help When:

1. Symptoms persist longer than a day (you will need a prescription for antibiotic drops or ointment).

2. Symptoms get worse instead of better despite treatment.

3. You experience pain in your eye.

4. The redness or irritation follows an injury to the eye.

5. There is severe swelling around the eye.

6. You are running a fever.

Rash

A rash can stem from almost anything—and, because a rash can signal a variety of problems, you should probably get medical attention for any rash that persists longer than a day. The most common causes of rash include:

Hives, or an allergic reaction of the skin, most often caused by allergy to food or medication. Hives can be small, reddened bumps that resemble insect bites, or they can become large welt-like raised areas that are extremely itchy.

Heat rash results from overdressing in the winter or persistent high temperatures in the summer. The skin, usually rough and reddened, is covered by many small pimples about the size of a pinhead.

Eczema is usually most severe behind the knees, in front of the elbows, and behind the ears, but it can occur on any part of the body. Eczema causes severe itching, and the rash is rough and sometimes weeping.

Contact dermatitis results when the skin comes in contact with something that irritates it; the rash is red, rough, and may be weeping or blistery. There is severe itching.

Impetigo is a highly contagious infection that looks like white-heads or oozing blisters; these blisters eventually scab over. There is severe itching. Antibiotic creams, available without a prescription, are effective in some cases; in more severe cases, you may require antibiotic medication either orally or by injection.

Viral diseases such as chicken pox or measles, most common in children, cause a rash that covers the entire body. Diagnosis by a physician should be made, and contact with others should be limited.

Scarlet fever causes a coarse rash that covers the entire body and is most dense in the groin and armpits. Scarlet fever, which responds to antibiotics, is accompanied by fever, swollen glands, sore throat, and nausea and/or vomiting.

Treatment

Treatment depends on the cause of the rash:

1. *Hives:* discontinue any new medication or food that may have caused the hives; bathe in lukewarm water and baking soda; apply calamine lotion to the hives; consult your doctor for an anti-histamine to stop the itching. Apply witch hazel or rubbing alcohol to relieve itching.

2. *Heat rash:* dust affected areas with cornstarch to absorb perspiration; use nonprescription hydrocortisone cream on stubborn areas; avoid wearing wool; dress in lightweight, loose-fitting clothing of natural cotton.

3. *Eczema:* consult your doctor for an antihistamine to relieve itching; wash infrequently to prevent drying the skin; apply cortisone creams if infection is not present; if infection is present, apply lukewarm compresses and antibiotic cream, such as those available without a prescription.

4. *Contact dermatitis:* wash the affected area thoroughly with plenty of soap and water; apply lukewarm compresses to relieve itching; use calamine lotion if limited areas are affected; apply cortisone-type creams; ask your doctor for an antihistamine to relieve itching.

5. *Impetigo:* wash the area gently with mild soap and water; do not pick off scabs; do not scrub the area; use nonprescription antibiotic creams; avoid contact with others; do not scratch the area.

6. *Viral diseases:* avoid contact with others; treat other symptoms.

7. *Scarlet fever:* consult a physician immediately for antibiotic treatment.

Seek Medical Help When:
1. Attempts at treatment do not improve the rash within twenty-four hours.
2. You suspect that you may have a contagious disease.
3. The rash from contact dermatitis affects a large area.
4. The rash from insect bite or sting is accompanied by breathing difficulties or fainting.

Sore Throat

Sore throat is most commonly the result of upper respiratory infections—most often, the common cold. Sore throat is also a symptom that accompanies a variety of illnesses, and occasionally is caused by a streptococcal bacterial infection (the renowned "strep throat"). Sore throat may also result from breathing through the mouth during sleep (usually caused during colds or allergies that cause nasal congestion), excessive talking over a prolonged period, or other irritations to the throat tissues, such as breathing in heavily polluted air.

Treatment
1. Take aspirin or a nonaspirin pain reliever once every three to four hours to ease discomfort.
2. Suck on a throat lozenge, piece of hard candy, or hard mint.
3. Gargle with hot salt water once every hour to cut phlegm and increase circulation to the tissues of the throat.
4. Take a heaping tablespoonful of honey to coat the throat.

Seek Medical Help When:
1. You know that you have been exposed to a diagnosed case of strep throat.
2. Your throat is severe enough to interfere with breathing.
3. Your glands in your neck are tender and swollen.
4. You run a fever of 101° F or higher for longer than twenty-four hours after beginning treatment with aspirin.
5. You have a rash.
6. You begin drooling.

Stomach Ache

Most commonly, stomach ache is the result of either a viral infection (which also may cause diarrhea or vomiting) or eating foods that are too rich or that upset the stomach. Most stomach ache involves nausea; some includes cramping. The most feared cause of stomach ache—appendicitis—is much less common and can be detected by noticing the general location of the pain. While a common stomach ache generally hurts in the area beneath the navel or causes cramping throughout the abdomen, the stomach ache associated with appendicitis is a sharp, stabbing pain or a dull intense aching in the lower abdomen (on either side).

Treatment

1. Eat a clear diet—clear soups, juices, tea, and water—until the stomach ache completely disappears. Follow the clear diet by a bland diet for eight to twelve hours—eat foods such as soft-boiled eggs, mashed potatoes, bananas, rice, or gelatin. Avoid foods that are heavily spiced, fried, or foods that contain milk.

2. Apply gentle heat to the abdomen with a heating pad or hot water bottle (especially helpful for soothing cramps) *only* if you are certain you don't have appendicitis.

3. If you develop diarrhea, eat only a clear diet until you pass firm stools again.

4. *Never* take a laxative for a stomach ache.

Seek Medical Help When:

1. You have a sharp, stabbing pain or an intense dull ache in your lower abdomen for longer than two hours—regardless of the side the pain is located on.

2. Your stomach ache is less intense and is located other than the lower abdomen, and it lasts longer than twenty-four hours.

3. You vomit up blood or mucous.

4. Your vomit contains black, gritty material that resembles coffee grounds.

5. Your diarrhea contains blood or mucous.

6. You vomit up green material or bile-stained material more than once.

7. You run a fever of at least 101° F for longer than twenty-four hours after beginning treatment with aspirin.

Sty

A pimple-like swelling of either the upper or lower eyelid, a sty is usually red and hot to the touch; extremely tender, a sty may or may not feature a whitehead.

Treatment

1. Soak the sty with a hot washcloth for thirty minutes at a time once every two or three hours, or as often as you conveniently can.

2. Eventually, the sty will come to a head and will burst and drain on its own as you soak it with the hot washcloth. Wipe drainage gently away with the corner of the washcloth and wipe the sty gently with first a soapy cotton ball and then one with clear water; take care not to get soap in your eyes.

3. *Never* squeeze a sty in an attempt to drain it.

4. *Never* lance a sty with a needle or other instrument.

5. Apply nonprescription antibiotic ointment to the sty once it breaks and drains (use prescription ointment if your doctor recommends it).

Seek Medical Help When:

1. The sty becomes so large that it interferes with vision.

2. The sty keeps increasing in size after two to three days.

3. The sty resists treatment, does not come to a head, and does not drain.

4. You develop unusual pain or a fever of more than 100° F.

5. You develop more than one sty on the same eyelid or a sty on the eyelid of each eye at the same time.

Urinary Pain

Painful urination can result from a number of conditions, including kidney infection, bladder infection, infection of the urinary tract, narrowing of the urinary tract, or irritation of the genitals. Accompanying fever generally indicates infection of the kidneys, and should be checked by a doctor immediately. A hot, burning sensation during urination generally results from infection of the bladder, infection of the urinary tract, or irritation of the genitals; straining during urination, much less common and generally more serious, can result from a narrowing of the urinary tract.

258

Treatment

1. Check for irritation of the genitals. If present, wash the genital area thoroughly and gently with mild soap and warm water; make sure you rinse all the soap thoroughly. Apply a protective zinc oxide ointment, such as an ointment used for diaper rash.

2. Soak in a warm tub to ease discomfort.

3. If pain has made it impossible for you to urinate, soak in a tub of warm water and urinate directly into the tub; shower afterward.

Seek Medical Help When:

1. You cannot clear up irritation of the genitals with the above-described treatment.

2. You run a fever of 100° F or higher for longer than twenty-four hours.

3. You experience painful burning during urination for longer than twenty-four hours.

4. You urinate more often than every two hours continuously over a twenty-four-hour period.

5. You have dull, throbbing pain in your lower back.

6. You must strain to urinate.

The general rule is this: if you suspect a urinary infection of any kind, be on the safe side. Have a doctor perform a laboratory test of your urine to rule out infection.

Vaginal Discharge

Vaginal discharge comes in many varieties: some is clear and odorless, but the more troublesome kind is very different. Ranging from frothy and foul-smelling to the consistency of cottage cheese, it can cause pain or, more often, severe itching. Most often, vaginal discharge is related to infection of the vaginal tract—often caused by an imbalance in the bacteria levels, resulting in the common "yeast" infection.

Treatment

1. Wash the genital area thoroughly with mild soap and warm water. Rinse and dry thoroughly.

2. Avoid nylon undergarments that trap perspiration; wear cotton undergarments that can absorb moisture.

3. To relieve pain and itching, sit in a lukewarm tub two to three times daily.

Seek Medical Help When:

1. Attempts at treatment as described above are not effective within forty-eight hours.

2. The discharge is frothy, foul-smelling, or curdled (with a consistency like cottage cheese).

3. You experience pain during urination.

Since vaginal discharge that persists can be a sign of infection, it is wise to check with a doctor; common treatments include vaginal creams or suppositories. Do *not* douche—douching can aggravate the problem rather than solve it.

Vomiting

You shouldn't try to stop vomiting—but you should pay attention to one of vomiting's most serious effects: dehydration. Vomiting is a symptom that accompanies a wide spectrum of diseases, and rarely occurs by itself. Sudden, acute vomiting in the absence of other symptoms or previous illness can be a sign of food poisoning and should receive immediate medical attention.

Treatment

1. Try to replace lost fluid by drinking clear liquids; ginger ale or cola drinks may help settle your stomach.

2. Eat a clear liquid diet for at least twenty-four hours.

3. Don't eat solid foods until eight hours after the vomiting has stopped.

Seek Medical Help When:

1. You have vomiting spells for more than twenty-four hours.

2. You vomit up blood or mucous.

3. You vomit up green or bile-stained material more than once.

4. You vomit up dark material that resembles coffee grounds.

5. The vomiting is sudden and intense without symptoms of disease.

6. You run a fever of 101° F or higher for more than twenty-four hours after beginning treatment with aspirin.

Symptoms of Common Diseases

Think you might be coming down with The Plague? Feel like—well, like you've never quite felt before? No two ways about it: most of us feel helpless when we start to feel ill. And then the imagination takes over: what *can* this be? Is it serious? Will I end up under the surgeon's knife?

Before you panic, take a few minutes to calmly assess. Most of the time, symptoms are simply signals that something isn't running smoothly in the body; almost always, they are the signs of mild illness or infection. Much less commonly, they might signal something more serious. Making some attempts at intelligent and moderate self-treatment and following up by seeing a doctor when necessary can take care of most problems.

If your symptoms persist, or if you notice definite patterns over a prolonged period of time, check this table of symptoms to see if you might have a more stubborn problem.

Remember: This list of symptoms is merely a suggestion; just because you have many or all of the symptoms listed under a certain illness does not mean you definitely have that illness. Use this list as a guideline as to when you should consult a doctor. Only a licensed physician can accurately diagnose and treat disease.

Anemia

Anemia is more common than you think: an estimated 22 million people in the United States suffer from the condition, in which not enough red blood cells or hemoglobin are present in the blood. Red blood cells are the body's oxygen transportation system—when their numbers are compromised, the body tissues don't receive enough oxygen, and serious illness can result.

Anemia can result from two conditions: internal prolonged bleeding or loss of blood (such as that from a bleeding ulcer), or not enough iron in the diet.

Symptoms

Some of the symptoms of anemia include:
- breathlessness
- fatigue or drowsiness
- pale coloring, especially the linings of the eyelids, mucous linings of the mouth, and the beds of the fingernails
- dizziness
- ringing in the ears
- muscle weakness
- pounding, racing heart

- swollen, flabby, sore tongue
- increased thirst
- mental confusion or loss of acuity

Treatment

Anemia is treated by eliminating the source. If the anemia is due to loss of blood, the source of the bleeding is detected and corrected. If the source of the anemia is dietary, you will need to follow your doctor's instructions for eating an iron-rich diet, including plenty of dark green leafy vegetables, eggs, molasses, liver, and whole grains.

Appendicitis

The appendix—a wormlike extension from the colon—lies in the lower right area of the abdomen most of the time, but is occasionally found on the other side or more toward the center in some people—so the traditional "pain on the right" doesn't always hold true. Medical reseachers know of no real purpose for the appendix, and once it's removed surgically, you continue to function as usual. When the appendix becomes infected, it gets swollen, tender, and can become gangrenous or can rupture. If the appendix ruptures, it can lead to peritonitis, a sometimes-fatal disease.

Symptoms

Appendicitis is usually accompanied by an elevated white blood cell count, something your physician can determine with the help of laboratory tests. Other symptoms include:
- pain in the abdomen, usually on the lower right side, usually severe, dull, and constant
- rigidity in the lower right side of the abdomen
- fever (usually 100° F to 101° F, but sometimes higher)
- loss of appetite
- indigestion, nausea, or vomiting

Treatment

The only acceptable treatment for appendicitis is surgical removal of the appendix; delay can result in rupture. If you suspect that you may have appendicitis, you should *never* take a laxative or give yourself an enema—you could cause your appendix to rupture if it is infected. You should not apply heat to your abdomen.

Asthma

Asthma—a disease in which the victim has to struggle for breath—can be caused by infection, allergy (to dust, insecticides, pollen, feathers, or mold), or emotional stress; in some cases, a predisposition toward asthma runs in families. For most people with asthma, the spells are broken up by long periods in which there is no problem. Usually, these problem-free periods become shorter throughout the victim's life; periods of asthma become longer and more frequent, as well as more intense. Unfortunately, some people with asthma also develop allergies or sensitivities to the drugs used in asthma treatment, including aspirin.

Symptoms
• tightness and a feeling of constriction in the chest
• severe difficulty in breathing
• noisy and wheezy breathing
• pale, bluish face
• violent coughing that produces thick, mucousy sputum

Treatment

Asthma treatment is complicated and requires a physician's supervision. Many cases of asthma can be controlled with medication; people with asthma must take extra measures to avoid colds and upper respiratory infections. Good general health is critical to the control of asthma.

Athlete's Foot

Athlete's foot, a common malady among men, is caused by a fungus that thrives in warm, damp places—such as between the toes. You are highly susceptible if the areas between your toes are damp for a prolonged period—such as when you swim frequently, or when your feet perspire in the summer. You can also pick up the athlete's foot fungus by walking barefoot in locker rooms, gymnasiums, and areas around swimming pools.

Symptoms
• severe itching
• redness of the skin
• cracking of the skin between the toes
• occasional white patches of skin
• occasional blistering

Treatment

Most cases of athlete's foot respond to a regimen of treatment that you can do at home. Once every two to three hours, wash your feet thoroughly with soap and warm water; rinse well, and make sure your feet are dried completely. Pay special attention to the area around your toes and between your toes. Sprinkle your feet liberally with an anti-fungal powder; you can get them without a prescription in most drugstores. If you can, wear sandals so your feet can be exposed to the air. If you have to wear shoes, sprinkle the inside of your socks with the anti-fungal powder. If your athlete's foot does not respond to the above-described treatment within a week, you should consult a doctor; you should also consult a doctor if your athlete's foot is so severe that the skin between your toes starts to decompose.

Bronchitis

Either bacteria or virus can cause bronchitis—a disease that causes the bronchial tubes to become inflamed. If you are healthy and in pretty good condition otherwise, the bronchitis probably won't be too serious; the disease is most serious for infants and the elderly. It starts with what seems to be a bad head cold: you'll have a slight fever, a runny nose, and general achiness. Bronchitis is much more common in the winter, in climates that are damp, and you are most susceptible to it if you are run-down, in a highly polluted environment, or in overcrowded conditions.

Symptoms

After the symptoms of the common cold, the symptoms of bronchitis set in, which usually include the following:
- pain in the back
- pain under the breastbone
- cough—usually violent—which is nonproductive at first, but which then brings up plenty of thick, yellowish phelgm
- fever (usually higher than 101° F)

Treatment

If the bronchitis is caused by bacteria, your doctor will prescribe an antibiotic; antibiotics are not effective against viral infections. Regardless of the source of infection, you should stay in bed, drink plenty of fluids, and keep the air warm and moist (use a humidifier or vaporizer). If the cough keeps you awake at night—and it usually

264

is much more severe at night—your doctor will probably prescribe a strong cough suppressant so you can sleep.

Bursitis

Sometimes called "tennis elbow," bursitis can occur in any joint, but is most common in the shoulder, elbow, and knee. Bursitis occurs whenever there is constant irritation to the bursa, or the membranous sac that lies between joints. This irritation can come from a calcium deposit, constant bruising (common when a person kneels frequently on a hard floor), or the improper grip of a tennis racquet. Your doctor will probably want to x-ray the joint to make sure there is no bone damage.

Symptoms
• severe pain upon movement of a joint
• dull aching while the joint is not being used
• a sensation of extreme tension in the joint

Treatment
The pain from bursitis can usually be partially relieved by cold packs and keeping the joint immobile; if calcium deposits are causing the irritation, they may need to be surgically removed or controlled by medication.

Cancer

Cancer is a complex disease that can manifest itself in any of hundreds of ways; to try to list its possible symptoms would be almost impossible. As a guideline, the American Cancer Society has listed what it calls the "seven warning signs" of cancer; according to the Society, the presence of any of these symptoms for a period longer than two weeks should be reason to see a doctor.

The Seven Warning Signs
1. A change in bowel or bladder habits
2. A sore that does not heal
3. An unusual bleeding or discharge
4. A thickening or lump in the breast or elsewhere
5. Indigestion or difficulty in swallowing
6. An obvious change in a wart or a mole
7. A prolonged cough or hoarseness

Treatment and Prevention

Cancer treatment usually consists of surgery, radiation treatment, and/or chemotherapy; while some forms of cancer do not respond well to treatment, medical researchers are gaining ground in the fight to cure an increasing number of cancers.

There are some things you can do to prevent cancer. The following may help to prevent certain kinds of cancer:

1. Get your weight to its proper level and maintain it there.
2. Avoid cigarette smoking.
3. Eat a well-balanced diet rich in foods that have natural fiber; get plenty of whole grains and eat vegetables with their skins and seeds.
4. Avoid excessive exposure to the sun.
5. Avoid unnecessary x-ray.
6. Get frequent check-ups.

Chicken Pox

The most contagious of the so-called "childhood" diseases, chicken pox does afflict adults who have never had the disease as children—even though three-fourths of all children get chicken pox before the age of fifteen. While immunizations have been developed against measles and the mumps, there remains no effective prevention against chicken pox. A viral disease, its symptoms last approximately two weeks.

Symptoms

In an adult, the following symptoms usually occur:
• rash, beginning as spots which turn into raised pimples and then teardrop-shaped blisters that eventually crust over
• high fever
• chills
• headache
• severe backache

Treatment

Because the chicken pox rash itches severely, most treatment is aimed at relieving the itch. You can use calamine lotion or zinc oxide, or you can add starch or baking soda to your bath water. Get plenty of rest and drink plenty of fluids. You are no longer contagious when *all* blisters have crusted over and no pimple-like rash remains. You should consult a doctor if your temperature is above 102° F or if the blisters begin bleeding or get infected.

Common Cold

There still is no cure for the common cold—a disease that can be caused by any one of more than forty viruses. The cold, unfortunately, is highly contagious—and your chances of picking up a cold are greater if you are worn out, depressed, or under stress.

Symptoms
Any of these symptoms may mark a common cold:
• sore, scratchy throat
• runny nose
• nasal congestion, stuffiness
• loss of sense of smell and taste
• sneezing
• headache
• mild fever (under 100° F)
• mild coughing
• mild aches and pains

Treatment
Since the cold is caused by a virus, there is no medication that is effective against it; some decongestants may provide temporary relief, but should be used with caution. Aspirin may be used for fever and aches; use nasal sprays with extreme caution, since they may actually worsen the condition. Bed rest and drinking plenty of fluids is the best treatment for a cold; most colds will clear up within two weeks.

Cystitis

Cystitis—a bacterial disease that causes inflammation of the bladder—is particularly common among women of child-bearing age, but can also affect men, particularly those with enlarged prostate gland. Cystitis, too, is especially common during pregnancy. If detected and treated early, cystitis is usually responsive to treatment.

Symptoms
• frequent need to urinate (waking up often during the night)

267

• burning or pain during urination
• scanty urine
• general fatigue and weakness

Treatment

Since cystitis must be treated with antibiotics, you should contact your doctor if you suspect that you might have cystitis.

Diabetes

There are approximately five million diabetics in the United States today—and almost one-third of them are unaware that they have diabetes. The disease occurs when the body does not produce insulin, a hormone necessary to digest fat, protein, and carbohydrates. As a result, the body cannot utilize sugar.

Symptoms

• unexplained weight loss
• excessive hunger
• excessive thirst
• excessive, frequent urination
• cramps in the legs
• dryness of the mouth and throat
• frequent skin infections, especially boils
• frequent vaginal infections
• numbness or tingling in the limbs

Treatment

Diabetes can in some cases be controlled by strict diet and exercise; in many cases, the diabetic must take insulin. Control of

---

Stocking Your Medicine Cabinet: Getting It All at Your Fingertips!

Want to be prepared for common medical problems that might crop up at home—but been confused about what to put in your medicine cabinet?

You really don't need much to have a well-stocked medicine cabinet. Part of your medicine cabinet should be your first aid kit; other than that, all you'll need is the following:

Aspirin or its substitute. If you prefer aspirin, buy it in the least expensive form possible: aspirin is just aspirin, and fancy labels and brand names simply drive up the cost. If you can't tolerate aspirin, go for acetaminophen. Aspirin or acetaminophen can be used to reduce fever, relieve aches and pains, and reduce swelling.

Dispose of your aspirin if the tablets start to crumble excessively or if the tablets accidentally get wet. If there are children in your family, buy aspirin tablets in bottles with tamper-proof lids.

Antiseptic. Ordinary rubbing alcohol is best; mercury antiseptics and tincture of iodine are less effective and have more limited uses.

Calamine lotion. Calamine lotion is great for use on minor skin eruptions that don't involve a large area—it can relieve the swelling and itching from insect bites, common rashes, and mild poison ivy.

Antacid. Keep a product on hand to fight indigestion. If you want to, you can use simple baking soda— it's inexpensive and effective against mild heartburn and indigestion. If you purchase an over-the-counter remedy, read the label carefully to make sure there are no added medications for headache or cold symptoms.

Decongestant. Again, look for a product that has no added ingredients for relief of headache or other disorders. Decongestants should be used carefully; follow instructions on the label, and take care not to overdose. The use of nasal spray is not recommended unless you do so at a doctor's direction: nasal spray can cause a "rebound effect," resulting in a worsening of the condition instead of improvement.

Diarrhea medication. A formula containing kaolin and pectin is generally effective in correcting mild diarrhea that results from eating the wrong kinds of food or simple indigestion. If the diarrhea is severe or does not respond to treatment within twenty-four hours, you should consult a doctor.

Laxative. You should keep a mild laxative on hand for occasional use. Don't rely on laxatives—remember that most cases of constipation can be relieved by getting plenty of rest, exercising, and drinking lots of fluids.

Vaporizer. For safety's sake, choose an electric vaporizer that releases cool mist; doctors have found little if any difference between the therapeutic value of cool and warm mist.

Electric heating pad. For times when you need to apply heat, an electric heating pad gives you the option of choosing the temperature and maintaining it—unlike the hot water bottle, which cools off and has to be refilled. Take care not to set the heating pad too high, and never use it without its protective cover. Make sure you never pierce the heating pad with pins.

Ice bag. There are plenty on the market—choose one that is relatively small, well insulated, and fitted with a tight cap.

A word about prescription drugs: Unless you have a chronic illness that requires constant medication, you don't need lots of leftover prescription drugs in your medicine chest. It's not wise: something your doctor prescribed for you under one set of circumstances may not work at all under another. Or, worse yet, it may prove to be unsafe. Some drugs even change character over time—some become toxic as they age. So here's the rule: when you've finished taking the drug—that is, when you have taken as much as your doctor recommended—flush the rest down the toilet. *Never* throw away prescription drugs in the garbage can; a child or pet might discover them. *Never* take someone else's prescription drug. And *never* switch containers; leave a prescription drug in its original labeled container until you no longer intend to use it.

diabetes is essential; if not controlled, the disease may lead to blindness, chronic kidney disease, coma, or death.

External Otitis

Sometimes called "swimmer's ear," external otitis is a fungal infection of the ear canal. Prolonged dampness of the ear canal—especially common among swimmers—results in the infection, which is easy to clear up with proper treatment.

Symptoms
• severe itching of the ear canal
• moderate to severe pain, especially when the ear is tugged
• mild fever (under 100° F)

Treatment
To begin with, keep water out of your ears: wear ear plugs or cotton plugs coated with petroleum jelly when swimming, showering, or washing your hair. Your doctor can prescribe ear drops that will usually correct the condition within a week.

Gastroenteritis

Gastroenteritis—the catch-all phrase that describes an inflammation of the stomach and intestinal lining—can result from food allergy, virus, intestinal flu, food poisoning, or too much food and/or alcohol. Gastroenteritis can also be brought on by allergy or sensitivity to medication—researchers have identified more than 200 medications that can bring on the symptoms of gastroenteritis. Because of the vomiting and diarrhea, it can lead to dehydration if not managed properly.

Symptoms
Gastroenteritis comes on very suddenly, with some of the following symptoms:
• cold, sweaty skin
• fatigue
• muscle weakness
• nausea and/or vomiting
• stomach and intestinal cramps
• diarrhea
• pain or tenderness in the abdomen

Treatment

You should avoid food and drinks while vomiting and diarrhea continue; once the vomiting and nausea have passed, eat only a clear liquid diet. If vomiting persists, you should immediately contact a doctor, who can prescribe medication or give intravenous liquids to correct dehydration.

Hay Fever

Hay fever—which can occur in the spring, summer, or autumn seasons—is an allergic reaction to wind-borne pollens. Hay fever differs from common allergy because it is seasonally occurring— unlike an allergy to cat fur or household dust, for example.

Symptoms

- headache isolated in the front of the head
- violent sneezing
- thin, watery nasal discharge (unlike the thicker discharge that accompanies the common cold)
- watering of the eyes
- itching of the eyes, nose, throat, and roof of mouth
- fatigue
- loss of appetite

Treatment

It's important to isolate the cause of the hay fever, usually determined by a skin patch test. Once the allergen, or source, is identified, some people can develop immunity with the help of a desensitization program. Your doctor can also prescribe antihistamines to relieve your symptoms; antihistamines are effective in about 85 percent of all cases.

Hemorrhoids

Hemorrhoids—very simply, varicose veins in the anus or rectum—can result from stress, chronic constipation, sedentary lifestyle, or, in some cases, heredity. People who are overweight or pregnant are much more likely to develop hemorrhoids. External hemorrhoids protrude from the anus and look like wrinkly brown folds of skin; internal hemorrhoids can't be seen without physician's tools.

Symptoms:
Hemorrhoids may cause the following symptoms:
- itching following a bowel movement
- pain during and following a bowel movement
- blood streaked on the stools
- bleeding or passage of clots following a bowel movement
- irritation or burning following a bowel movement

Treatment
Only the most severe hemorrhoids require surgery; your physician can help you treat less severe hemorrhoids in a variety of other ways. One of the most important keys is to avoid straining during a bowel movement; you should drink plenty of fluids and eat foods rich in fiber so you can keep your stools soft. Even though hemorrhoids themselves are not life-threatening, you should see a doctor if you notice bleeding during or following a bowel movement so that he or she can rule out other possibly serious conditions.

Hepatitis (Infectious)

Infectious hepatitis (as differentiated from serum hepatitis caused by dirty needles) can result from poor sanitation, infected food, or can be spread from person to person. The intensity of the disease varies greatly: some are decapacitated, while others may have such a mild infection that they are not even aware of it.

A viral infection affecting the liver, hepatitis occurs in phases; it is only during the later phases of infection that the characteristic yellowish skin (jaundice) occurs. Recovery from hepatitis is generally very slow; some victims are fatigued for months after other symptoms disappear.

Symptoms
Depending on the severity of the disease, hepatitis brings the following symptoms:
- nausea and/or vomiting
- intestinal cramping
- diarrhea
- loss of appetite
- pain and tenderness on the right side below the ribcage
- high fever (102° F and up)
- dark urine
- light-colored stools

272

- yellowish coloring of the skin and the whites of the eyes (jaundice does *not* occur in all cases of hepatitis)
- extreme fatigue
- general weakness

Treatment

There is currently no effective treatment against the hepatitis virus. Your doctor will advise you to stay in bed until most symptoms have disappeared and then to slowly rebuild your strength with moderate activity. You should eat a well-balanced diet to provide strength.

Since hepatitis is contagious during the first two to three weeks of the illness, you should take extreme caution not to spread it to others. Wash your hands well in soap and hot water after using the bathroom, and dispose of any waste matter properly. Towels and bedding should be laundered in hot soapy water.

Once symptoms have disappeared, you may suffer a relapse of the disease if you become extremely fatigued or if you catch influenza, a cold, or other generalized infection.

Hypoglycemia

Hypoglycemia results when the body produces too much insulin, with the result that the body can't handle sugars normally. Most common in women—especially young women who are suffering from obesity or extreme stress—hypoglycemia can also result from other disorders, such as liver disease.

Symptoms

Most symptoms of hypoglycemia occur after eating food rich in sugars. These symptoms can include:
- dizziness
- shakiness
- inability to concentrate
- mild to severe headache
- excessive sweating
- fatigue and general body weakness

Treatment

After confirming a diagnosis of hypoglycemia with a glucose tolerance test, your doctor can advise you about a diet and exercise regimen that can help control the hypoglycemia. Generally, you should eat foods that are high in proteins and low in carbohydrates or sugars. Instead of eating three large meals a day, many doctors advise eating smaller quantities six times a day to keep the blood sugar level constant and avoid stress on the pancreas.

Impetigo

Caused by the staph and strep bacteria, impetigo most often strikes children, but can also strike young adults. Highly contagious, it is an infection of the skin, usually around the mouth and nose; you should take extreme care not to spread the infection. Avoid scratching the lesions; wash all towels, washcloths, bedding, and clothing in hot water with a germicide.

Symptoms
Symptoms can include the following:
• red patches around the mouth and nose
• tiny watery blisters around the mouth and nose
• blisters that break and form a yellowish crust
• tiny blisters surrounded by a red ring
• severe itching

Treatment
In severe cases, your doctor will probably prescribe an oral antibiotic. In other cases, you should wash and soak the area until the crusts fall off; use an antibiotic cream on the underlying skin. If the impetigo does not respond to treatment within a week, consult your doctor.

Infectious Mononucleosis

Called the "kissing disease," infectious mononucleosis is a viral infection that affects mostly young adults. Even though the disease is contagious, reseachers are unsure of how it is transmitted—there is little evidence that kissing is actually the culprit. "Mono," as it is called, can vary in severity; mild infections may last only a week or two, while severe infections can last for months. Since the spleen becomes enlarged during mononucleosis, you should not engage in strenuous exercise that could lead to rupture of the spleen.

Symptoms
• low-grade fever (usually around 100° F), which may last for weeks

274

- headache, mild to severe
- loss of appetite
- nausea and, less commonly, vomiting
- extreme fatigue
- extreme weakness
- enlarged, tender lymph nodes in the neck, armpits, and groin
- sore throat (often severe)
- general body rash (uncommon)
- yellowish coloring of the skin and eyes (uncommon)

Treatment

Doctors advise bed rest during the active stage of the illness, when the most symptoms are present. Aspirin or nonaspirin medication can be used to reduce fever if it is troublesome; if nausea is severe, your doctor can prescribe medication to correct or ease it. As mentioned, you should avoid strenuous physical activity. While you cannot be reinfected with mononucleosis after your original infection (it brings immunity), you *can* suffer a relapse if you become exceptionally fatigued or ill with another infection.

Influenza

Influenza, or the "flu," is a viral disease that can be brutal but is usually short-lived among healthy young people; most deaths from influenza occur among infants, the elderly, or those with chronic disease (such as respiratory, heart, or kidney disease).

Symptoms

Symptoms of the flu can include:
- high fever (102° F to 104° F)
- chills
- muscle and joint aching
- nausea and/or vomiting
- diarrhea
- sore throat
- coughing
- flushed skin
- runny nose
- severe fatigue

Treatment

Bed rest is the best treatment for influenza; stay down and get plenty of fluids. Since the flu is highly contagious, take care not to spread the disease. If fever persists for longer than three days and is accompanied by persistent sore throat or coughing for more than three days, consult your physician to rule out the possibility of a bacterial infection or pneumonia.

Kidney Infection

Kidney infection—which can be caused by a variety of things, including something as simple as a boil—is really quite common, with close to ten million Americans suffering from kidney infection at any one time. Bacterial infection of the kidney responds well to antibiotics; neglect or failure to treat kidney infection, however, can lead to long-term damage of the kidneys.

Symptoms

Besides feeling very ill, a person with a kidney infection may have the following symptoms:
• scanty, cloudy urine
• burning, painful urine
• urine that contains pus
• pain in the abdomen and groin that radiates from the lower back
• urine that is foul-smelling
• high fever (up to 104° F)
• chills
• nausea and/or vomiting
• severe headache

Treatment

If you suspect that you might have kidney infection, you should see a doctor immediately—kidney infection can only be diagnosed by a doctor. Treatment of kidney infection usually involves antibiotics and bed rest, with plenty of fluids.

Kidney Stones

Ranging in size from that of a grain of sand to that of a large walnut, kidney stones have been described as one of the worst afflictions known. Formed by either calcium or uric acids, kidney stones form in the kidneys and can be lodged anywhere along the urinary tract: in the kidneys themselves or in the ureter, bladder, or urethra. As the stones pass through the urinary tract, they cause excrutiating pain; in some cases, they can become lodged where they will interfere with the flow of urine.

Symptoms

Symptoms depend on the size and smoothness of the stone, and can include the following:
- incredible pain, radiating across the back
- bloody urine
- fever and chills
- nausea and/or vomiting
- pain in the groin and genitals

Treatment

Stones must either be passed out of the body through the urinary tract or removed surgically. Your doctor can administer pain medication that will ease the pain and will recommend therapy to help in passage of smaller stones.

Migraine Headache

Most migraine headache victims are women who are under stress, but migraine headache can also afflict men and is known to occur in people of all ages. Triggered most often by stress, migraine headaches can also be caused by foods high in certain chemicals (most notably cheese, chocolate, and cured meats). The pressure from a migraine headache results from too much blood circulation to the brain.

Symptoms

Prior to onset of the actual headache, some victims will see flashing lights, spots before their eyes, or other visual patterns; some experience ringing in the ears, sudden or violent changes of mood, or an impending sense of doom. Symptoms of the headache include:
- severe, throbbing pain on one side of the head
- pain that radiates to the eye
- nausea and/or vomiting
- visual difficulty (blurred vision, double vision, spots or colors)
- dizziness
- chills

Treatment

A migraine headache may be as brief as a few hours or may last for as long as forty-eight hours. Bed rest in a dark, quiet room can help, as can aspirin or other pain relievers and a cold pack on the head. For severe or repeated headaches, your physician can recommend a prescription medication for control of pain.

Mumps

A contagious viral infection that is now preventable with immunization, the mumps usually attack children, but can affect adults who did not have the disease as a child. Mumps is not serious in a child, but can have lasting complications in adults or older adolescents; if you are exposed to mumps and have never had them, you should contact your physician.

Symptoms

Symptoms of mumps can include:
- painfully swollen glands in front of the ear, below the ear, and below the jaw
- pain upon opening the mouth
- fever (sometimes high)
- abnormal salivation (either scant or profuse)
- swollen glands in the neck
- furry tongue

Treatment

The mumps usually last about ten to twelve days; while there is nothing you can do to treat the mumps themselves, you can lessen your discomfort by eating soft foods that don't need to be chewed very well. Aspirin can relieve some of the pain; you can also relieve some pain by applying heat or cold to the affected areas. Rest in bed for the first eight days, and get plenty of fluids. You should check with your doctor to rule out the possibility of complications if you are over the age of fifteen.

Otitis Media

Otitis media—infection of the middle ear—can be caused by either a virus or bacteria, or can occur as a complication of a cold, flu, tonsilitis, pneumonia, or other infection. While most cases of otitis media respond well to treatment and do not cause complications, occasionally an untreated infection can wreak havoc, possibly even leading to permanent deafness.

Symptoms
- persistent stabbing earache
- ringing in the ear
- high fever (up to 105° F)
- sensation of fullness in the ear
- sensation of fluid in the ear
- radiating throbbing pain in the ear that may come and go
- throbbing pain in the ear that may spread to the other ear
- tenderness in front of the ear

Treatment

If caused by bacteria, your infection will respond to treatment with antibiotics. In other cases, the symptoms will disappear as the secondary illness (such as cold) disappears. In severe cases, involving large amounts of pus that threaten to invade the inner ear, your doctor may need to surgically drain your ear, although this is not common.

Perforated Eardrum

An eardrum that perforates—or ruptures—can result from a foreign body (such as a cotton swab or bobby pin) in the ear, suction on the ear, a blow to the side of the head, or a severe infection in the middle ear. Perforated eardrum is serious: it can lead to permanent deafness.

Symptoms

The symptoms of a perforated eardrum include the following:
- a sudden, severe, agonizing pain in the ear
- a hollow sensation
- nausea and/or vomiting
- dizziness
- drainage from the ear (blood or pus)

Treatment

Do *not* put any kind of drops in your ear if you suspect that your eardrum has ruptured. Place a small plug of sterile cotton loosely in the opening of your ear and call a doctor immediately. If a doctor acts quickly, he or she can take steps to promote complete healing even in the case of a large rupture.

Pinkeye

Conjunctivitis, or pinkeye, can be caused by virus, bacteria, or irritating chemicals in the eye. Pinkeye caused by virus or bacteria is highly contagious: wash your hands carefully with hot water and soap after touching your eyes, and use a separate towel and washcloth.

Symptoms

Symptoms of pinkeye include:
• redness of the eye
• redness and irritation of the lining of the eyelids
• burning and itching of the eye
• discharge (either watery or thick)
• swollen eyelids
• visual disorders, especially blurred vision

Treatment

Treatment depends on the cause of pinkeye; your physician can prescribe drops or ointment that not only relieve pain but also ease symptoms. Avoid touching the eye—be especially careful not to rub it. After applying medication, wash your hands thoroughly and dispose of tissues by flushing them down the toilet. Launder handkerchiefs, towels, washcloths, and bedding in hot water with a germicide.

Pneumonia

Pneumonia, an illness that causes inflammation of the air cells in the lungs, is most commonly caused by bacteria, but can also result from virus or chemical irritants. Pneumonia caused by bacteria or virus is contagious, of course, and is spread through the air by coughing or sneezing. You can be exposed to pneumonia without developing the disease yourself, but you are at high risk if you haven't been eating properly, have been in bed for a prolonged period from another illness, have recently had the flu, or are overtired; the elderly and infants are at particular risk.

While pneumonia used to have a high mortality rate, improved medical care and the use of antibiotics have led to much better rates of recovery. Several strains of pneumonia still claim many victims.

Symptoms

Pneumonia begins with an upper respiratory infection that is much like the common cold; symptoms that follow include some of these:

- violent, shaking chills
- extremely high fever
- flushed skin
- eruptions of cold sores around the mouth
- hot, moist skin
- profuse sweating
- rapid pulse
- severe fatigue and weakness
- pain in the chest
- rapid breathing with wheezing
- painful, persistent coughing that produces bloody or rust-colored sputum

Treatment

If you suspect pneumonia, you should alert a doctor immediately. If caused by bacteria, he or she will prescribe antibiotic therapy. Bed rest is essential until the fever has eased completely. In severe cases, the doctor may need to administer oxygen.

Sinusitis

When the sinuses in the skull that are usually filled with air become filled with fluid or pus due to infection, sinusitis is the result: the sinuses can no longer drain as intended, and the dark, warm spaces encourage the reproduction of bacteria that worsen the condition. Sinusitis is more common among those who suffer from frequent head colds, allergies, or those who have a deviated septum.

Symptoms

Symptoms of sinusitis can include the following:

- severe, constant headache
- tenderness around the eyes
- pain or tenderness in the face
- toothache in one or more upper teeth
- mild to severe fever
- chills
- sore throat (caused by pus drainage)

- nausea and/or vomiting
- dizziness
- thick, yellow, foul-smelling nasal discharge

Treatment

Sinusitis must be treated with antibiotics. Your doctor may need to drain the sinuses; most procedures used in drainage are painless and effective. You can relieve pain with aspirin and heat packs over the affected sinuses. Do *not* use nasal sprays. Sinusitis usually persists for about four weeks, even with treatment.

Strep Throat

Caused by invasion of streptococcal bacteria in the throat, a strep throat can lead to possible complications if left untreated; with antibiotic treatment, most strep throat is responsive and disappears without complication.

Symptoms

Strep throat usually causes you to feel quite ill; specific symptoms may include some of the following:
- severe sore throat
- painful swallowing
- dry, burning sensation in the throat, as if there was a lump in the throat
- fever
- chills
- swollen lymph glands in the neck and, occasionally, the armpits
- general weakness
- fatigue

Treatment

Strep throat is generally successfully treated with antibiotics; as mentioned above, failure to treat strep throat can lead to complications, such as abscess or rheumatic fever.

Tooth Abscess

Usually caused by bacteria but occasionally due to fungus, tooth abscess is a pocket of infection at the end of a tooth's root. Untreated, a tooth abscess can lead to serious complications as pus spills over into the bloodstream and circulates throughout the body.

Symptoms

Symptoms of a tooth abscess include the following:

- relentless, gnawing toothache
- severe pain during chewing
- swollen gum surrounding the tooth
- swollen jaw

Treatment

Your dentist will probably prescribe oral antibiotics to remove the threat of generalized infection. If the abscess is still in its early stages, the dentist will probably treat it with a root canal: the tooth is opened, the nerve is cut out, and the abscess is allowed to drain completely before the tooth is packed and sealed. If the abscess is too large or has done too much damage, the dentist will, as a last resort, pull out the tooth.

Trench Mouth

Trench mouth, which is mildly contagious, is caused by bacteria and can be triggered by poor nutrition, untreated dental cavities, diabetes, insufficient sleep, or undue stress. If left untreated, trench mouth can loosen all the teeth and may cause damage to the bones of the jaw.

Symptoms

Symptoms of trench mouth may include the following:

- a dirty, gray membrane over the mouth that can be removed
- foul-smelling breath
- bad taste in the mouth
- red, spongy gums
- bleeding gums
- sore gums
- painful swallowing
- sores on the gums and inside of the cheeks
- fever
- general fatigue

Treatment

You should stop brushing your teeth until you get the go-ahead from your dentist. Avoid smoking, drinking alcoholic beverages, and eating spicy foods; strive for a well-balanced, nutritious diet of soft foods. Rinse your mouth every two hours with a mixture of hydrogen peroxide diluted with two parts of water. If you are unable to clear up the trench mouth within a week, consult your doctor; trench mouth generally responds well to antibiotics when needed.

Ulcer

Usually the result of prolonged stress or frustration, peptic ulcer occurs most frequently among professionals who are fiercely competitive. Ulcers, or perforated sores in the lining of the stomach, occur most often in men who are middle-aged and have O blood type. If left untreated, peptic ulcer can perforate through the stomach wall and cause uncontrolled bleeding.

Symptoms

The symptoms of peptic ulcer can include the following:
• steady abdominal pain, least severe in the morning before breakfast and most severe after going to bed
• cramping in the abdomen
• nausea and/or vomiting
• blood in the vomit (dark and gritty, like coffee grounds)
• blood in the stools (black and tarry)

Treatment

In an otherwise healthy individual, an aggressive treatment program should lead to healing of an ulcer within about five weeks. Your doctor will advise you to eat regular meals to keep something in your stomach; most doctors advise bland foods and avoidance of spicy foods, foods high in fiber, or very hot or cold foods. Your doctor can also recommend a good antacid to coat the stomach lining, cut down on the hydrochloric acid secreted by the stomach, and help heal the ulcer. You will need to avoid situations that cause stress and begin to exercise more regularly.

T ransportation can come in all sizes and shapes—from a shiny new car to a well-traveled bicycle—but it's critical that your transportation be reliable. If you've ever been stranded at the edge of a dusty road as traffic screeches past unrelentlessly, you know the wisdom of proper maintenance!

In the two charts that follow, you'll find tips to keep your bicycle and your automobile in good running condition.

Bicycle

Selecting size	As a general rule, you should be able to straddle the horizontal bar with 1 inch of clearance as you stand on the ground. If your legs are between 30 and 34 inches long, you need a frame between 21 and 22 inches.
Adjusting the seat	Before you ride, adjust the seat so that the heel of your foot barely reaches the low pedal. In this position, the ball of your foot should rest on the pedal with your knee slightly bent.
Nuts and bolts	Quickly check all nuts, bolts, and other hardware items before you begin riding to make sure they are tight. Keep an eye out for damaged or worn parts.
Brakes	Make sure brakes are in good condition by squeezing them; they should come no closer than halfway to the handlebar. Quickly check the brake cables for fraying, and check to make sure the brake pedals are not worn.
Front wheel	The front wheel should be centered between the fork; check to make sure the fork is not bent or broken. Make sure the axle nut is tight.

Rear wheel	The rear wheel should be centered within the chain stays; keep the spoke tight. Both the rear and the front wheels should rotate smoothly without wobbling.
Cables	Check for fraying and wear.
Chains	Check for damage and stress; keep chains lubricated with a lightweight oil (apply once every three months).
Sprockets	Check to make sure sprockets are tight on the cranks. Replace the sprockets if teeth are bent or broken.
Handlebars	Make sure they are tightened securely; replace worn tape or grips. Adjust handlebars for comfort if necessary.
Tires	Each time you ride, check both tires thoroughly. They should be fully inflated according to specifications; check to make sure they are not splitting, tearing, or pulling away from the rims. Check for bulging or nails.

Note: Carefully study the owner's manual for your bicycle before you ride it. Keep the manual handy as a guide to repair and maintenance.

Automobile

Each time you get in the car, check the following:

Headlights	Check to make sure the headlights on both sides are working, are of uniform brightness, and are clean (snow and mud can cut down on headlight efficiency). Check to make sure high beams are working.
Signal lights	Check to make sure that signal lights on both sides are working, both front and rear.
Brake lights	Make sure that brake lights are working and are clean.

286

Windshield wipers	Windshield wipers should be working; if worn, they should be replaced.
Brakes	Test to make sure brakes are working; when you press the brake pedal, it should come no closer than two to three inches from the floor.
Steering	The steering wheel should function smoothly; if your car has automatic power steering, you should be alert for a groaning sound (a signal that the car is low on steering fluid).
Tires	Check to make sure that tires are all fully inflated; check carefully to make sure that there are no bulges, splits, or nails and that the tires are not pulling away from the rim.
Jack/flares	Check the trunk to make sure you have the jack and a set of flares.
Spare tire	Check to make sure that you have a spare tire and that it is in good condition and fully inflated.

To keep your car in good condition, perform the following general maintenance:

Oil	Engine oil should be changed every 2,000 to 3,000 miles.
Oil filter	The oil filter should be changed every other time you change the oil.
Spark plugs	Replace every 15,000 miles if you use leaded gasoline or every 30,000 miles if you use unleaded gasoline.
Fuel filter	Replace every 15,000 miles.
Power steering fluid	Check every time you change the oil; replace when level is low.
Air conditioning	Check operation of controls, belts, and hoses for leaks, tears, or brittleness every six months.

Hood and door hinges	Lubricate every six months.
Tires	Rotate every 10,000 miles.
Seat belts	Check for fraying or fuzzing; check to make sure the buckles totally engage and disengage as designed. Check to make sure retractor locks.
Defroster	If weather conditions indicate, check to make sure defroster works.
Horn	Sound the horn to make sure it works.
Windshield washer fluid	If your car has windshield washer fluid, check to make sure you have plenty of fluid and check to make sure that the sprayers are not clogged. Make a quick overall check of the system to assure proper function.

INDEX

fudge
cake, 181
creamy, 212
fantastic, 211
five-minute, 212
icing, 182
peanut butter, 211
Virginia, 213
fudgesicles, 210
fuel filter (automobile), 287
furniture polish, 51, 52

G

garlic cloves, how to store, 32
garlic powder, 5
gastroenteritis, 270
gelatin salad
cherry, 121, 122
fruit, 121, 124
raspberry, 121
tuna, 131
vegetable, 122
ginger, to use in place of sugar, 8
gingerbread, apple, 176
glaze
basic, 184
definition of, 48
lemon, 184
graham cracker crumbs
crust, 188
substitution for, 44
grains, whole
as source of protein, 2
as source of vitamins, 4
grain-cereal food group, 11
granola
apple, 68
nutty, 68
grapefruit
how to select, 22
how to store, 22
grapes
best time to buy, 15
how to select, 22
how to store, 22
grate (cooking term),
definition of, 48
gravies, 174
green beans, best time to buy, 15
green pepper
how to select, 22
how to store, 22
grill (cooking terms),
definition of 48
grits, fruited, 68
grocery stores, 13
guacamole dressing, 136
gumdrops, 214

H

halibut steaks, 138
ham
casserole, 142
Hawaiian, 147
how to roast, 53
pie, 157
salad, 133
sandwiches, 81
substitution for, 46
hamburger
casserole, 141, 144,
154, 161, 163
patties, 146, 155
pie, 141, 154
sloppy joes, 158
stew, 142, 158
stroganoff, 144
hamburger buns, 110
hamburger pie, 141, 154
hamburger soup, 91, 95
hamburgers
best-ever, 83
making them juicy, 58
handlebars, bicycle, 286
Harvard beets, 167
hay fever, 271
headache, 250–252
caused by allergy, 251
caused by eyestrain, 251
caused by infection, 251
migraine, 251, 277–278
tension, 251
heat rash, 254, 255
heating pad, electric, 269
Heimlich maneuver, 238
hem, how to repair, 232–233
hemorrhoids, 271–272
hepatitis, infectious, 272–273
hives, 254, 255
holiday candy logs, 213
hominy, substitution for, 46
honey
how to store, 32
substitutions for, 44
honey butter, substitutions for, 43
honeydew melon
how to select, 22
how to store, 22
horn (automobile), 288
hot chocolate, 113
hot dogs, 83
casseroles, 145
corn dogs, 150
how to select, 31
how to store, 31

in biscuits, 145
in soup, 95
with potatoes, 145, 153
with barbecued beans, 146
with corn, 144
hush puppies, 109
hypoglycemia, 273–274

I

ice, grapefruit, 114
ice bag, 269
ice cream, how to store, 32
icing
chocolate, 182
coconut, 183
fudge, 182
penoche, 183
impetigo, 255, 274
infectious hepatitis, 272–273
infectious mononucleosis,
274–275
influenza, 253, 275–276
instant onion, substitution for, 44
iodine, 9–10
iodine (antiseptic),
stains, 223–224
iron (mineral), 8–9
deficiency of, 261
ironing, 222
Italian dressing, 134

J

jack (automobile), 287
jam
as source of carbohydrates, 3
how to store, 32
muffins, 107
jaundice, 272
jello
hints on using, 56
how to store, 32
jelly
as source of carbohydrates, 3
how to store, 32

K

kidney infection, 276
kidney stones, 276–277
knead, definition of, 48

L

labels
as source of sugar content, 8
how to read, 36–38

293

298

Please ask your local retail Gift or Bookstore about other fine products

ASPEN WEST
PUBLISHING & DISTRIBUTION

"Where's Mom Now That I Need Her?" Surviving Away from Home. Frandsen, B.R.   356 pages of hints on nutrition, grocery shopping, laundry and clothing with a stain removal guide, first aid and recipes for quick, easy meals, plus lots more.

0100 Vinyl Three-ring	ISBN 9615390-0-3	$21.95
0101 Paperback	ISBN 9615390-1-1	$12.95

"Where's Dad Now That I Need Him?" Surviving Away from Home. Frandsen, B.R.   350 pages with hints on budgeting, credit cards, balancing a check book, buying and maintaining cars, home maintenance, crimes prevention, and more. Also includes recipes such as Dutch-oven, BBQ, fish ,beverages, soups and pancakes!

0102 Vinyl Three-ring	ISBN 9615390-2-X	$21.95
0103 Paperback	ISBN 9615390-3-8	$12.95

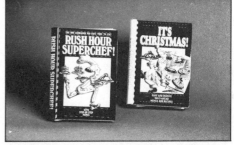

"A Pinch of This A Dash of That" Conversations with a Cook. Johns, K.   Ever asked a good cook for the recipe to one of her most treasured dishes? Chances are she whispers, "Oh, I just put in a pinch of this, and a dash of that." This attractive collection features treasured recipes passed down from one generation to another.

0106 Vinyl Three-ring	ISBN 9615390-5-4	$22.95
0107 Paperback	ISBN 9615390-6-2	$14.95

"Rush Hour Superchef" The One Cookbook You Have Time to Use! Mayes, D.   Meals in less than 20 minutes for the person who either doesn't have time to spend in the kitchen, or doesn't want to! "It's Christmas" Easy and Festive Do-it-ahead Menus and Recipes. Mayes, D.   Take the hassle out of the holidays and do it ahead!

0108 Rush Hour	ISBN 0-9611588-4-0	$16.95
0110 It's Christmas	ISBN 0-9611584-1-7	$16.95

"After the Wedding..." A Guide for the Bride. Collins, S. 200 pages with information no communication, physiological insights, social etiquette, entertaining ideas, and easy recipes. A very helpful and informative guide for the newly married couple.

0113 Hardback
ISBN 0-96275260-6

$21.95

"Laundry 101" A simple "How To" book for doing laundry. Great for anyone faced with the unfamiliar task of doing laundry. A 6 x 9 booklet with 22 pages. "Every Woman's Reference Guide" Haskins, J.   Contains 276 pages of sensible, practical and often inspirational advice. Great for every woman!

0112 Laundry 101 (sold in 24 pack only)	$3.70
0109 Every Woman's Reference Guide	$10.95

PILLOWTALK DIVISION Pillowcases

*4213

*4514
*4515 other side Please more sex

*4202
*4201 I LOVE YOU!

*4216
Tomorrow Night on reverse.

*4500

*4189

*4502

*4203
*4509 I Love You w/ rose

*4520

*4220
*4221 Some things are perfect
just the way they are.

*4512

*4218

*4214
reverse side has two aspirin
tablets

*4224
*4225 Hugs and Kisses

*4550
*4551 Jingle My Bells!

$12.00 each

PILLOWTALK DIVISION Laundry Bags

$14.95 each

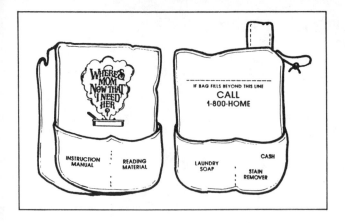

Extra Large Laundry Bags with Pockets

Available in either blue or white cotton twill. The size is 20"x 30" with a 6" gussett and pockets for laundry essentials. All bags have a strong nylon drawcord at the top. Available stock, or blank for custom prin Order in multiples of 6.

2000 XLG Laundry Bag, white $_____
2001 XLG Laundry Bag, blue $22.00

ORDERING INFORMATION

Sold to: _____   Date _____

_____   Customer rep. _____

_____   Day tel. no. _____

_____   Eve. tel. no. _____

ITEM DESCRIPTION	PRICE	QTY	TOTAL

Shipped via UPS. Figure shipping rates according to the following schedule:
If your order totals up to $10.00 ADD $2.57

$10.01 – $25.00	$4.95
$25.01 – $40.00	$6.60
$40.01 – $55.00	$8.90
$55.01 – $75.00	$10.50
$75.01 – $200.00	$12.50
$200.00+ additional charge	

Outside the Continental U.S. Special Quote.

Total for Merchandise	
Sales Tax x.0625 (UT)	
Shipping/Handling*	
TOTAL ENCLOSED	

*MY METHOD FOR PAYMENT IS: *ALLOW 10 - 15 DAYS FOR DELIVERY
☐CASH   ☐ CHECK NO. _____   ☐ MASTERCARD   ☐

Credit Card No. _____   Exp. Date _____   Home Tel _____

I agree that I have ordered the above items and have approved the above method of payment for the merchandise purchased. This form must be filled out completely for the order to be processed. All sales are FINAL. Prices subject to change without prior notice.

_____   _____   _____
Customer Signature   Print Name   Date

ASPEN WEST PUBLISHING CO., INC.

P.O. Box 1245/8385 Sandy Parkway, No. 129/Sandy, Utah 84070/801-565-1370/TOLL FREE 1-800-222-9133